Rock Reef Publishing House
President Daniel Barth
Art Director Charles Marin
Cover Design Steve Barth
Copy Editor Catherine Smith
Typography Charles Marin

First published in the United States of America by
Rock Reef Publishing House
4530 Pauling Ave San Diego, Ca
92122

ISBN 0-9670339-2-6

Price:$24.95 (U.S.)

OCEANS

the Photography of Sean Davey

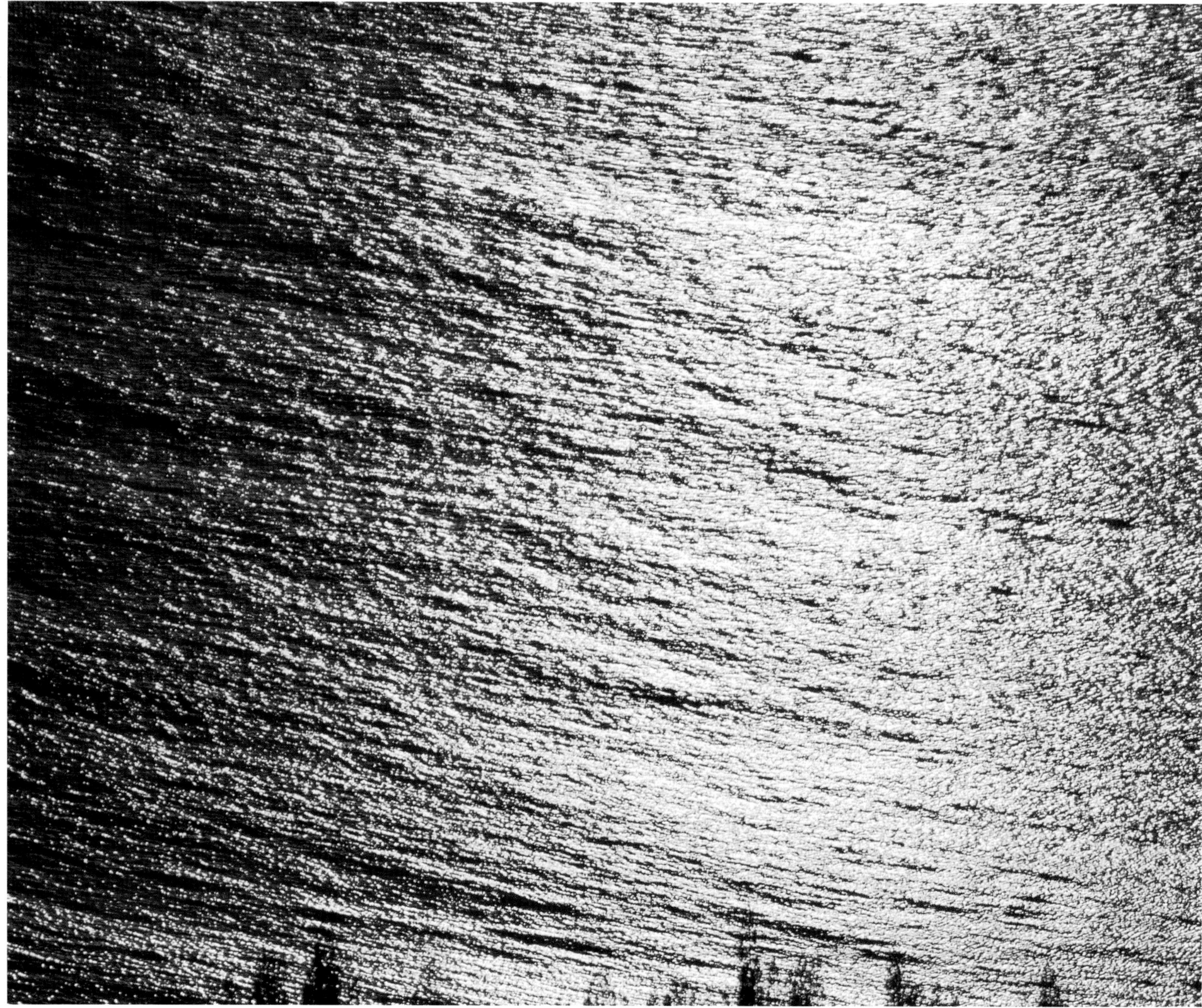

"I dedicate this book to my beautiful wife Lane. Without you, this book would not have been possible, let alone much of its content."

Sean Davey

OCEANS
the Photography of Sean Davey

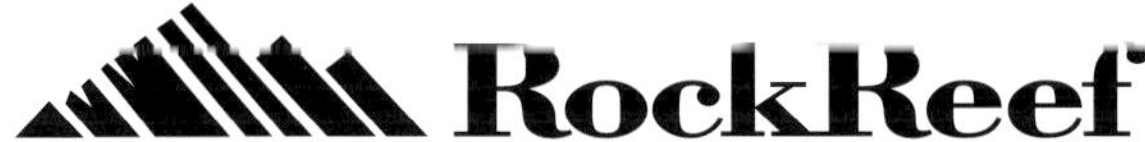

RockReef

Rock Reef Publishing House
San Diego, California
USA

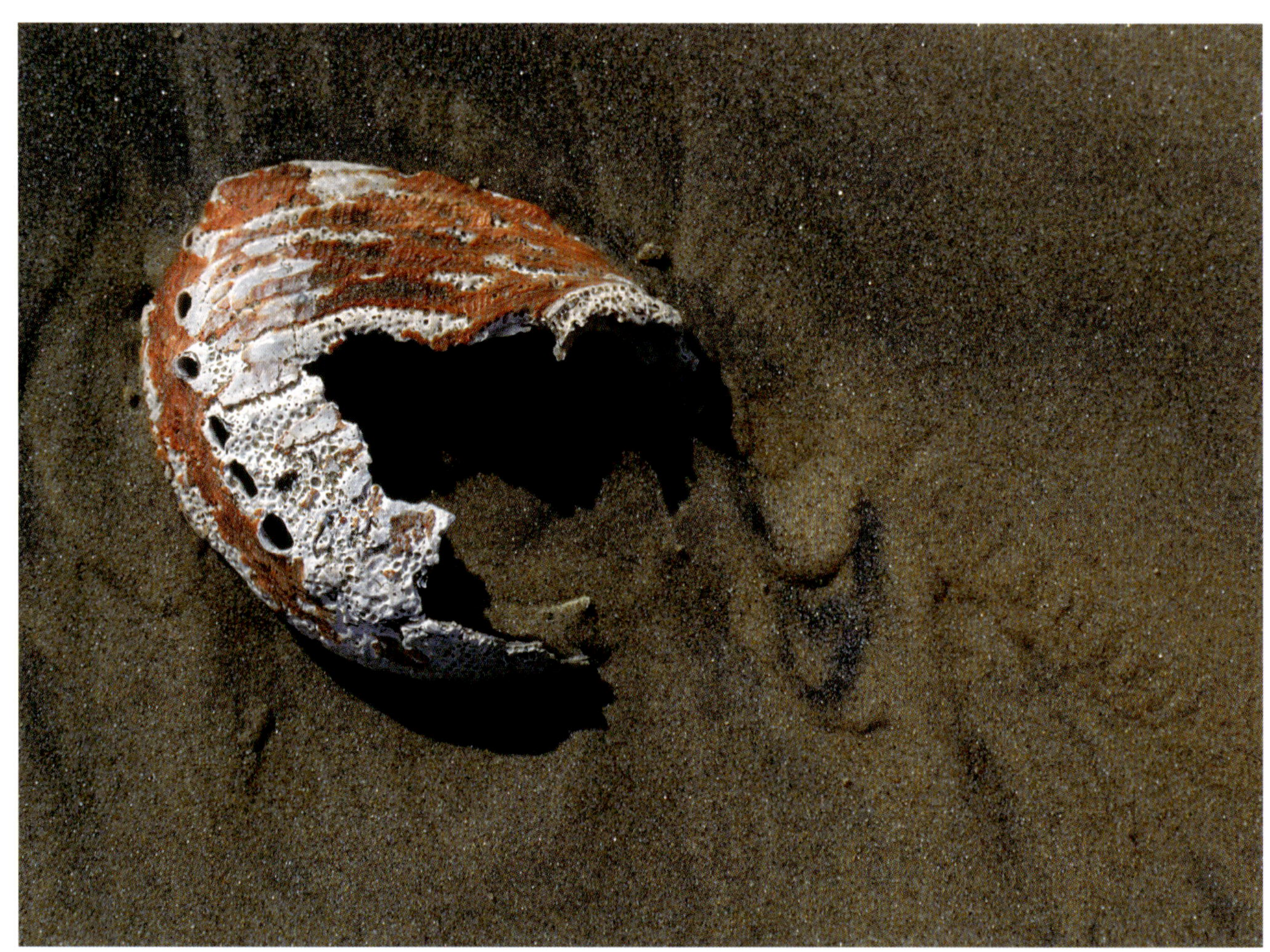

Thanks to the following people:

Kirk Wilcox who, as the then editor of Tracks Magazine in Australia, was the first person to publish my work and really see my potential as a photographer. Alan Waugh and Fotoforce (Hobart, Tasmania, Australia)—thanks for all the free hours in the darkrooms over the years Alan, not to mention the countless times that I borrowed your camera gear. Alan Love and Aquatech water housings for custom building me perfect water proof housings for my camera equipment—time and time again without ever grumbling about my often highly customized demands. To the many photographers who have inspired me over the years, both in and out of the surf scene. (You all know who you are.) To all those people over the years who have directly or indirectly helped in some way to develop my skills as a photographer, I thank you very much. Aloha and Mahalo

Sean Davey

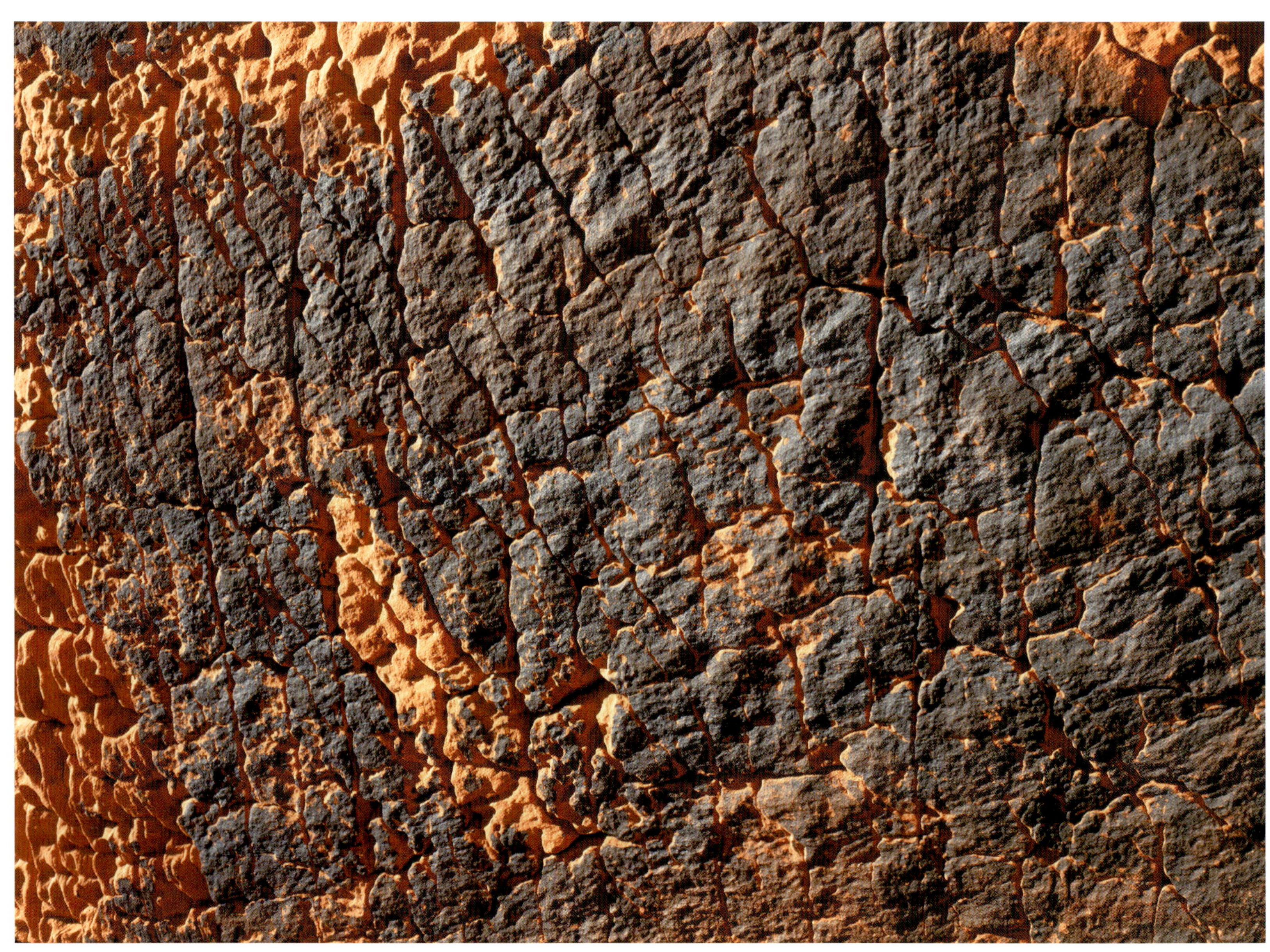

I can recall a trip that I took when I was 16 years old with five friends of mine, deep into Baja California, to Mexico.   It was to be a two-week trip to unspecified places to ride waves, dive, and do other 16-year-old things. The trip turned into our baptism into the world of wave travel: nothing goes as planned.   It was one crisis after the other, but was, luckily, limited to transportation problems. The car broke down five times and if it weren't for two brothers, both with the name Francisco, we would still be there.   This was the lure and the nearly deadly hook that wave exploration contained—it didn't matter what happened, just find the waves.

Myself and one of my compadres, Norvin, were reading a magazine while sitting near a Saguaro Cactus, yet again trying to figure out how we were going to fix the car, and Norvin came across an article that was entitled, 'You Know You're Hardcore When.'   Hardcore being defined as going to any length in exploration for waves.   The article was a point by point analysis.   Norvin and I read each one aloud in unison, typically laughing maniacally after each point. Then we read, 'If your car or boat was to break down you would die and no one would ever hear of you again.' We didn't laugh. We put the magazine down and started walking towards a nearby fishing village. Fast.

This is what Sean Davey has endured year after year, through disease and heat, more or less fire and rain—all in pursuit of collecting images of waves and Oceans from all over the globe.   I can identify with Davey, but only on a smaller level, for he is the one that has presented all of the wonderful images in this book. Without Davey we would not have the privilege of seeing a piece of our world that it takes a mad man with the temperance of an angel to go after.

Dan Raymond.

Introduction

The world's oceans contain saltwater. It is odd that the water has salinity to it. Salt, for its basic function, is for flavor. Religious Texts such as the Bible make philosophical reference to salt. A staple in the human diet is salt, we see it on every table of every restaurant; salt sustains us. In the mixture of the saltwater of the Oceans of the Earth are a taste and a feeling we can hardly savor because the moments and the locations go unnoticed. Sean Davey has noticed them for years and it is to our benefit that he has dedicated himself to capturing these moments for us. A man. An arsenal of cameras. A lifetime of skill. An unbreakable determination. The combination of those flavors might just make salt a bit jealous. Sean Davey. OCEANS.

Oceans are activity; they are life; they are a complete measure of the health of our planet. But, the world's oceans, beneath the surface, contain their unique aqueous existence. Free from the confines of the air that we humans breathe, the world's oceans survive within a space of sparsely distributed land that we consider to be continents. Whether the Indian, Atlantic, Arctic, or Pacific Ocean are the reference, it matters not--for each of these produce waves. Waves are pure oceanic energy. Energy that is released upon the shore of the landmasses that populate Earth. Through these waves we can see its beautiful strength.

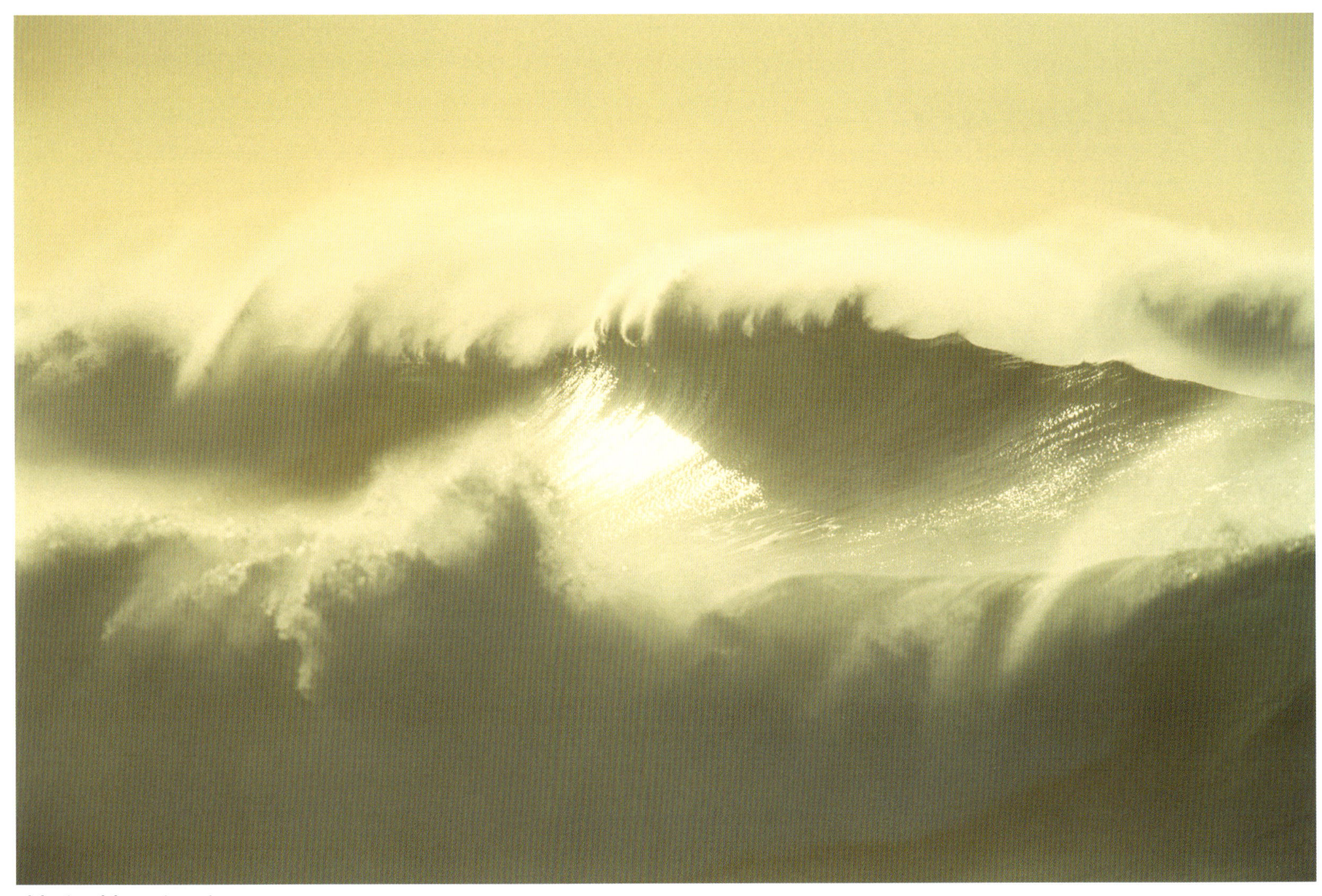

Misty Mountaintops
Parade through a golden afternoon in the South Pacific.

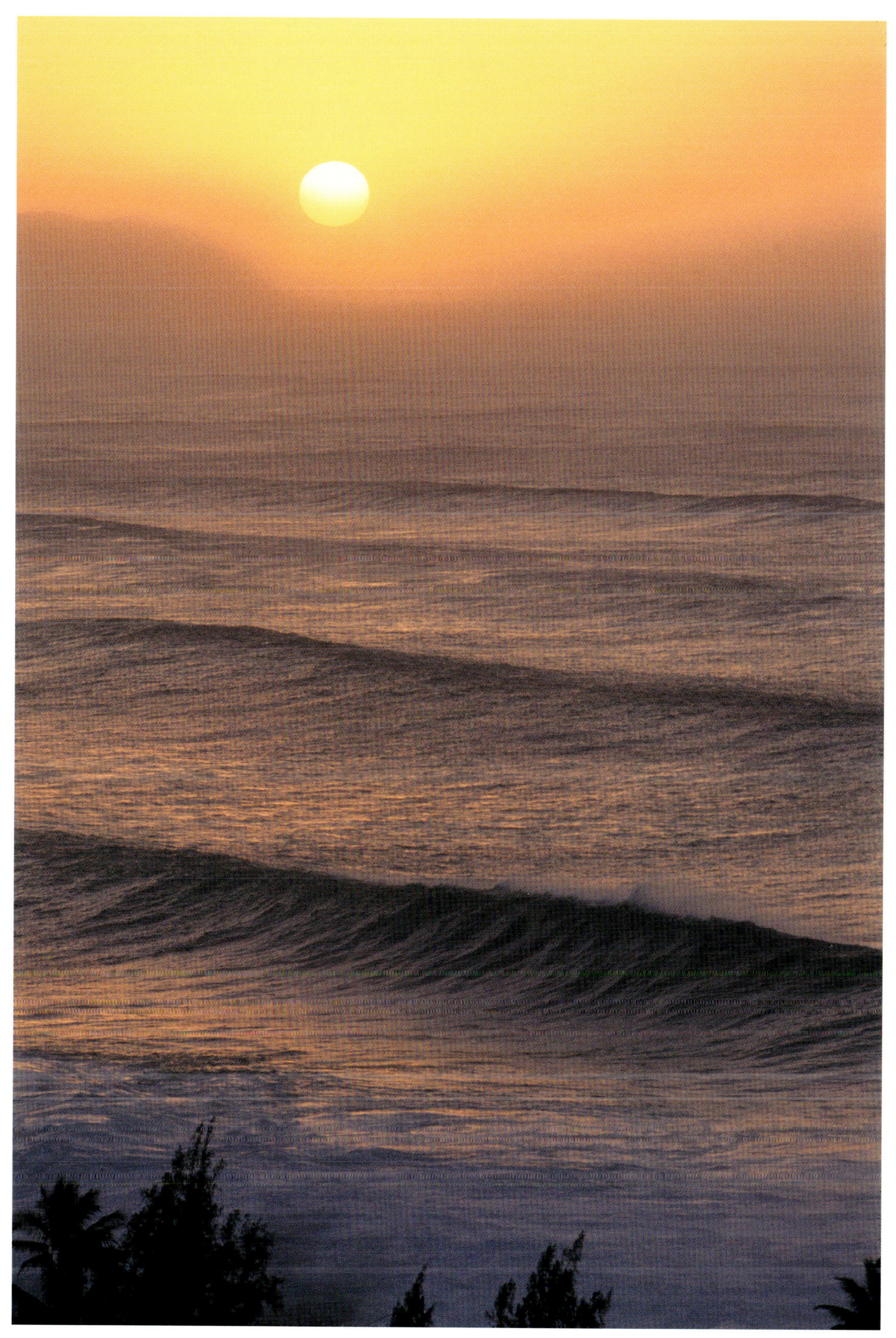

A Purple Haze of the Dusk
paints vivid lines on top of the Pacific Ocean's surface.

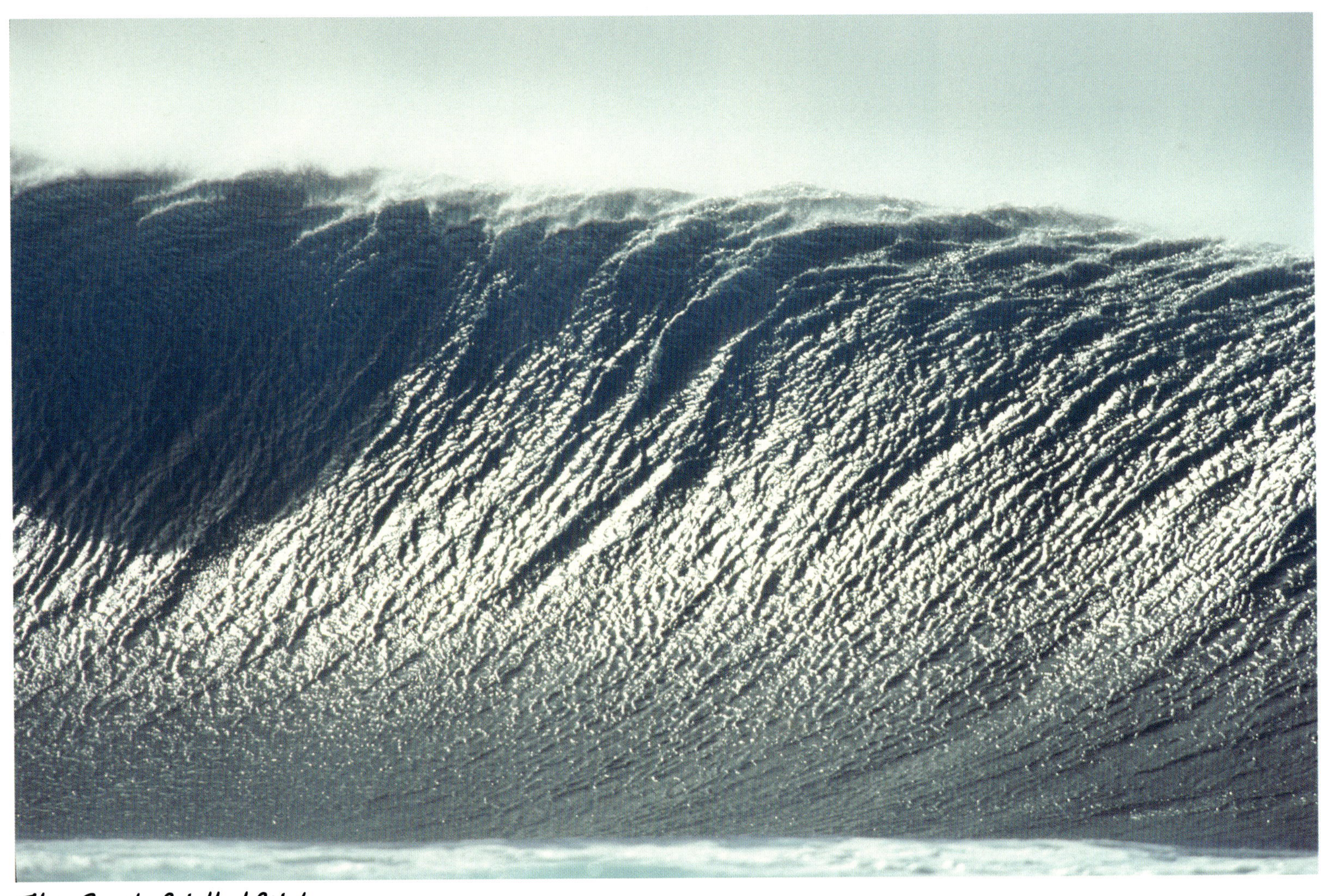

This Frosty Wall of Water

that is perpendicular to the Island of Oahu's sea-
floor must collapse—it has no choice.

An abstract Wave Shadow moves with stealth across a plane of speckled water. South Tasman Sea.

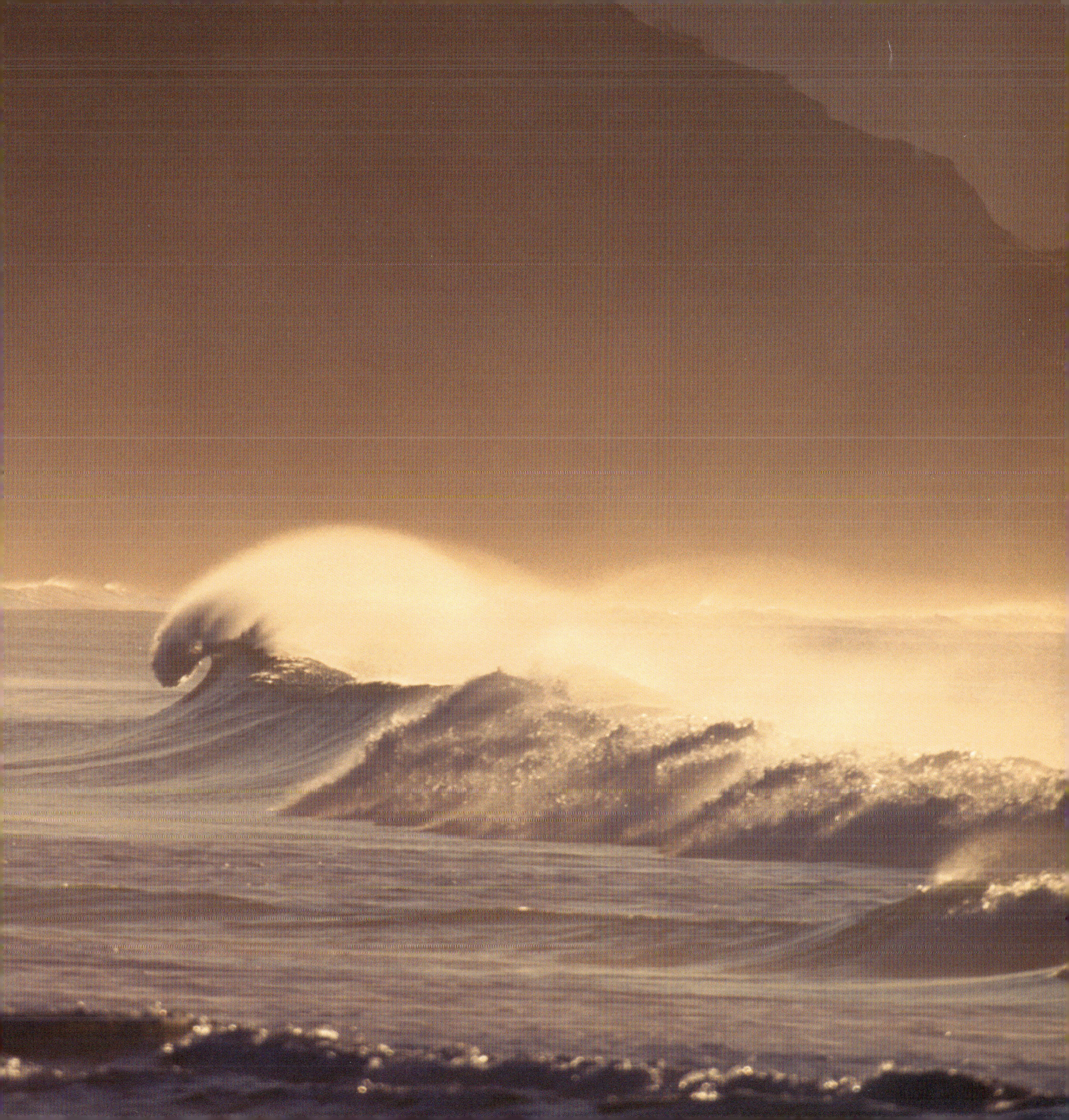

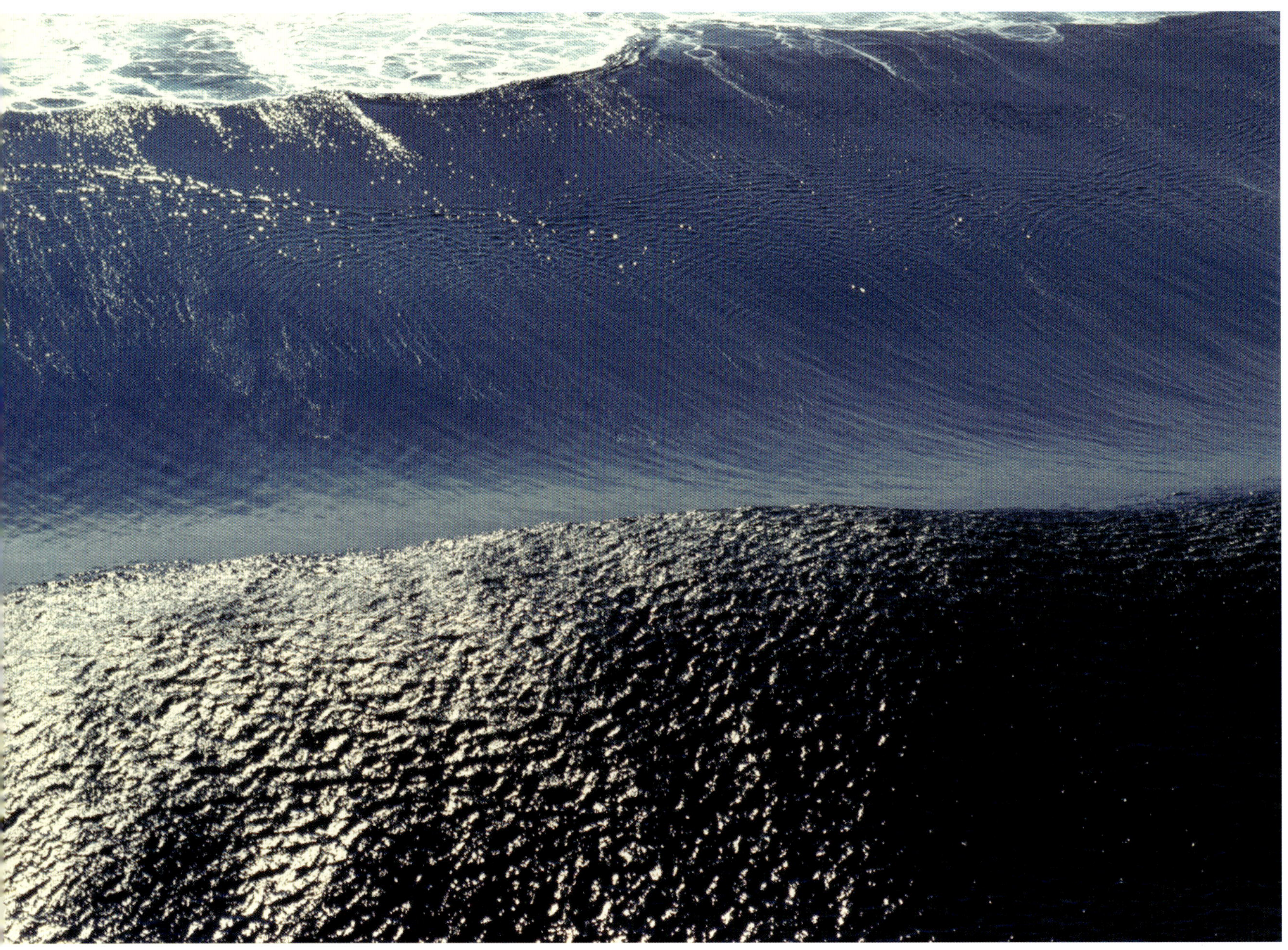

Cresting,

Above and Behind the Slope of a surge of saltwater. This view shows what a wave looks like just before it breaks, only we get to see it from the back. North Pacific Ocean.

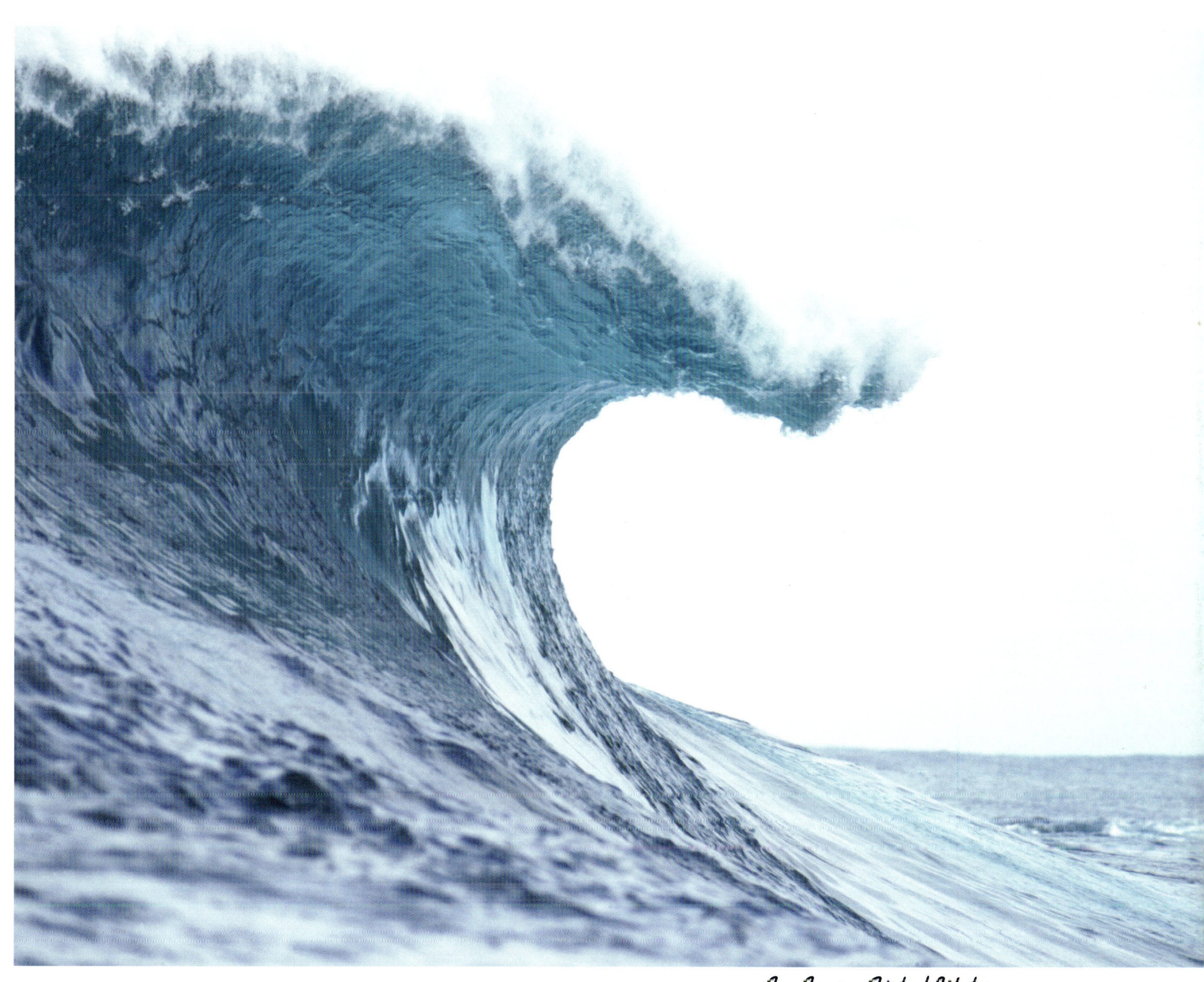

An Angry Fist of Water
about to land with a mighty blow to the innocent beneath it.

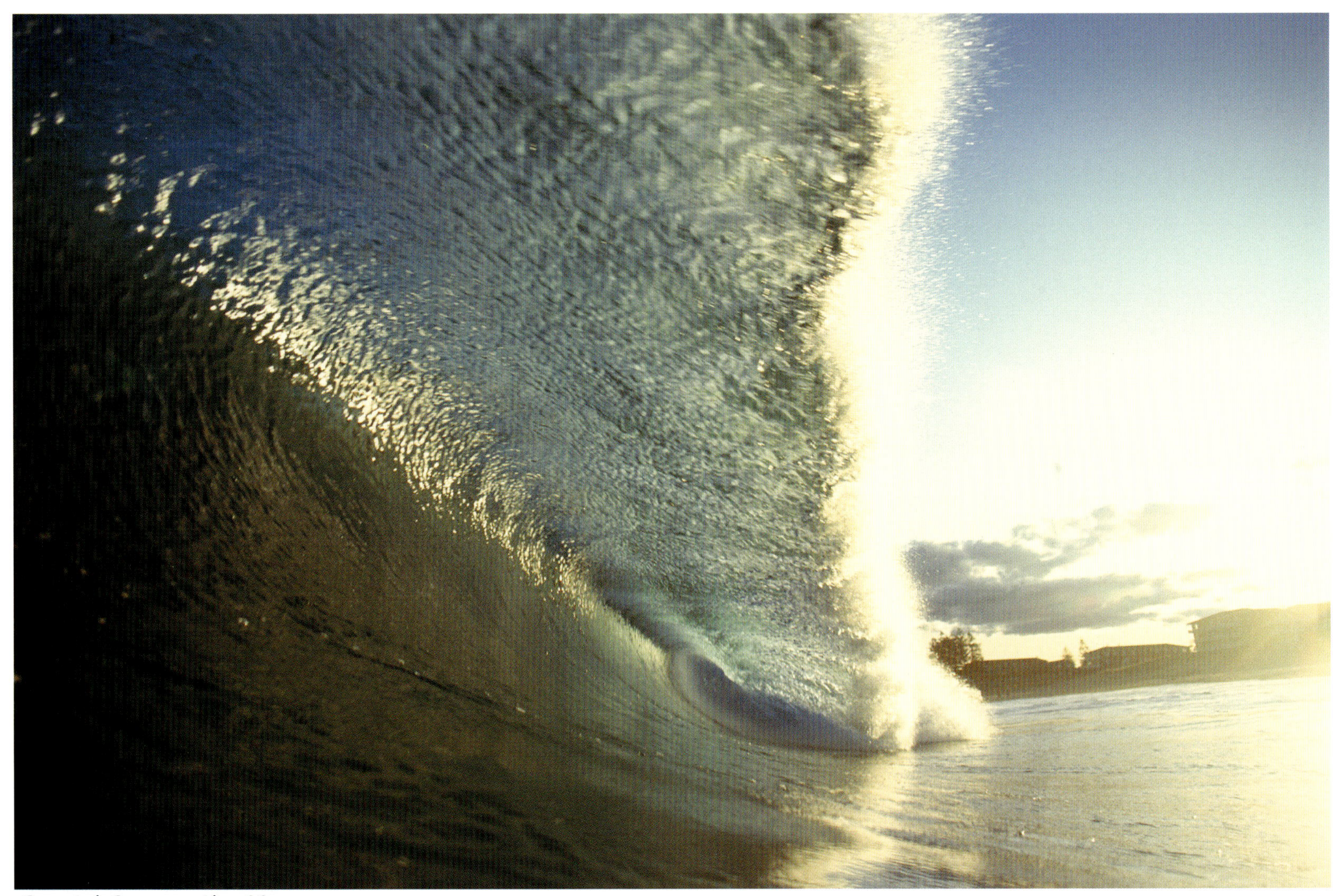

Crystal Cave in the Morning
A wave which is tossing out the 'lip' of itself
towards the horizon's sunlight. Australian Coast.

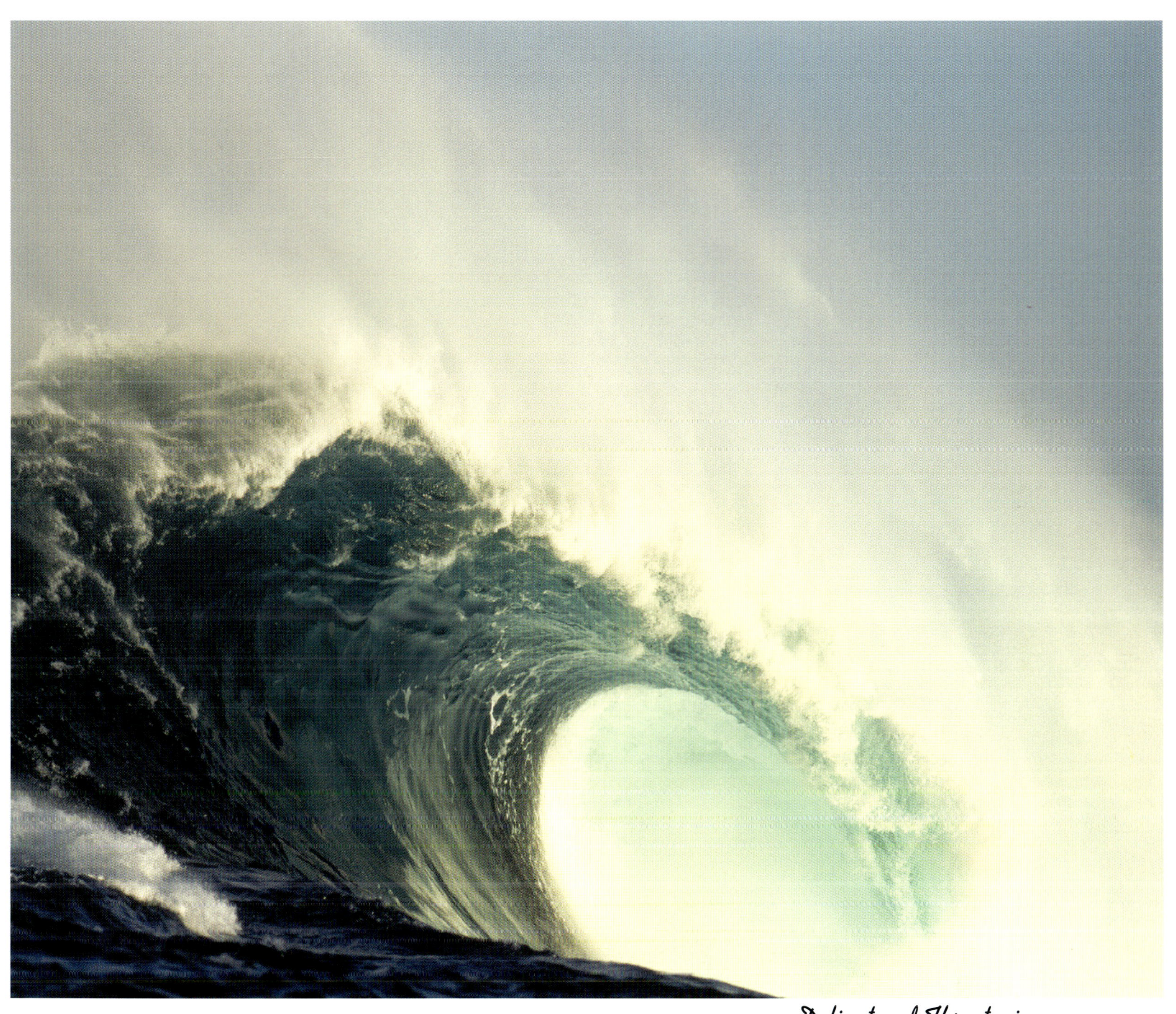

Defiant and Threatening,
this one is screaming to be left alone.

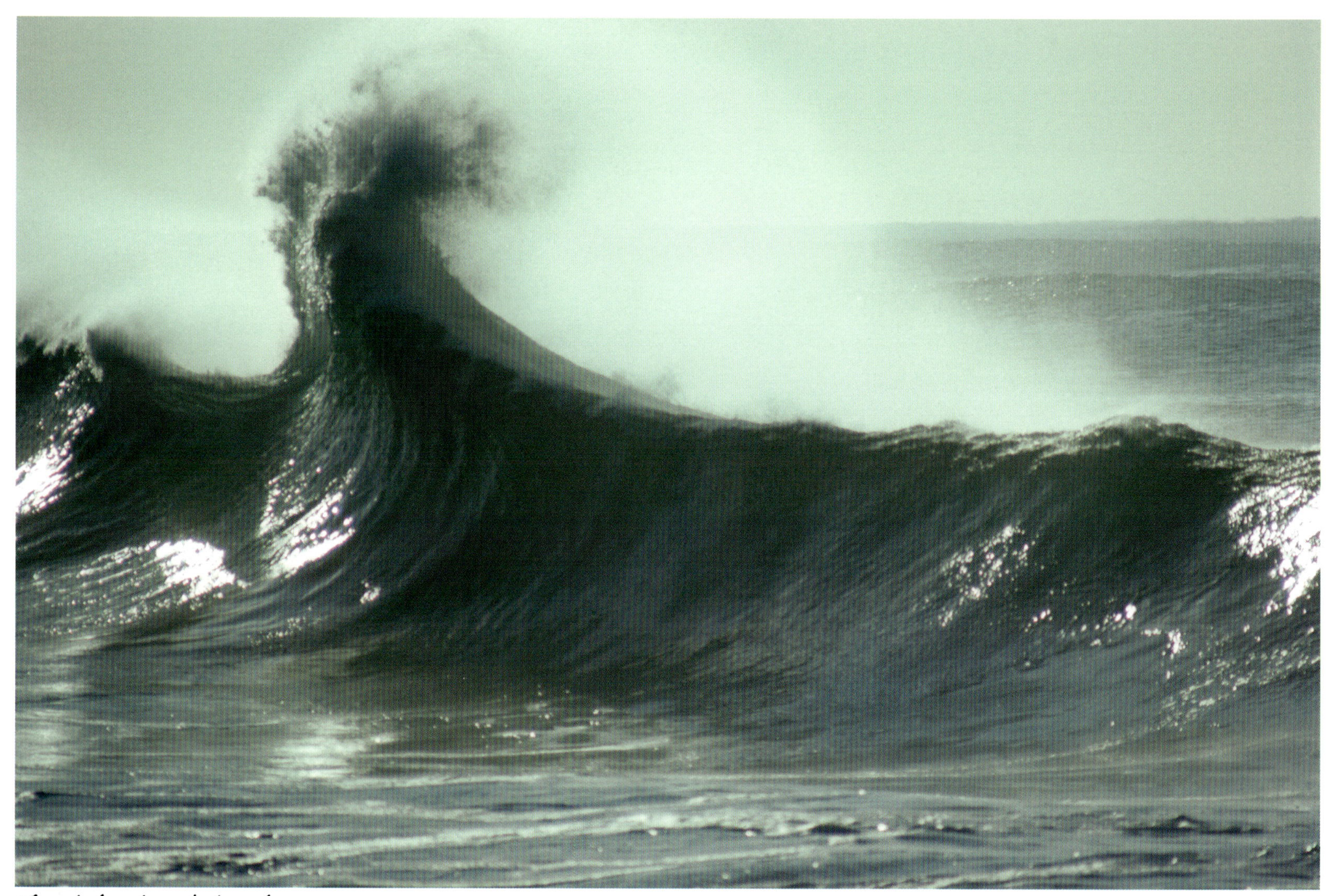

Twisted yet sculptured,
a wave that should be considered a monument
to the Ocean's creativity. East Indian Ocean.

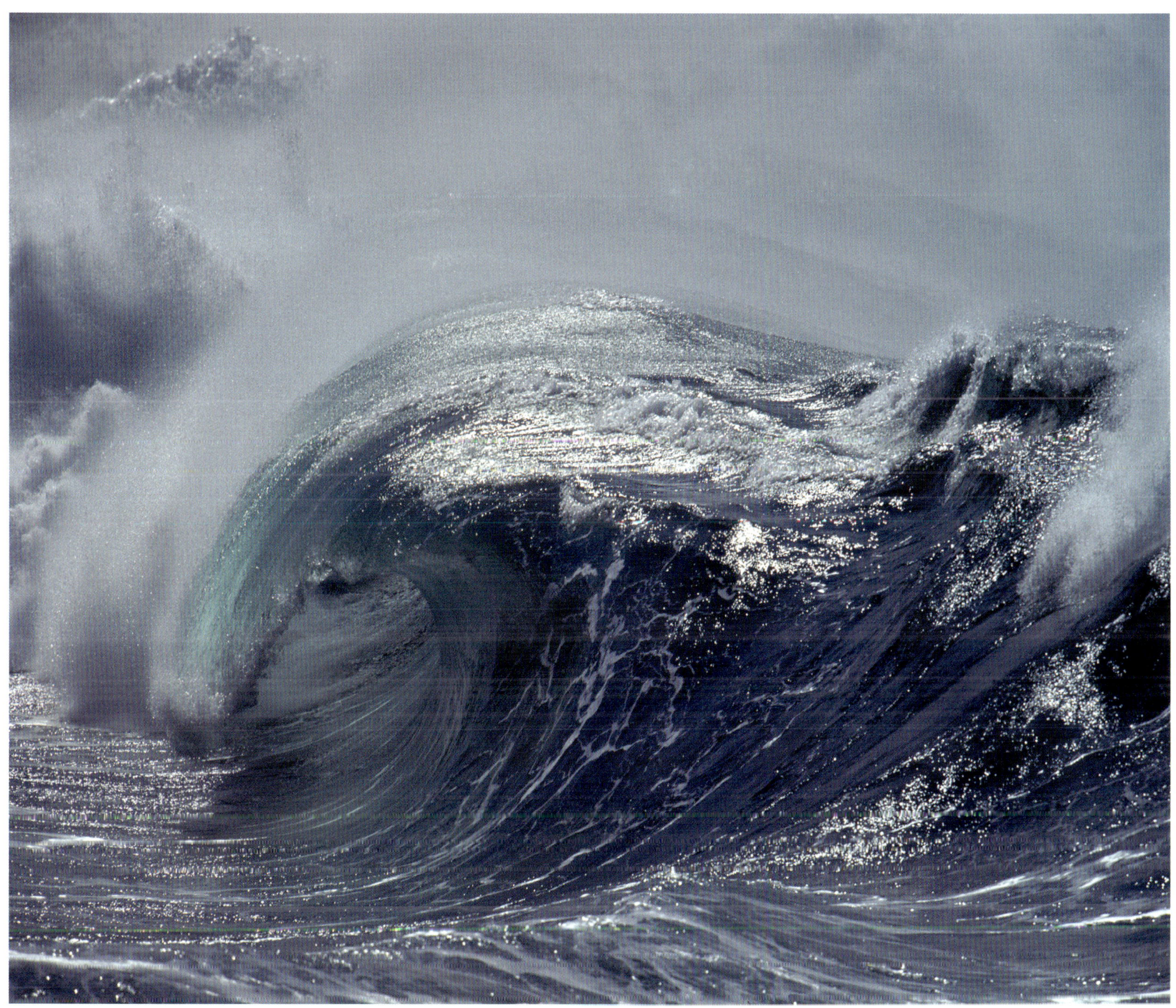

Gentle Sea,
quiet in its own grace and balance.

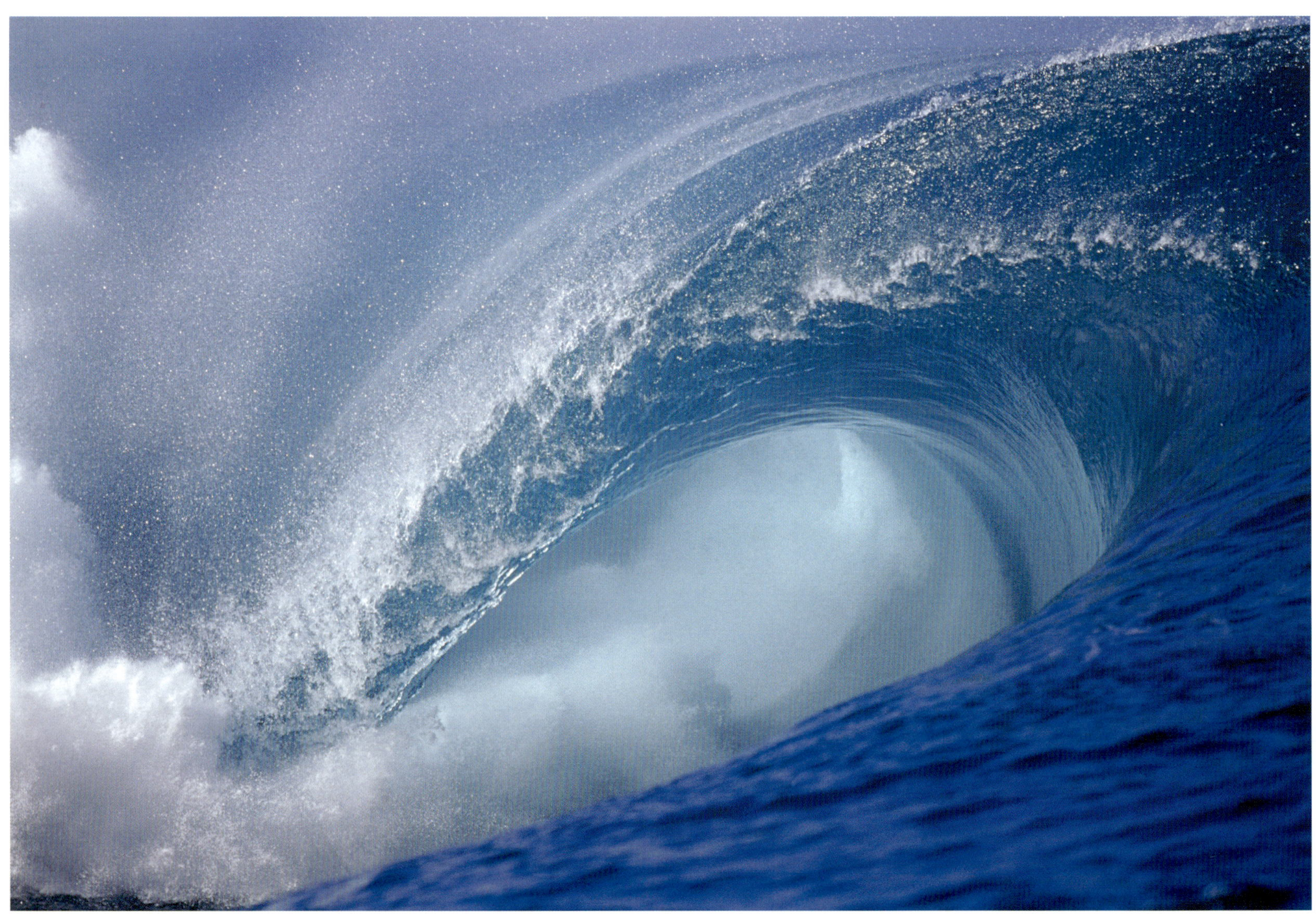

The Quiet
inside of a Loud Monster.

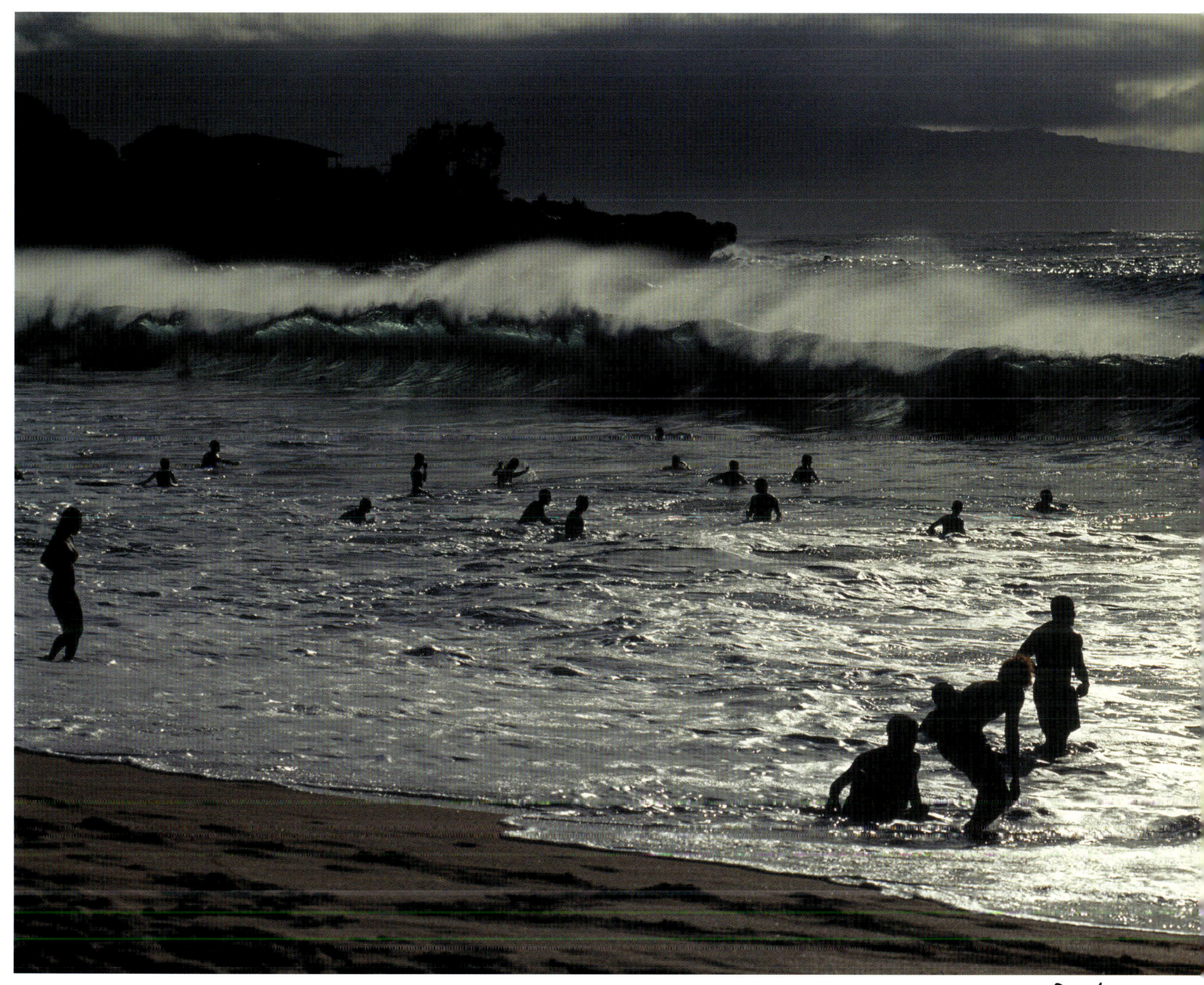

Dark,
Human Forms

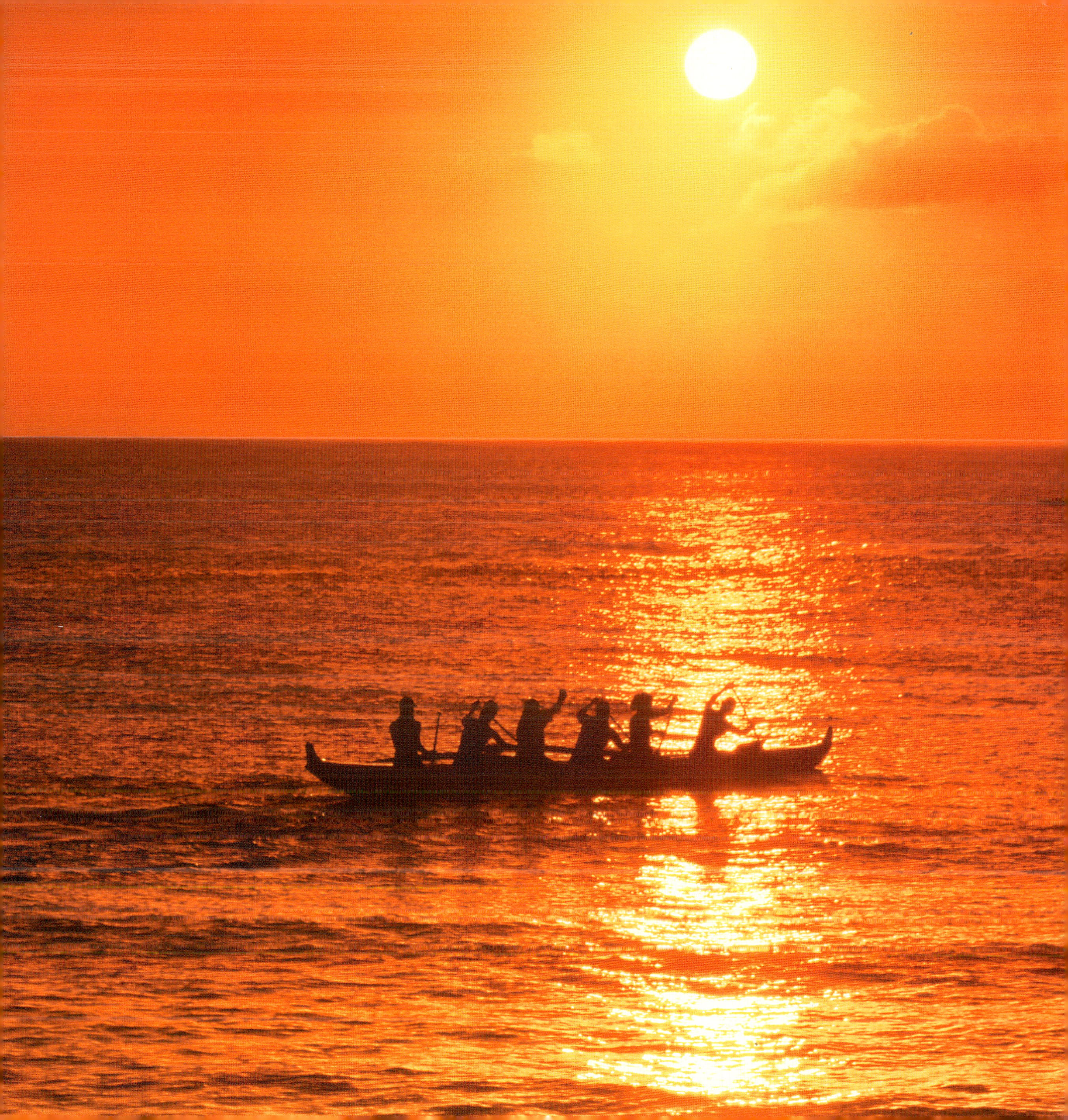

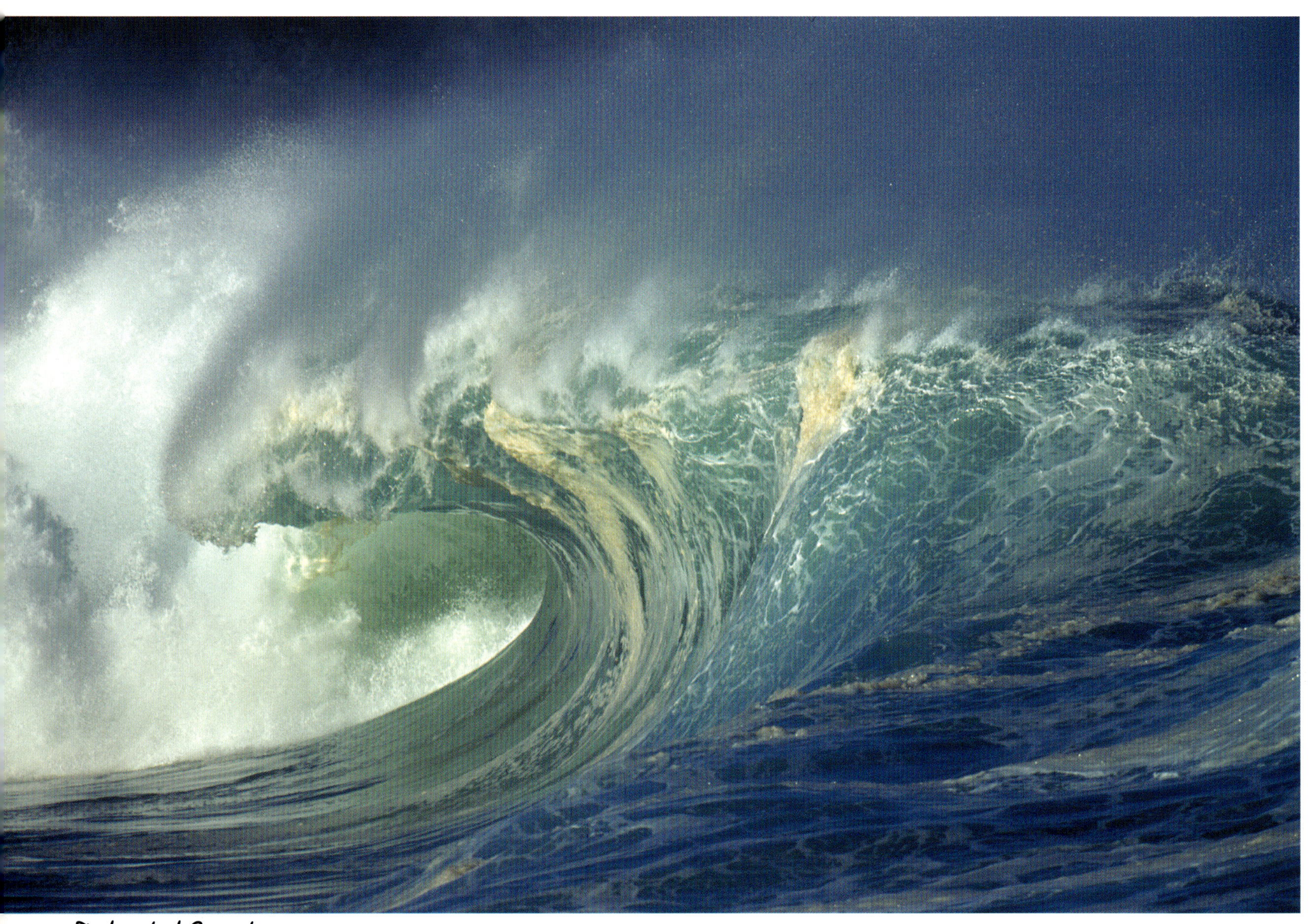

Defiant of Gravity,
a wave holds itself up—quite a ceiling—above
the same saltwater it consists of. Arctic Ocean.

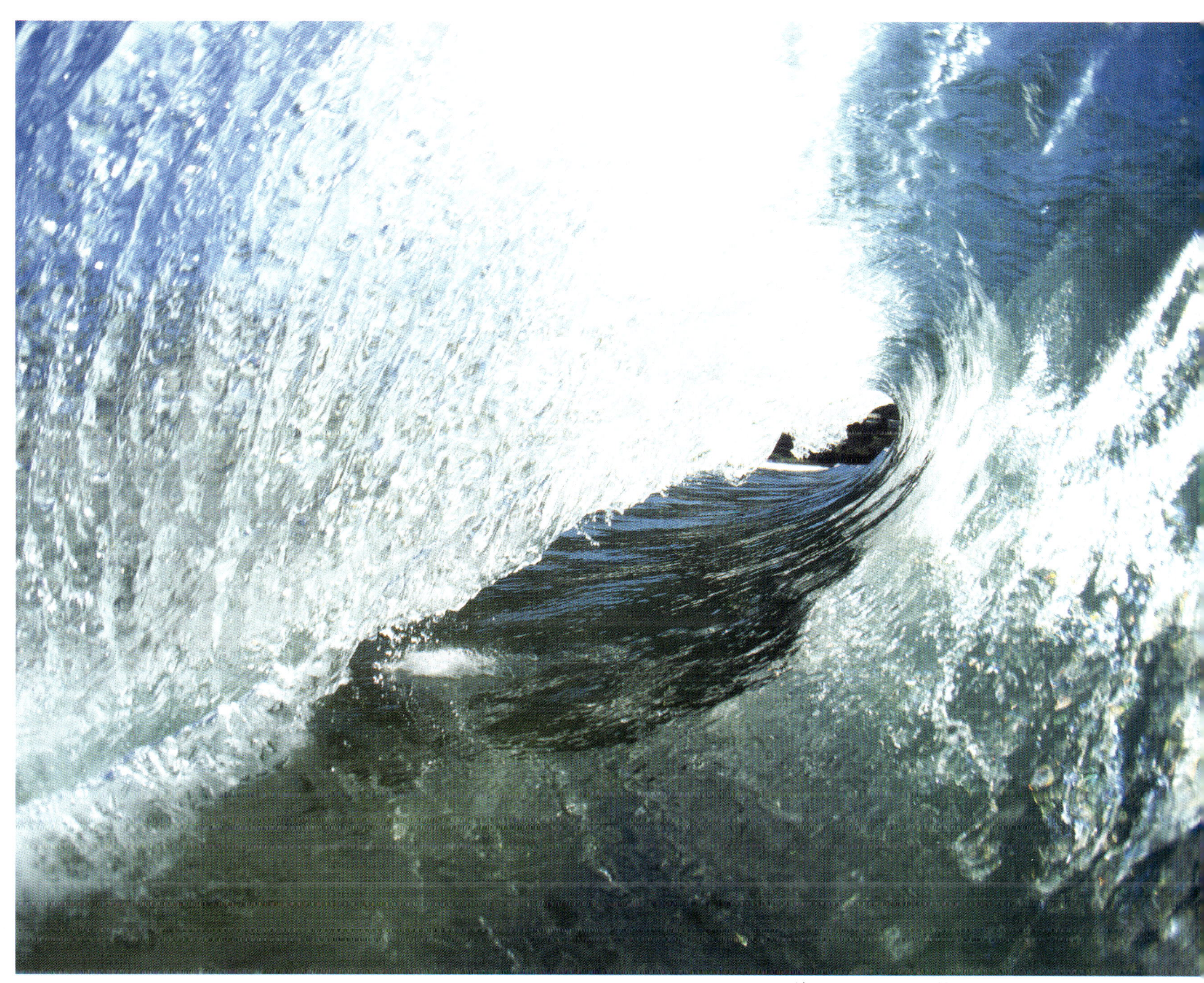

The Curtain Falls
over a wave that has traveled thousands of miles
across the Pacific Ocean, only to conclude its final
act on an island near the Equator.

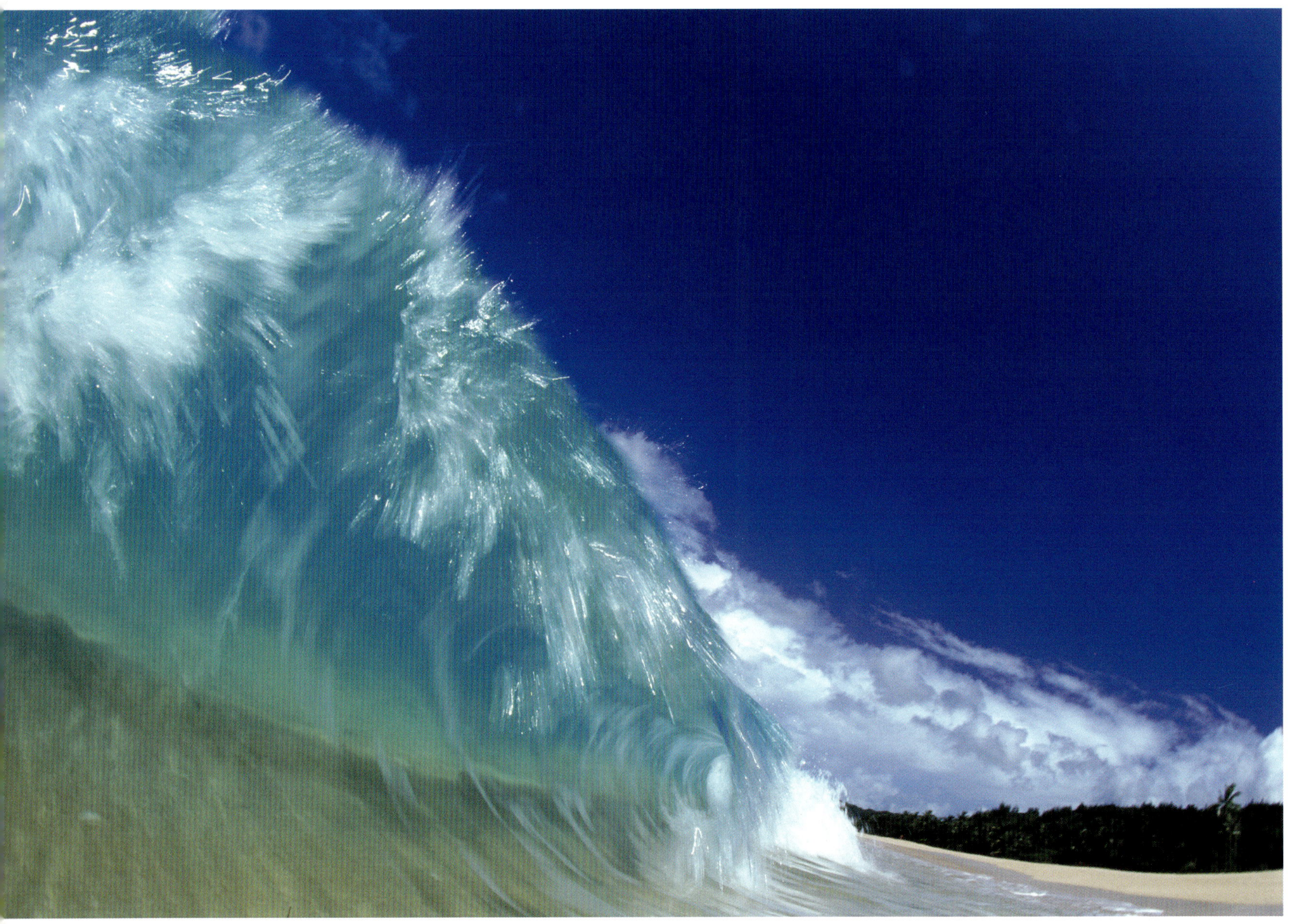

WaterColors on the Sand

The shorebreak caught, in its guilty stage, of moving grains of sand onto shore. The Island of Maui.

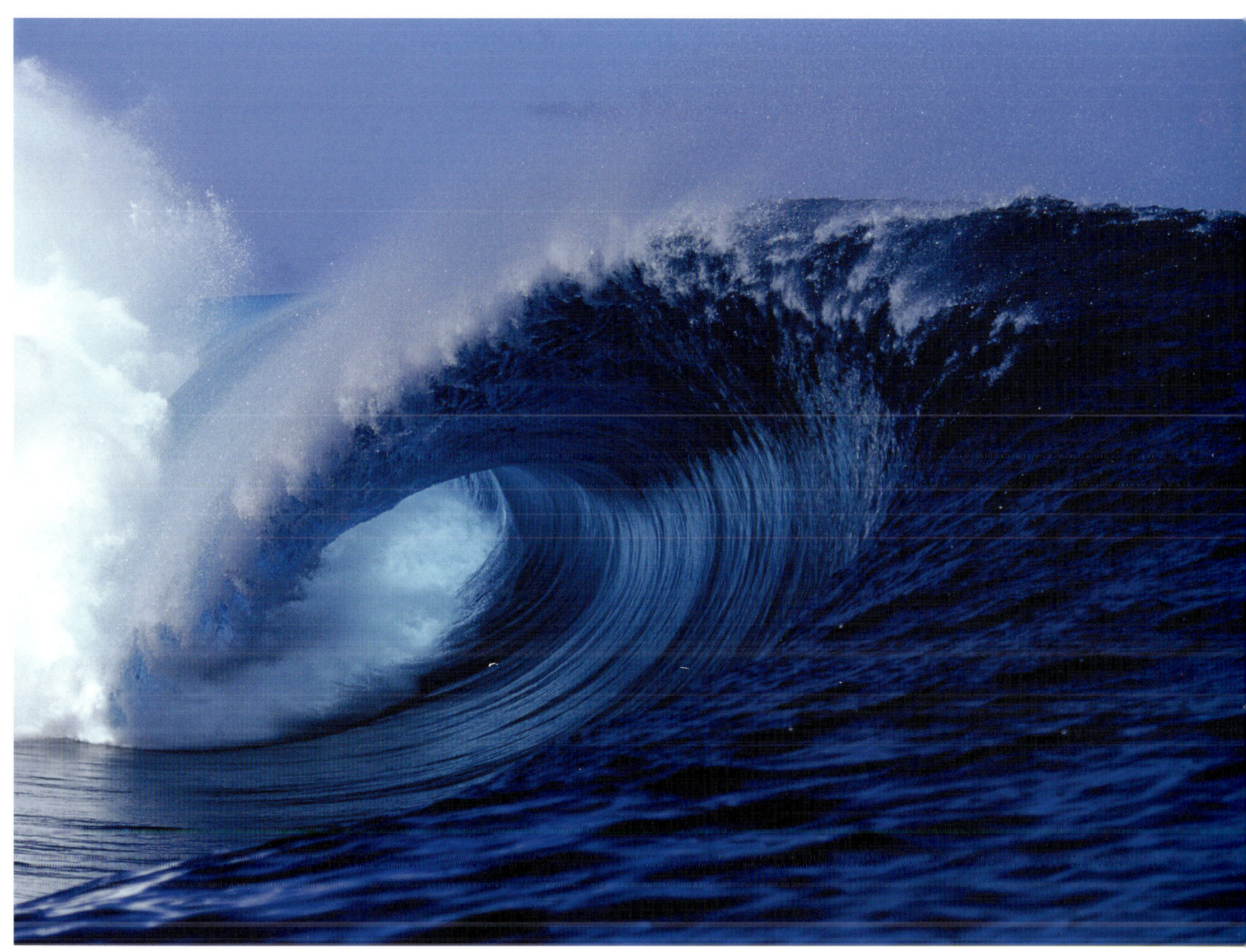

Blue Thunder
in the Fijian Islands.

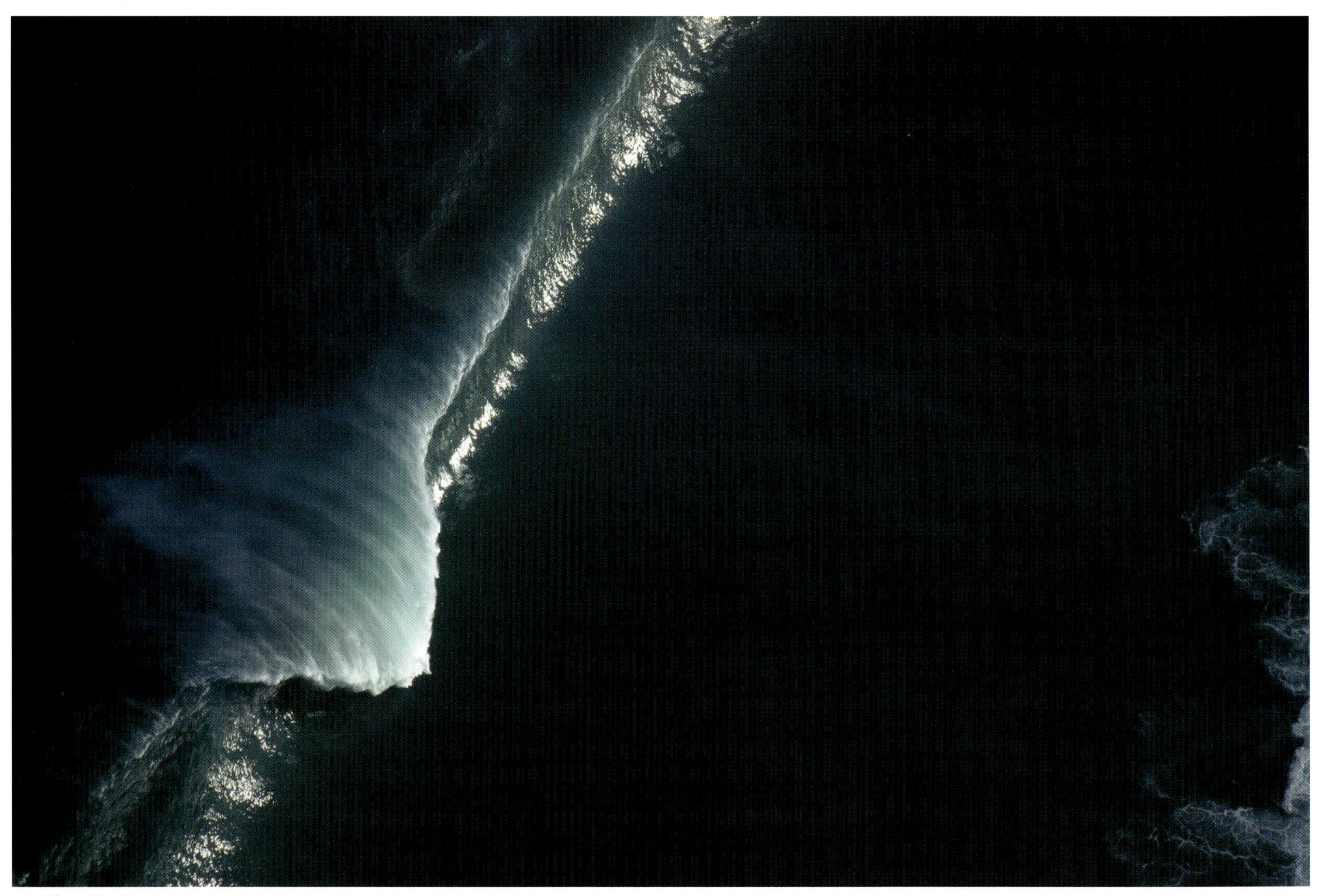

A Bird's Eye View of a Wave
A helicopter was used to take this photograph.
Birds don't realize the luck that was bestowed
upon them. North Pacific Ocean.

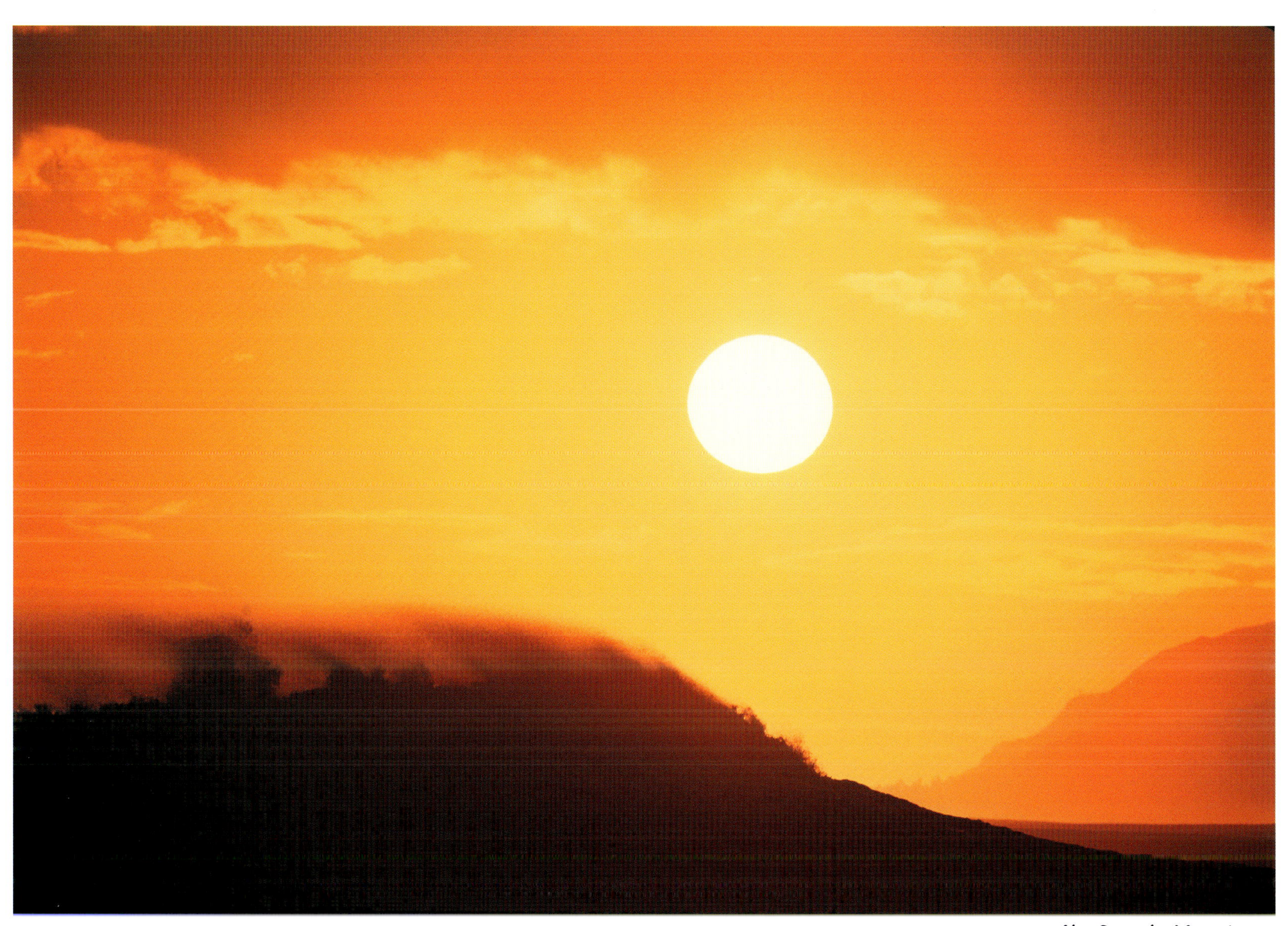

The Dusk Monster
of the North Atlantic Ocean.

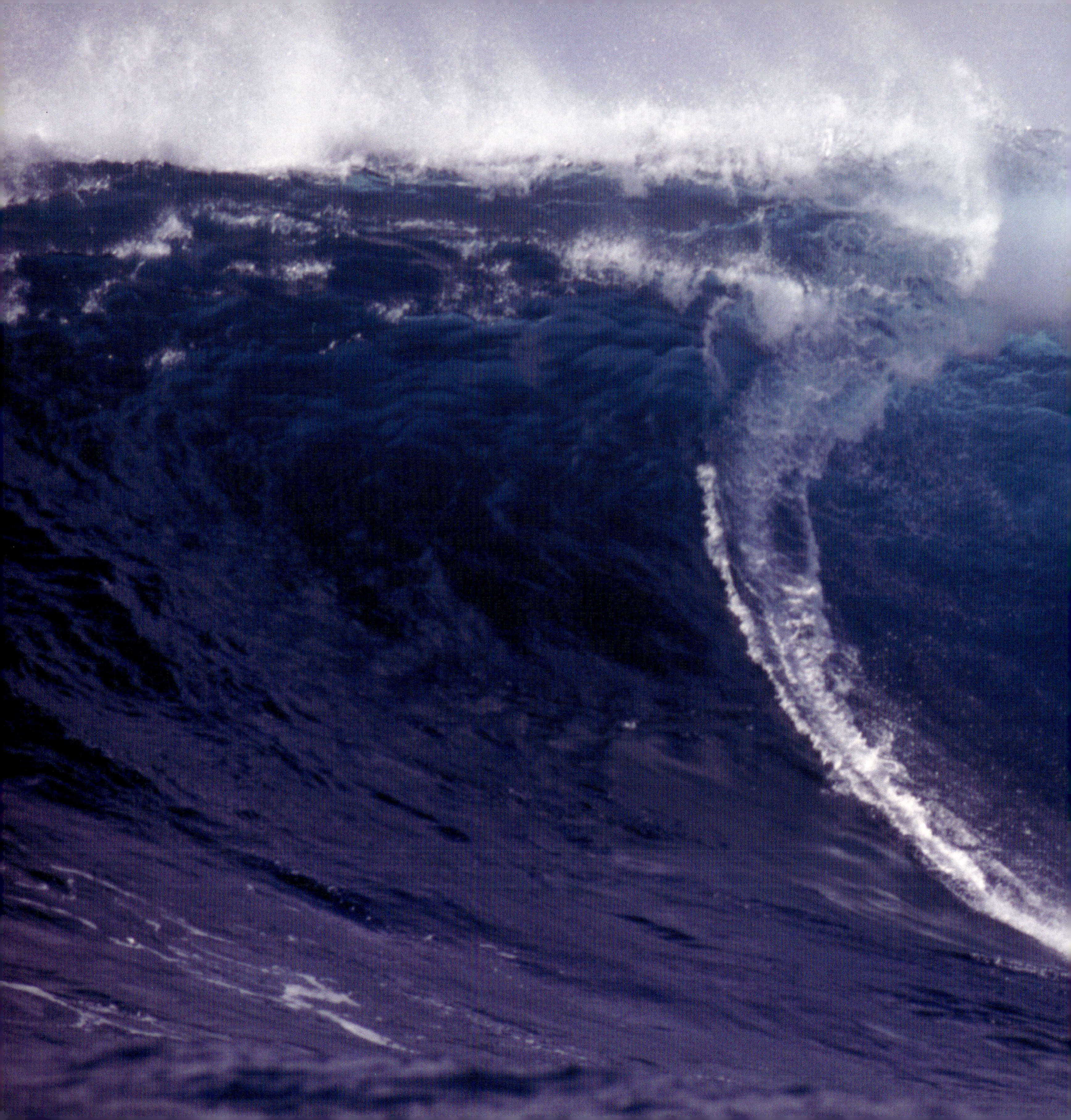

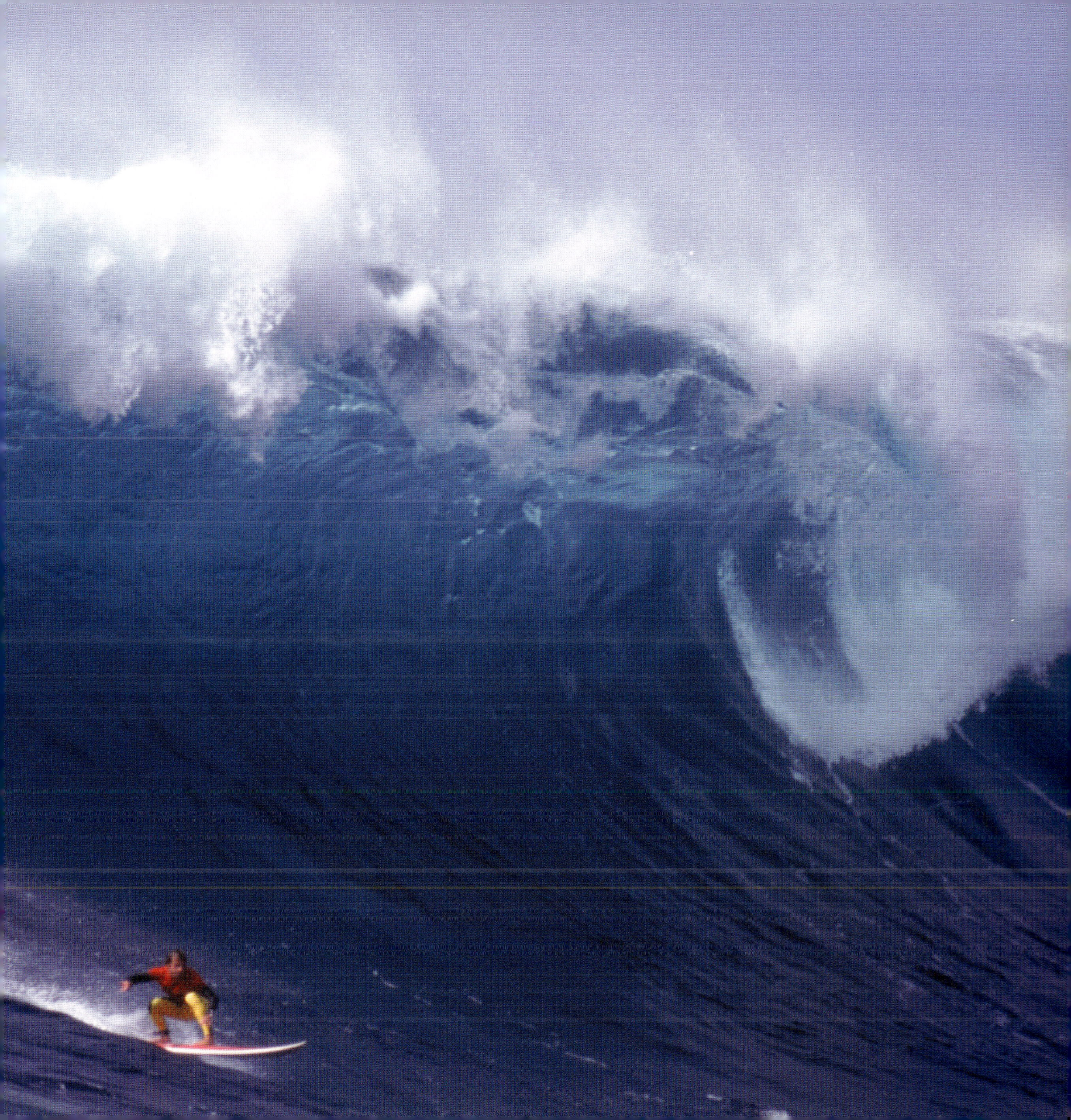

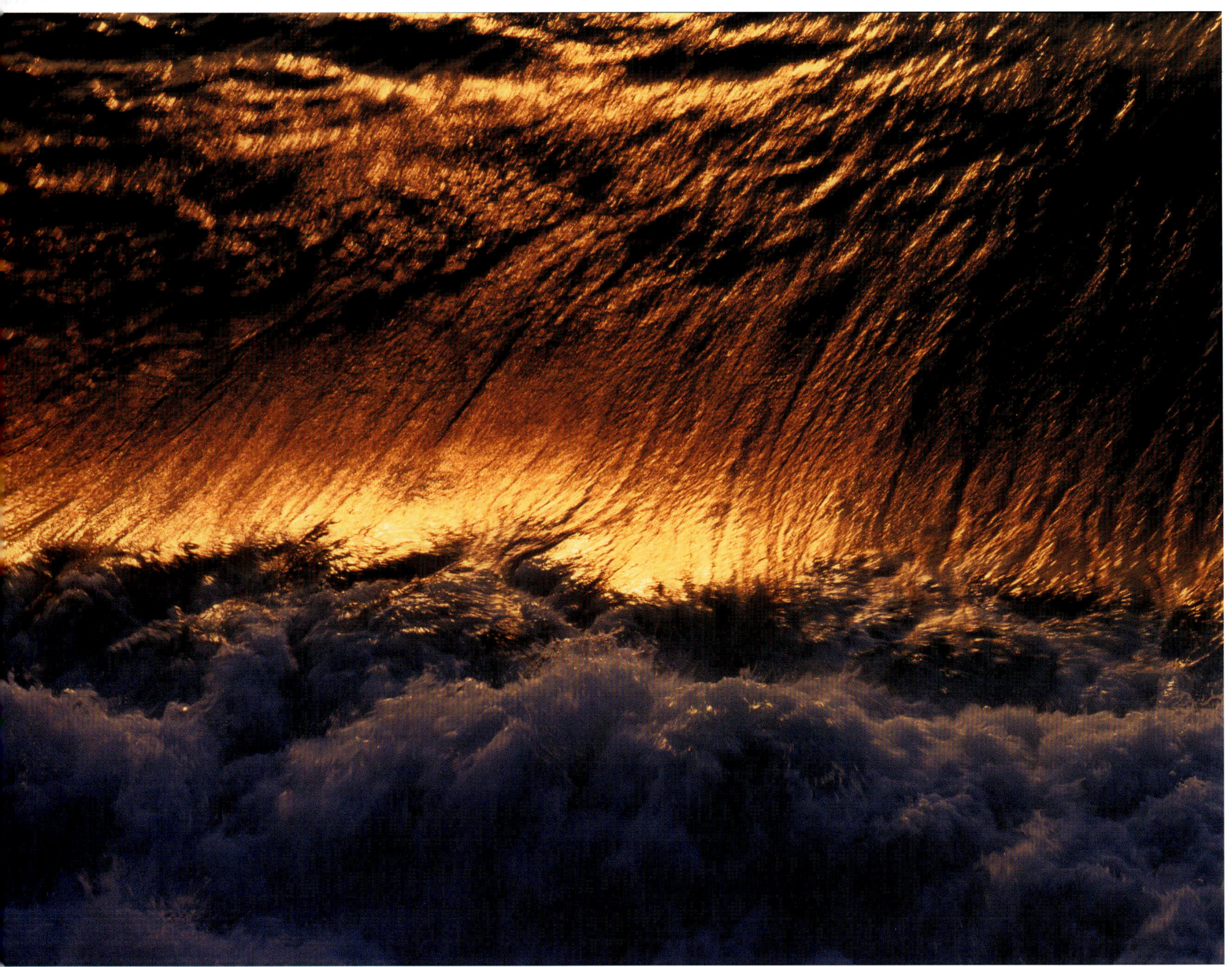

A Sheet of Gold
is cast as foam from a passing wave
rushes towards shallow saltwater.

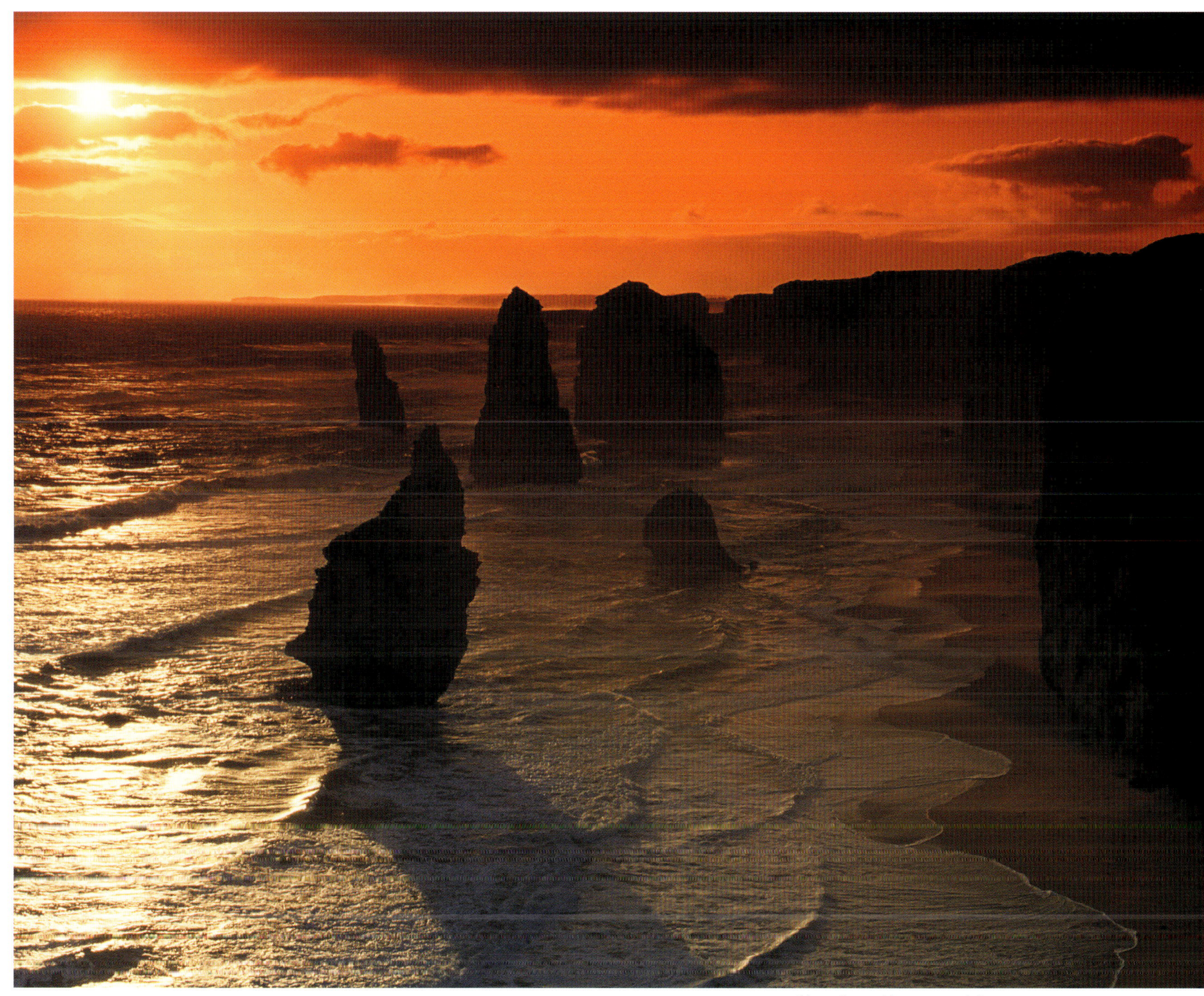

The Apostles caught
as they stand hard against the erosion and decaying forces that the ocean brings with it. The Apostles take in a sunset during it all.

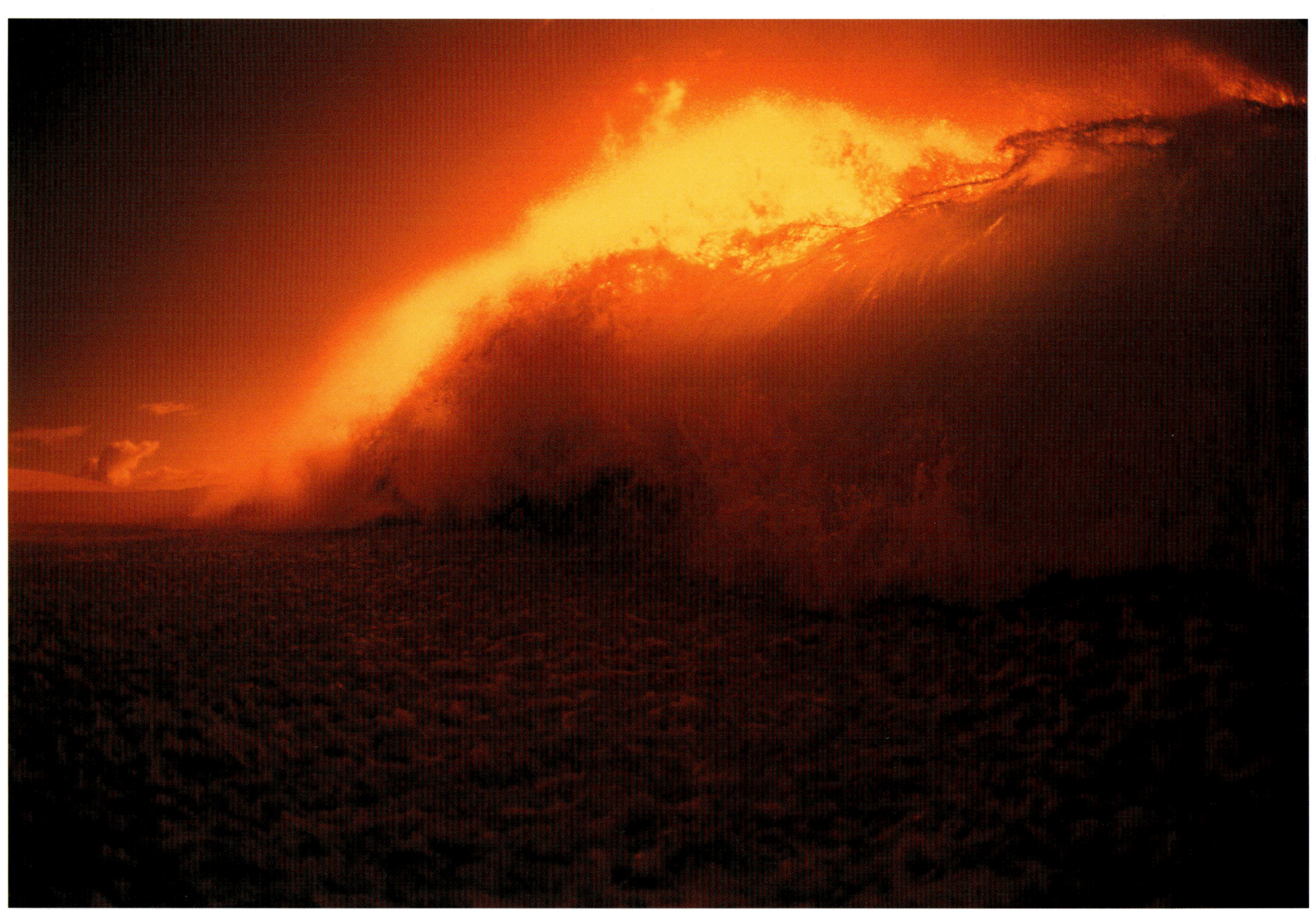

Fireball
of Saltwater. Flames seem to erupt from
this wave as it burns through shore.

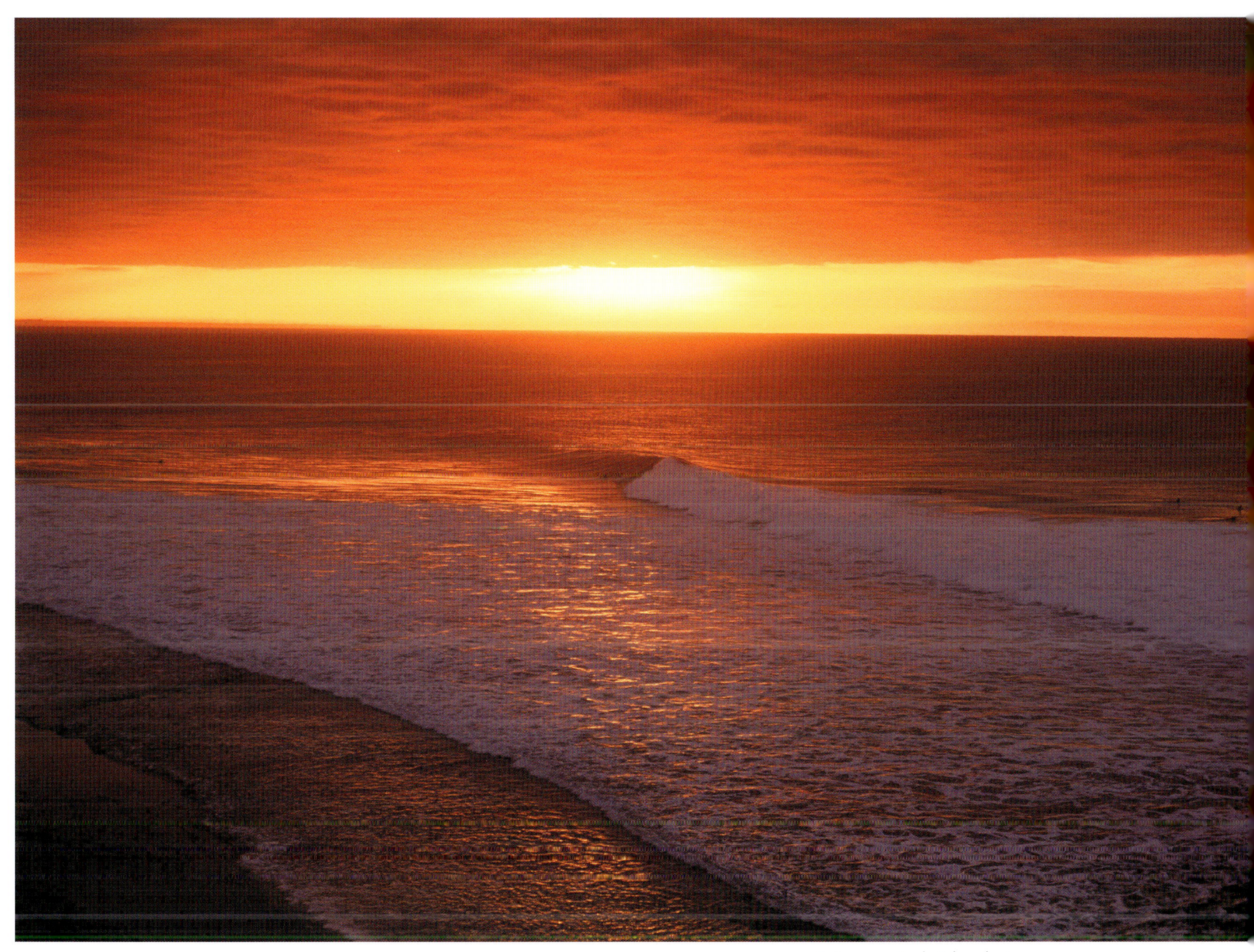

Warm, Red Blanket
finishing the Light of Day. Jefferey's Bay, South Africa.

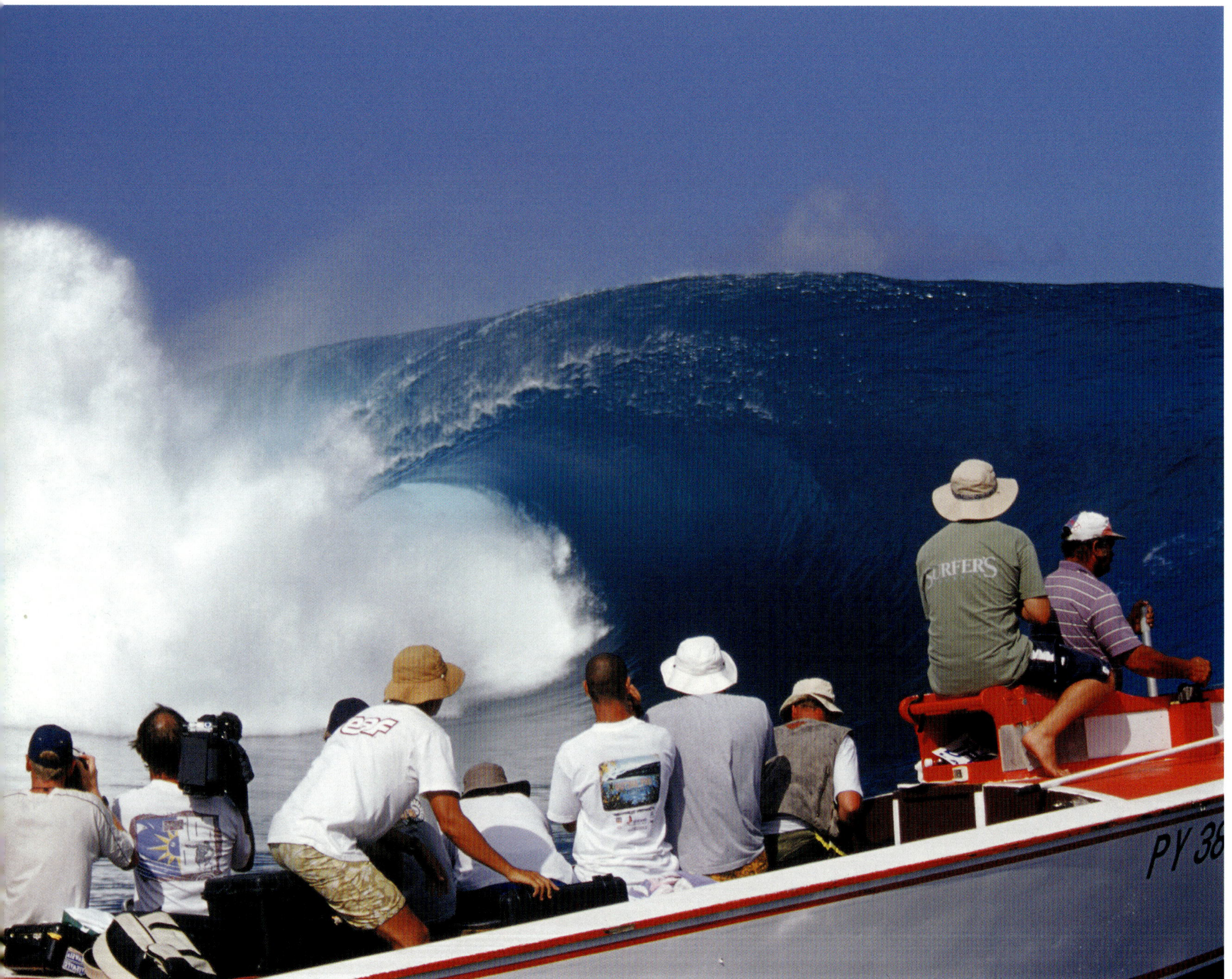

Fascination and Fear,
much like that of a car accident, humans are drawn
to watch from a distance which is considered safe.
Yet, look at the man with the tan hat. He is ready to
jump ship.

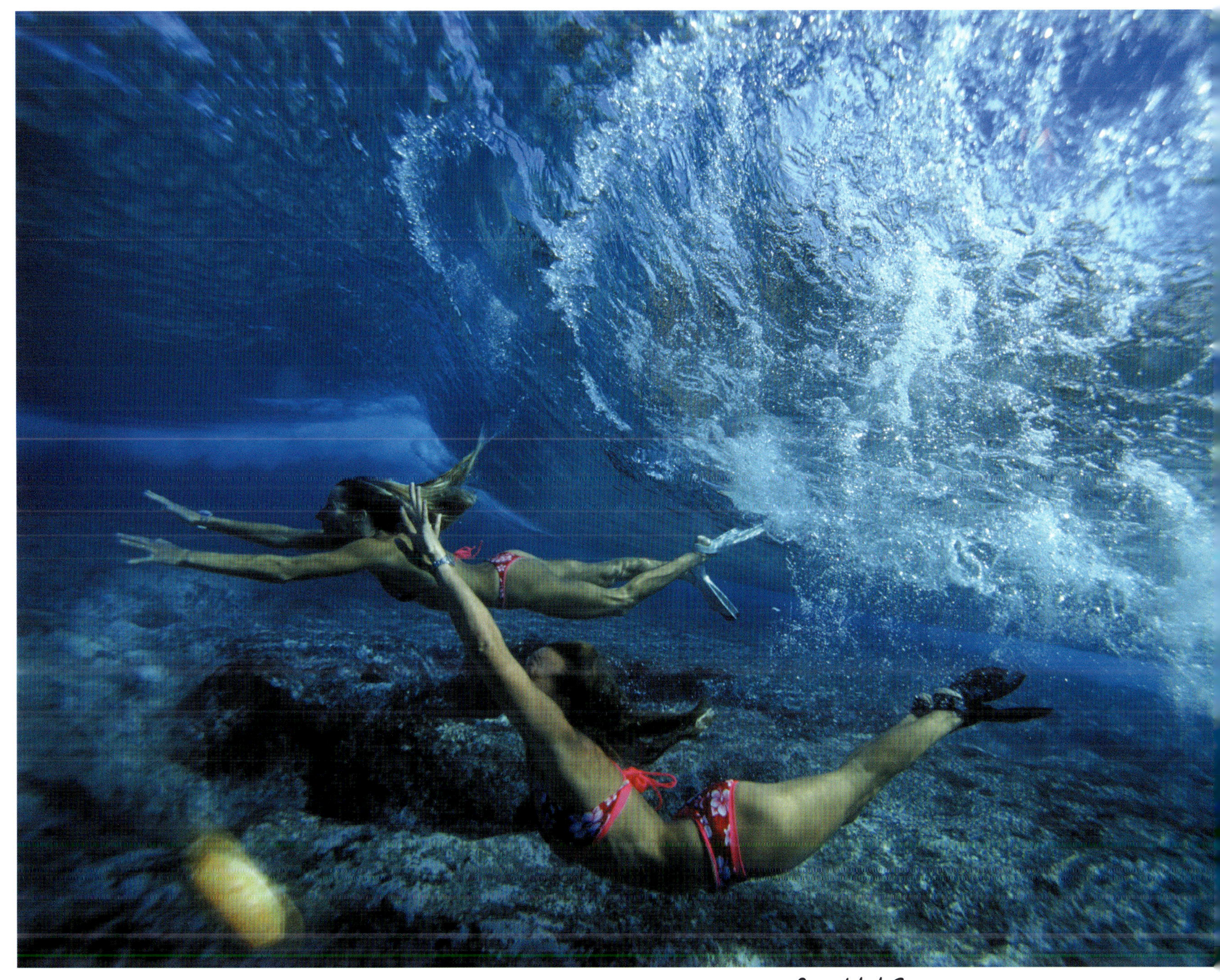

Beautiful Form:
the women and the wave. South Pacific Ocean.

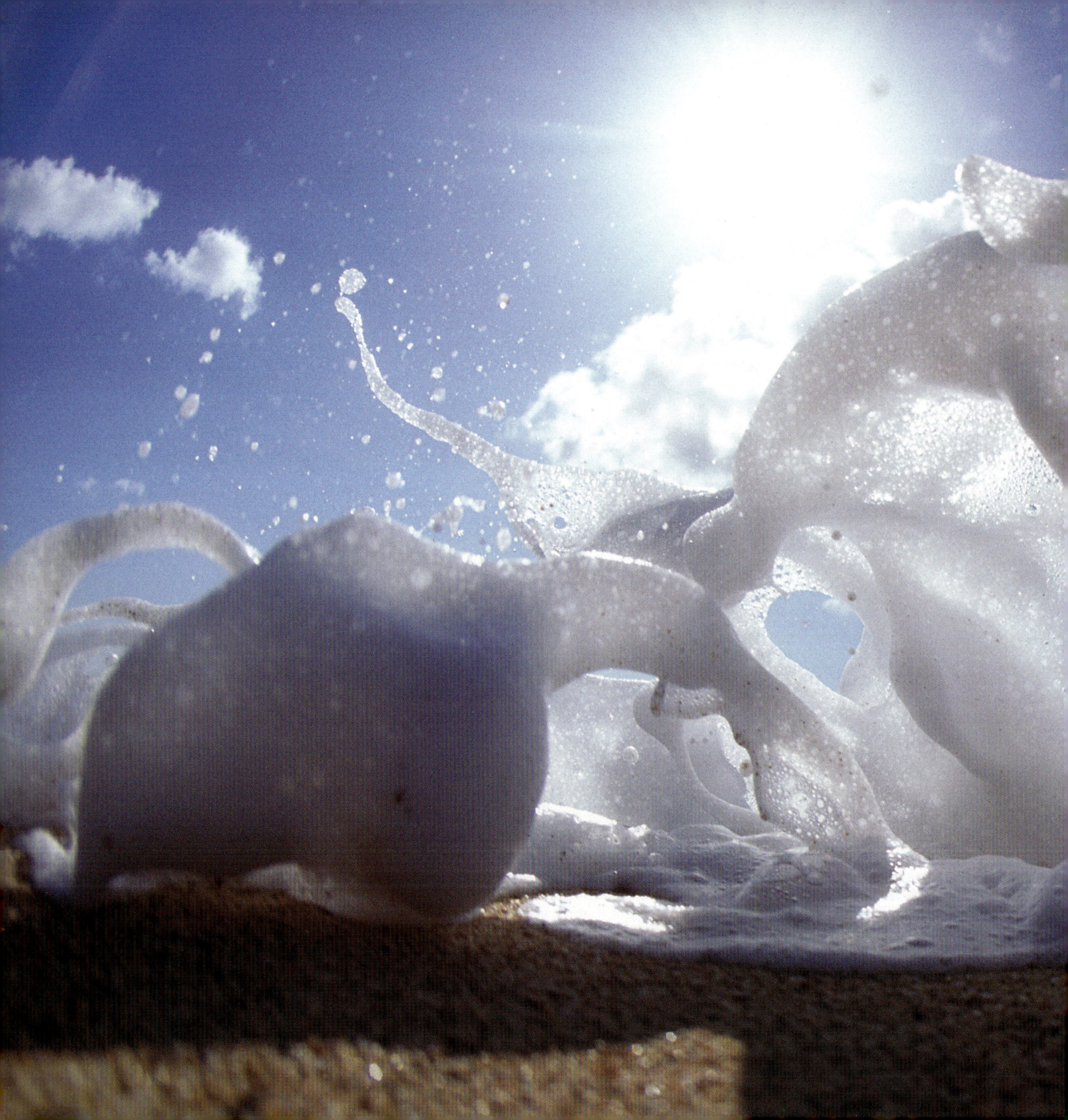

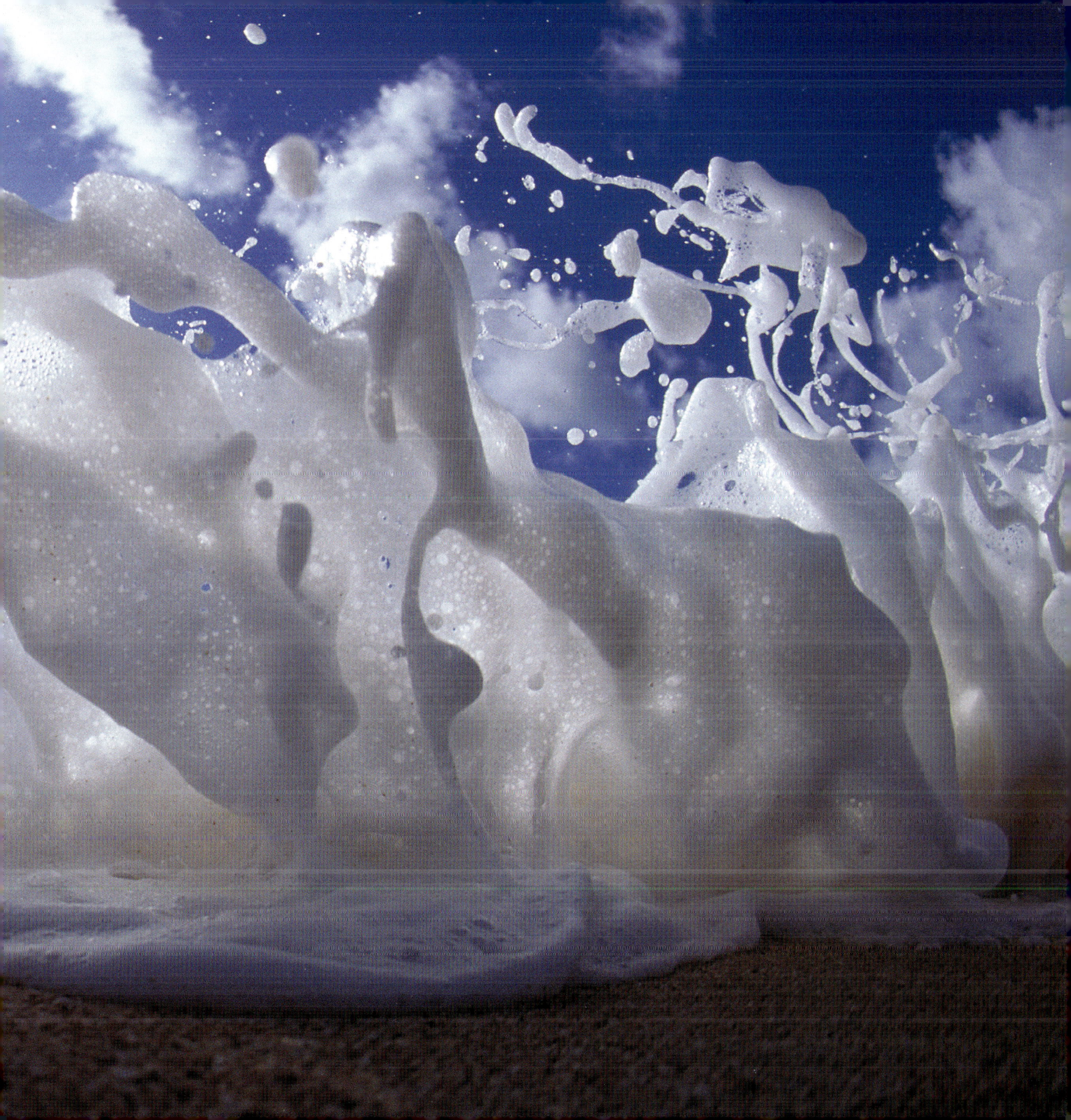

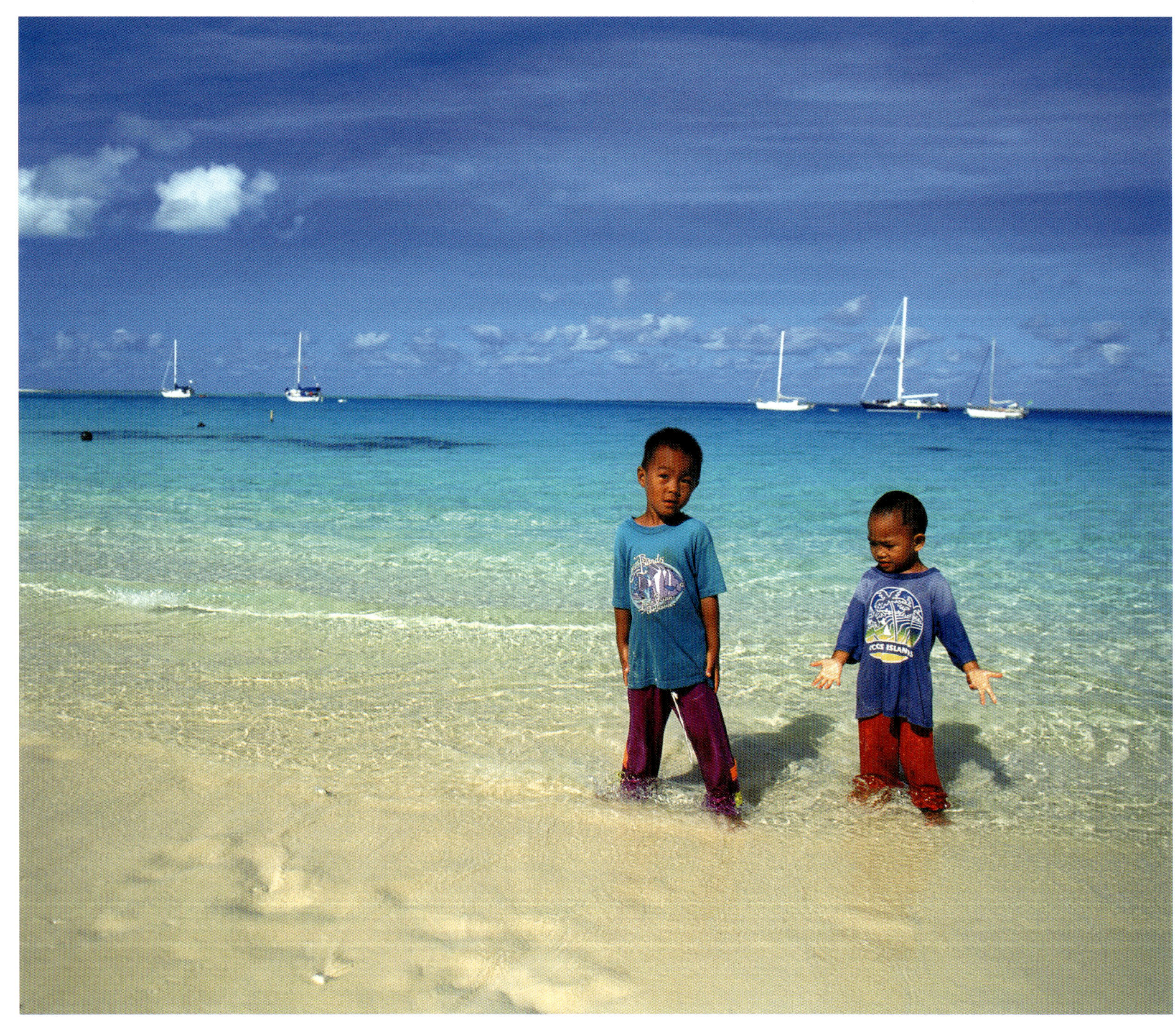

Two Boys,
anchored in the Sand, just like the Boats. Carribean Sea.

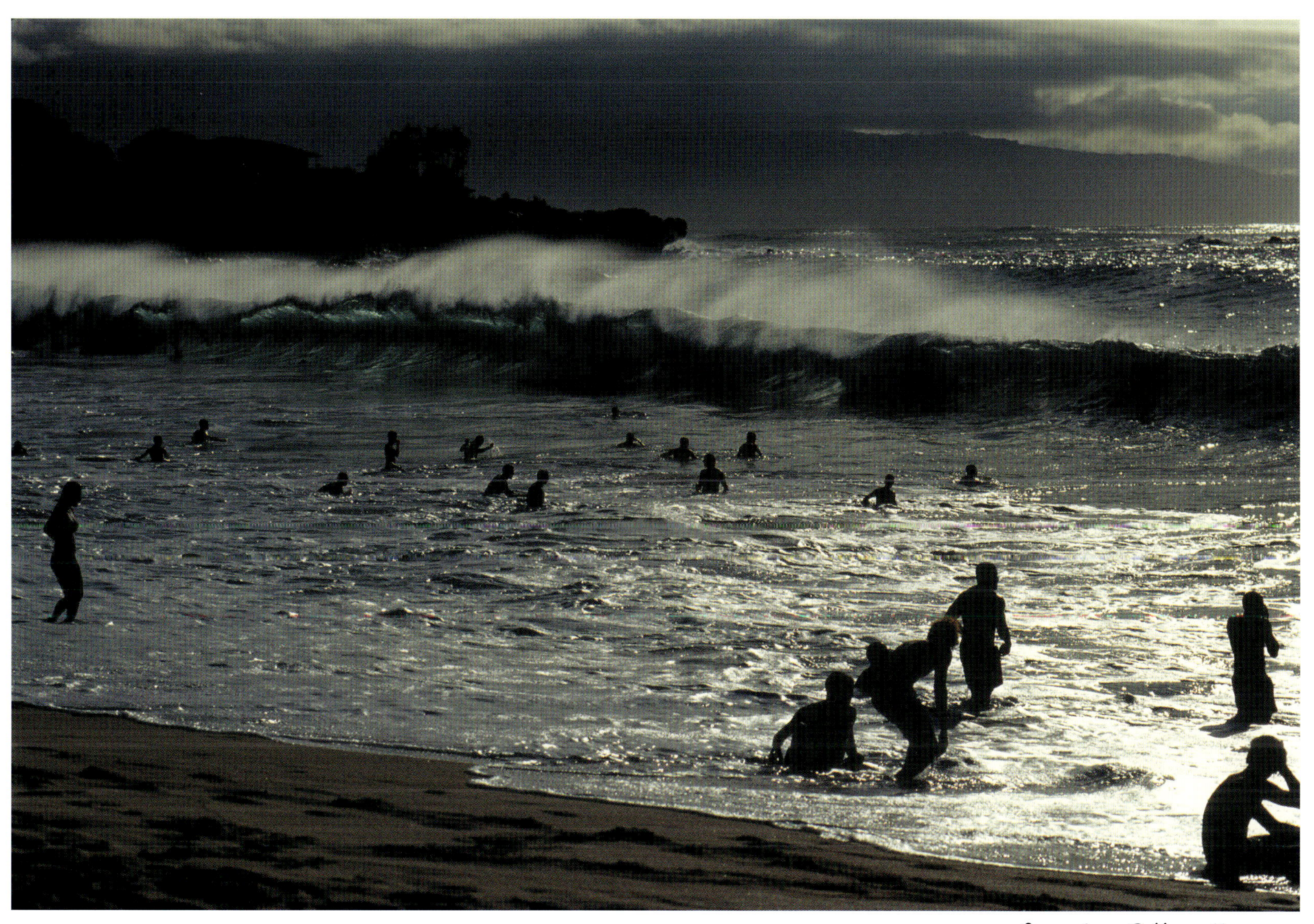

Primitive Silhouettes
move into the saltwater of the ocean.

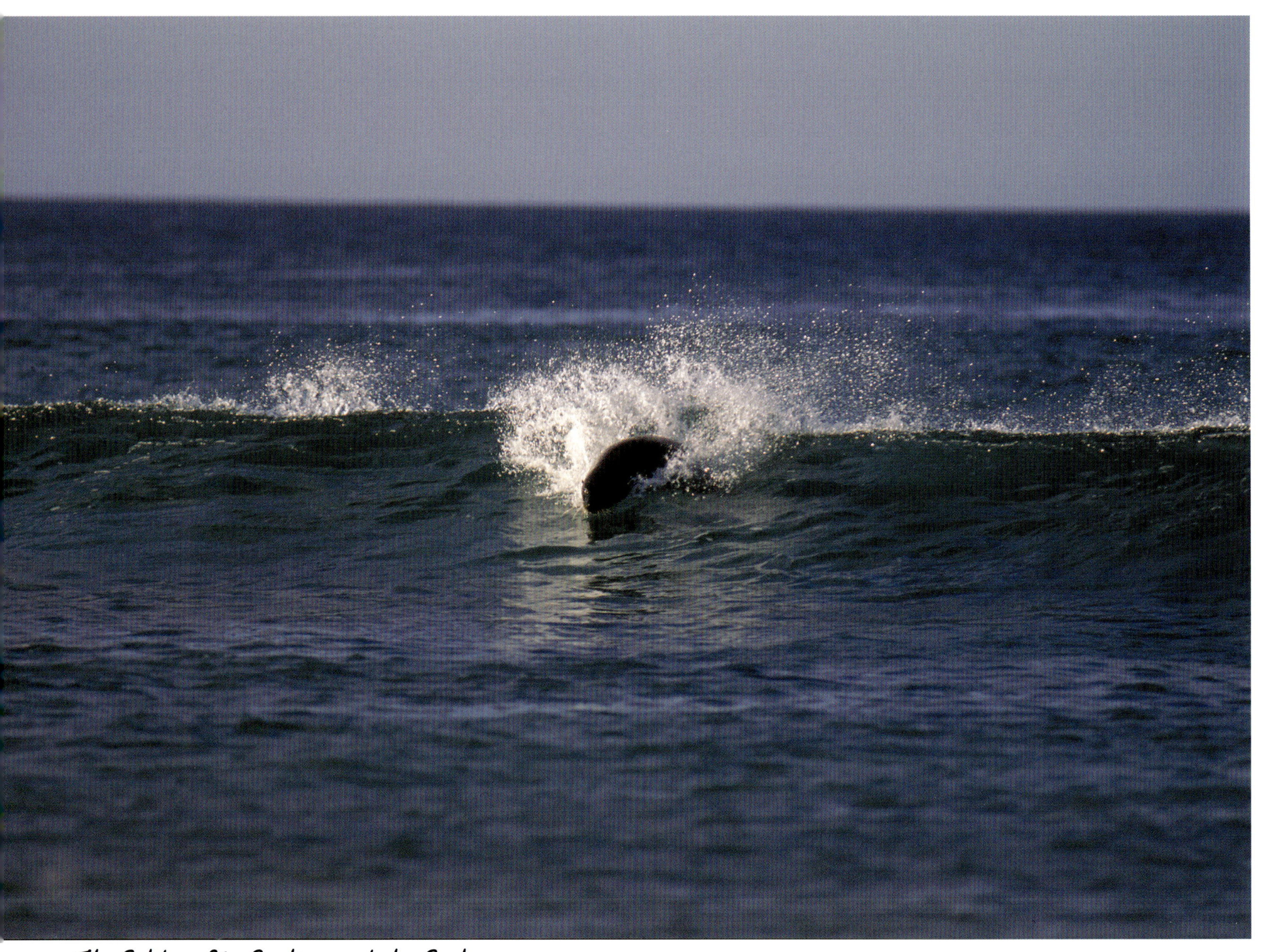

The Solitary Un-Confinement of a Seal

Seals will regularly use the energy of waves, riding
them for what can only be seen as amusement.

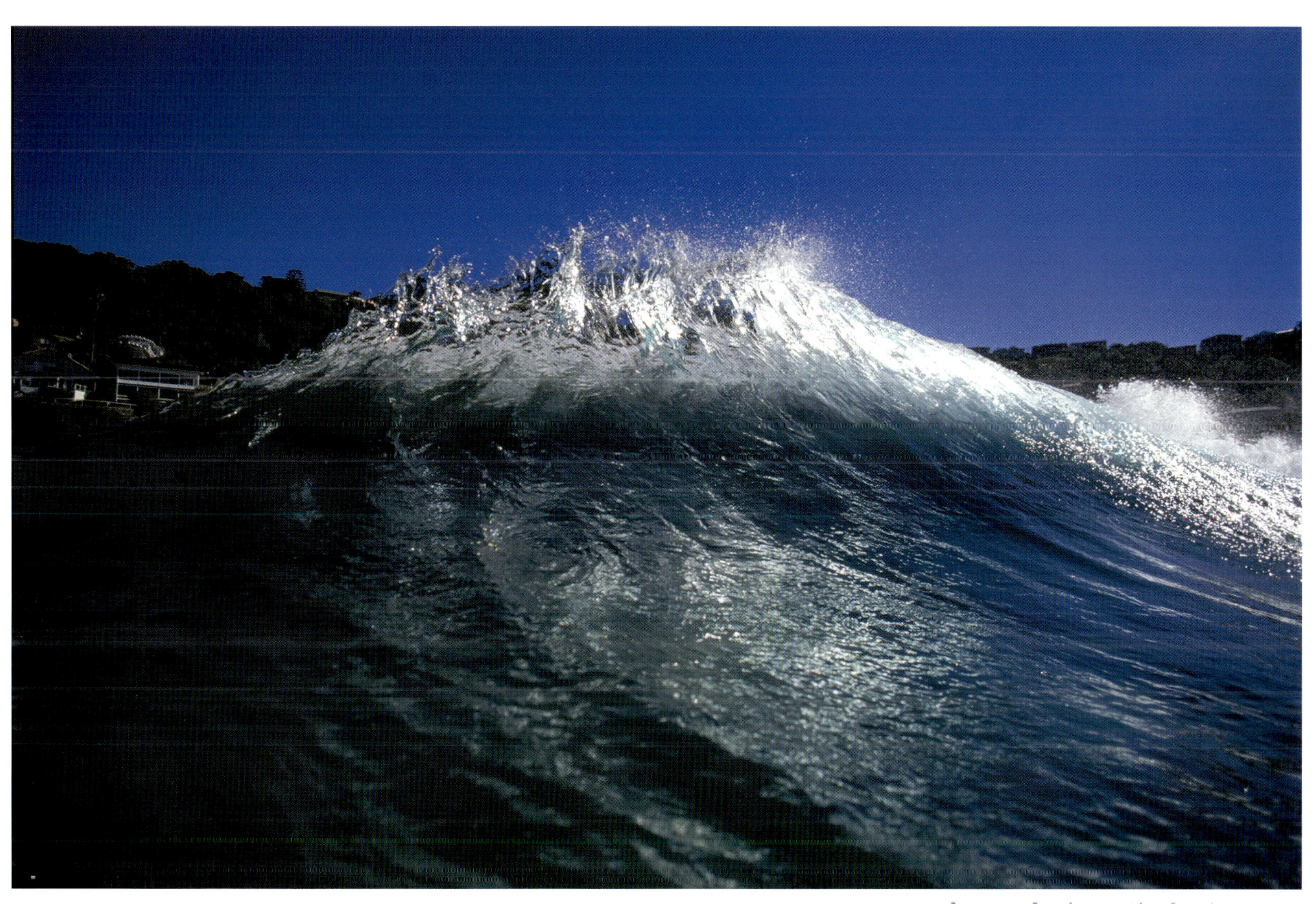

Precise Peaks in the Water,
jagged and mean. A wave that forms a volcano.

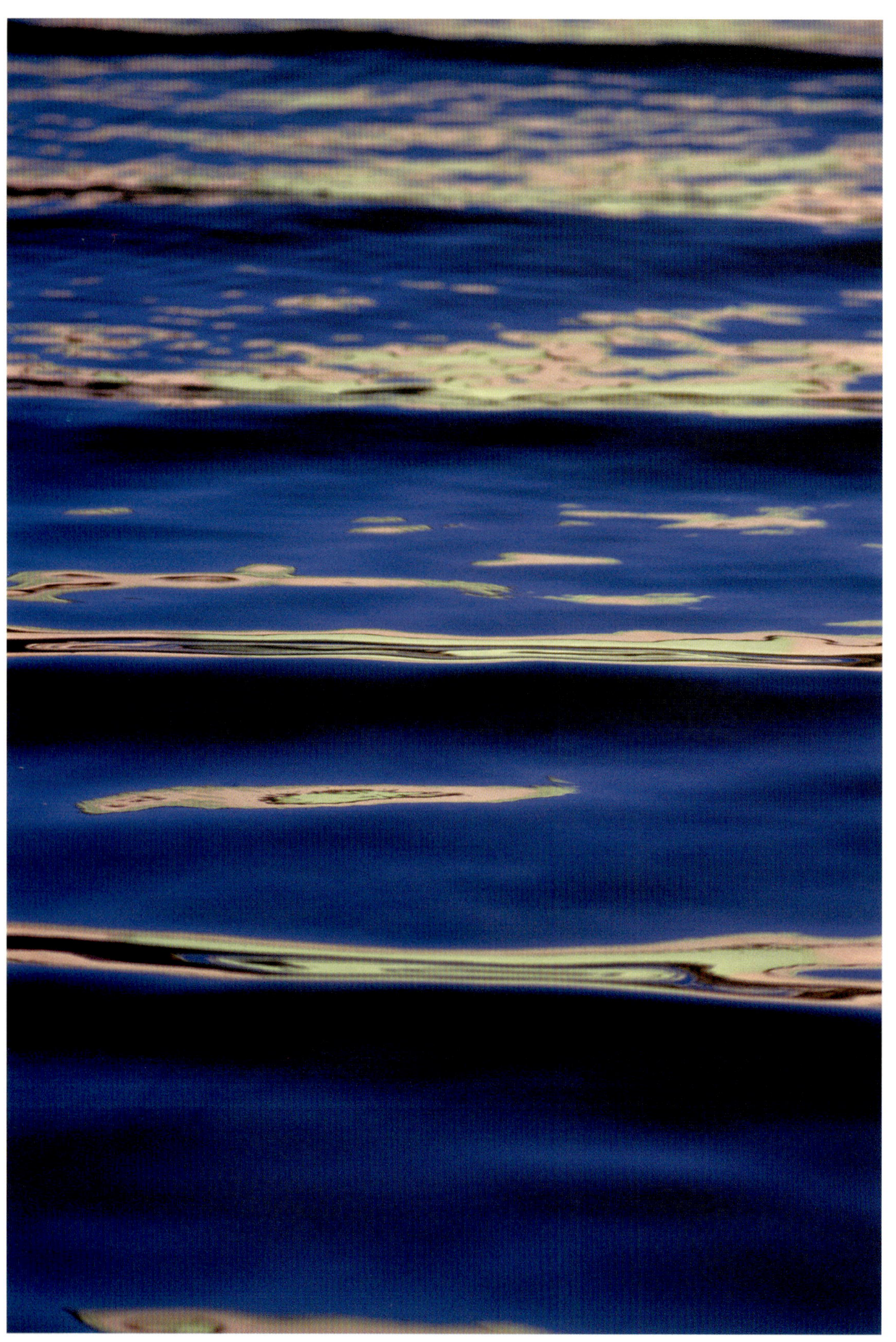

Corduroy
The even patterns of waves as they march forward.

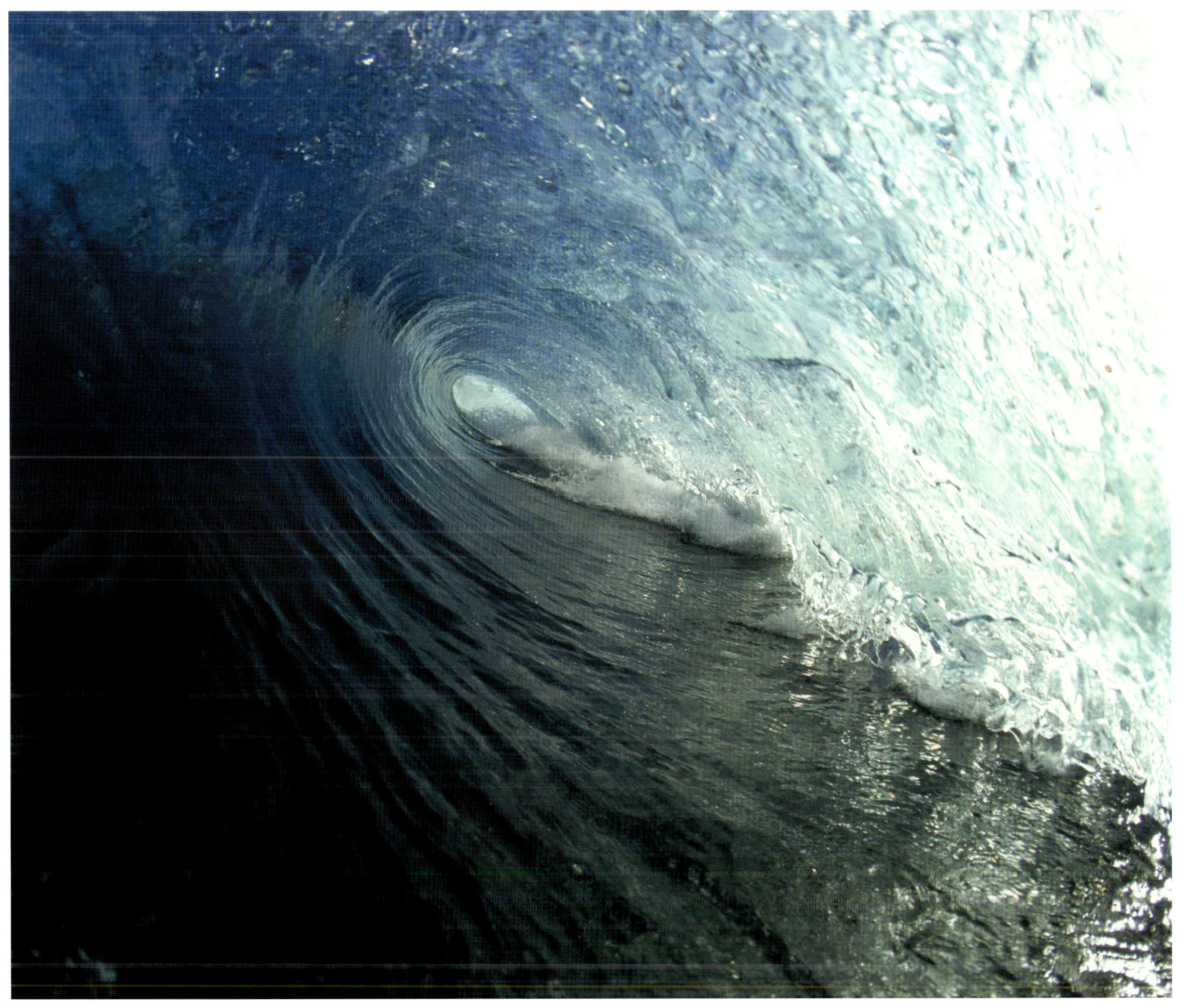

Inside the Womb of a Wave
But this womb is not giving birth, only finishing itself as it falls. South Atlantic Ocean.

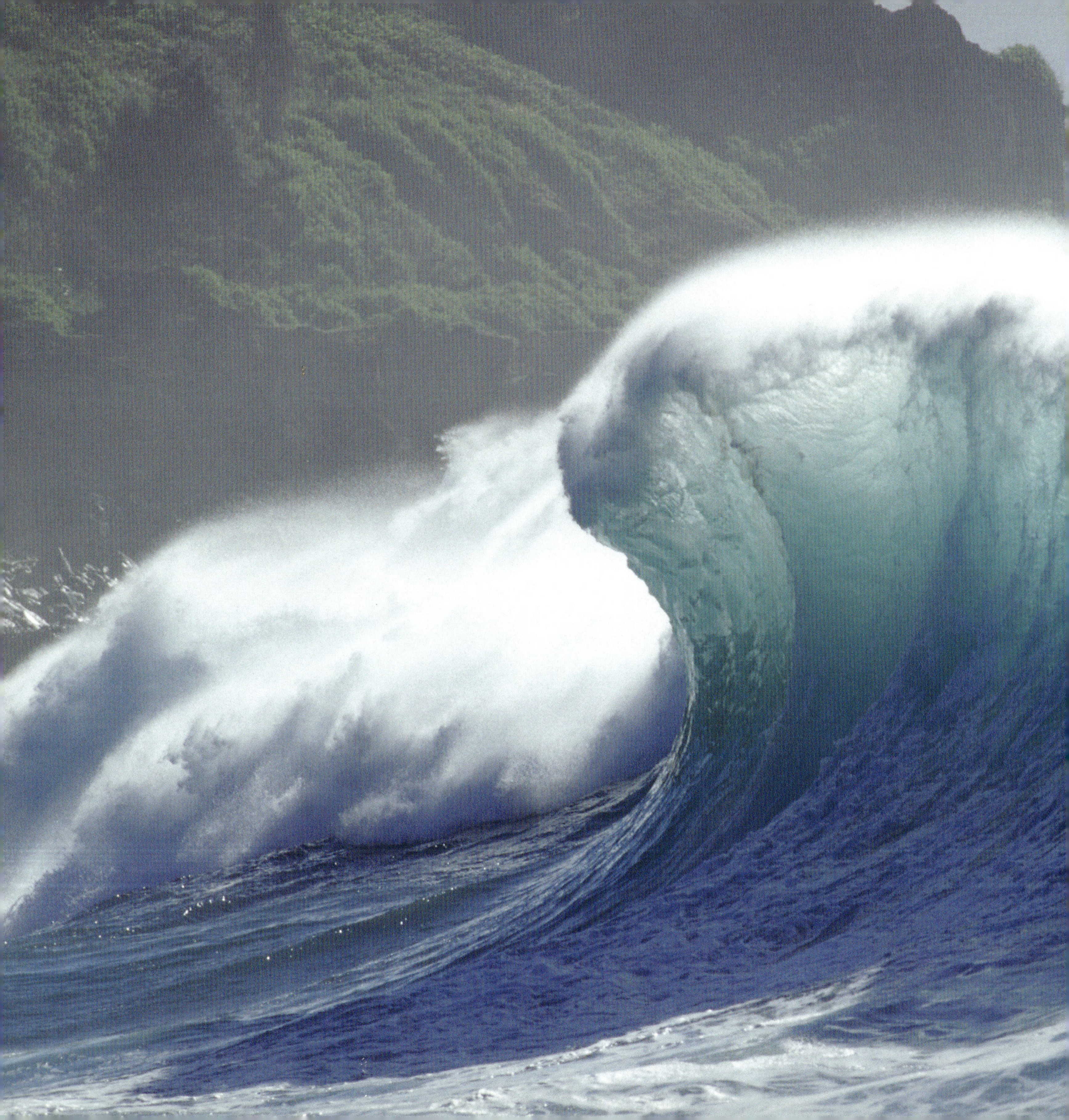

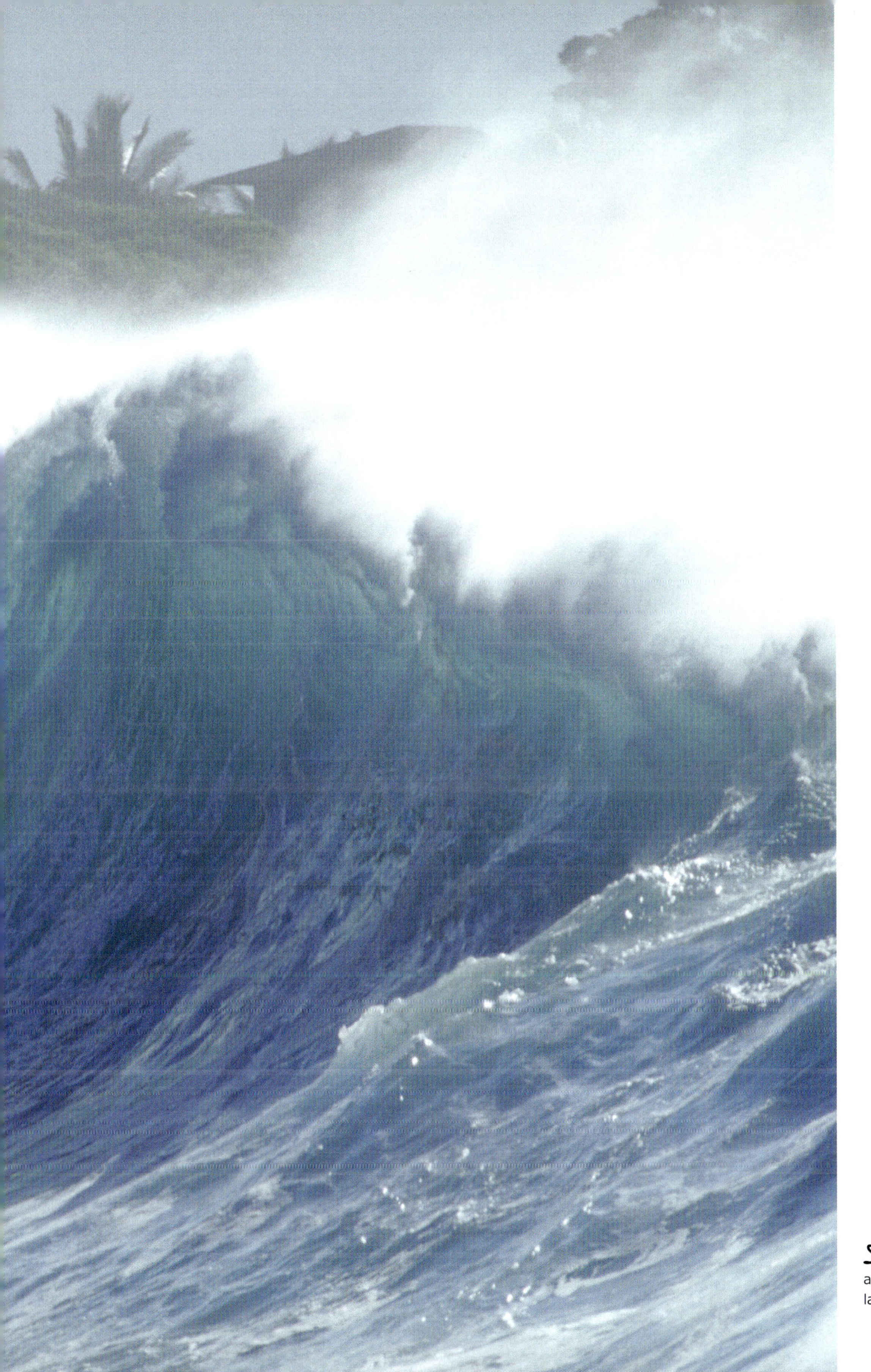

Disorganized and Full of Froth,
a wave that is haphazard and about to offer its
last breath of muscle: stopped for our evaluation.

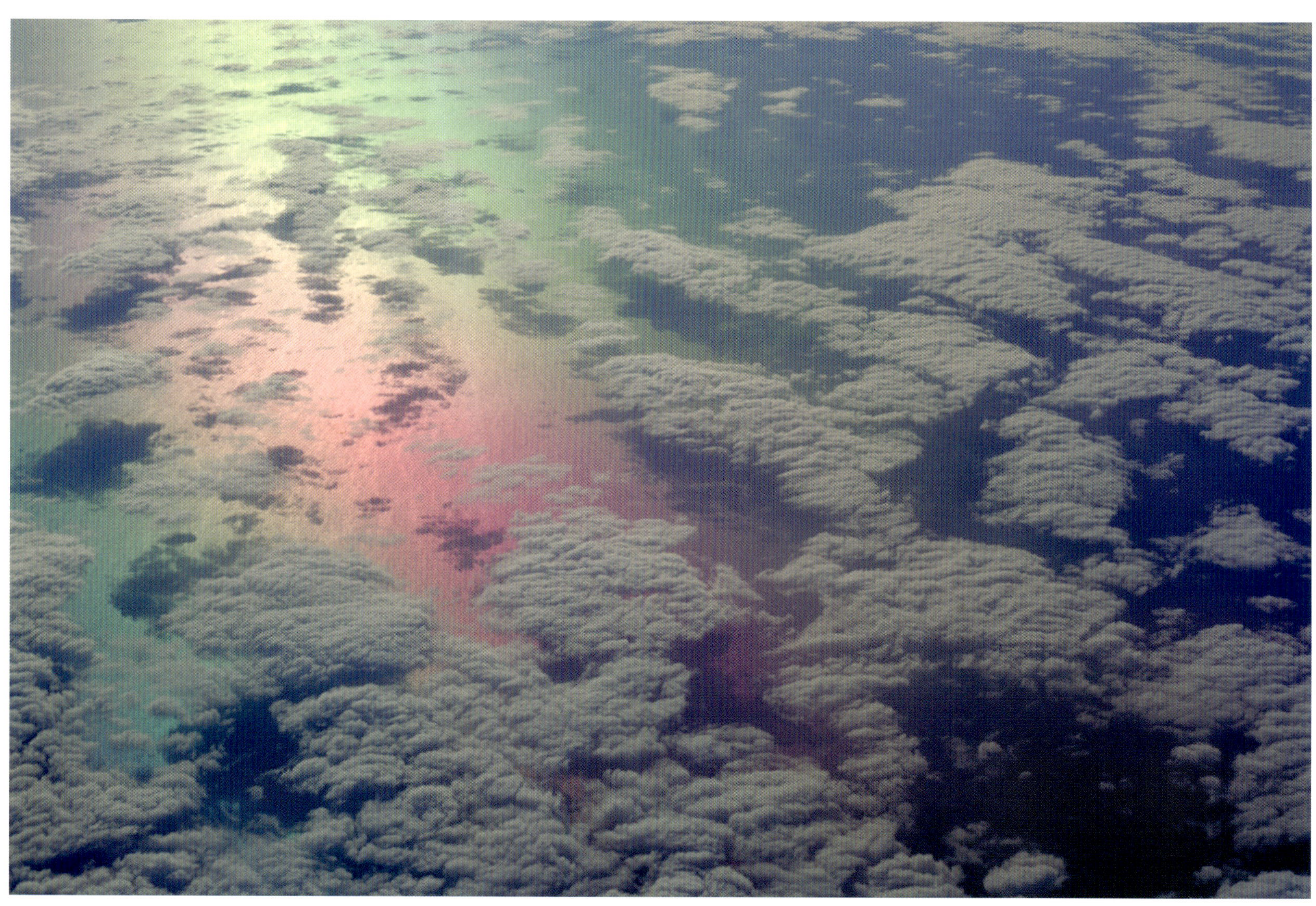

A View from the Heavens
Rainbow on the water and puffs of cotton-like
clouds are the foundation for which it stands.

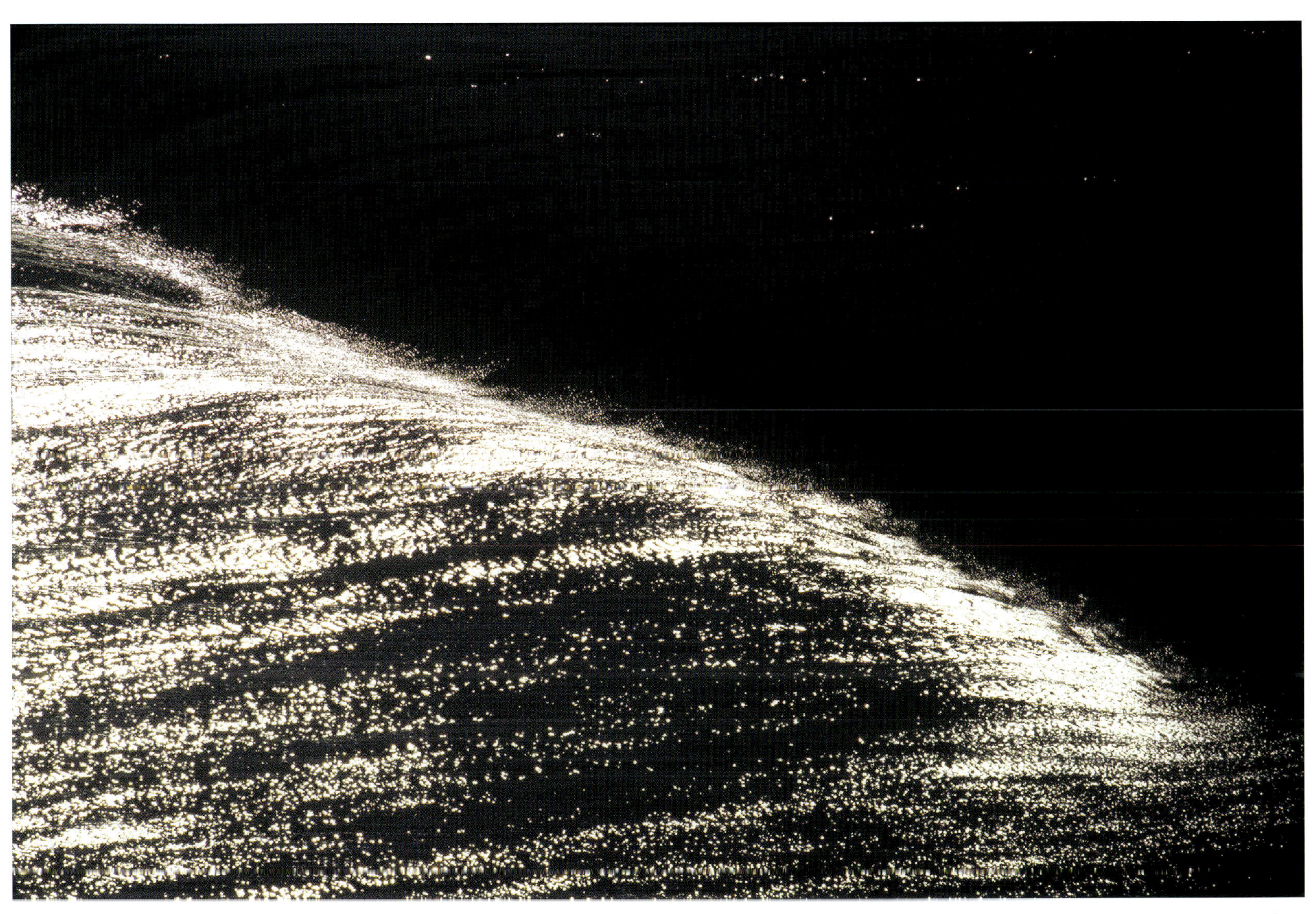

Contrast of White & Black in Symmetry
As if there wasn't enough distinction between the two colors,
this photograph shows the beautiful mesh of the two.

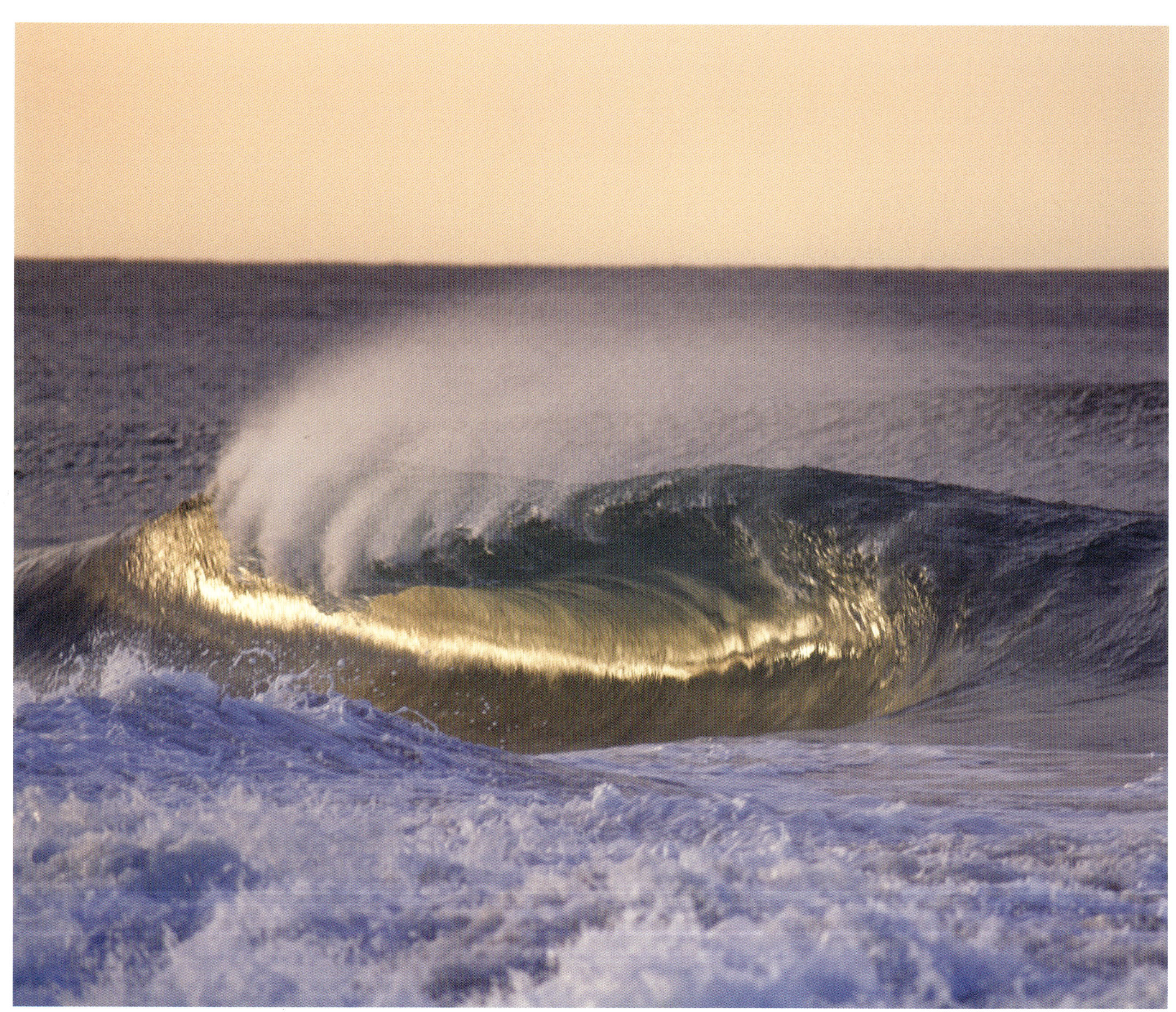

Vein of Gold
in an Australian morning.   A wave with thickness
and a concentrated effort takes center stage.

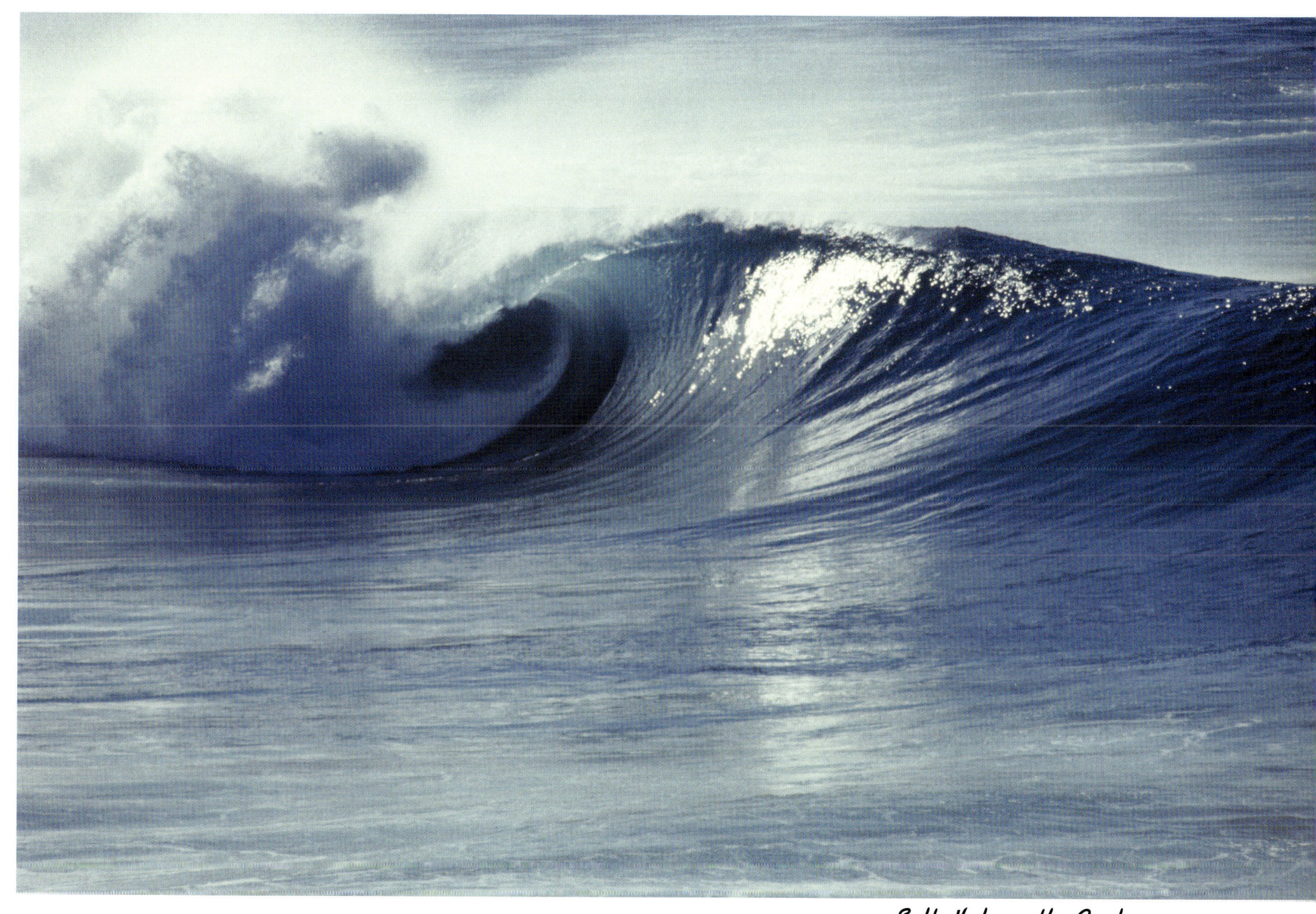

Soft Halo on the Curl

of the breaking wave. '...Angels fear to tread,' not
in the least when it comes to a wave like this.
North Pacific Ocean.

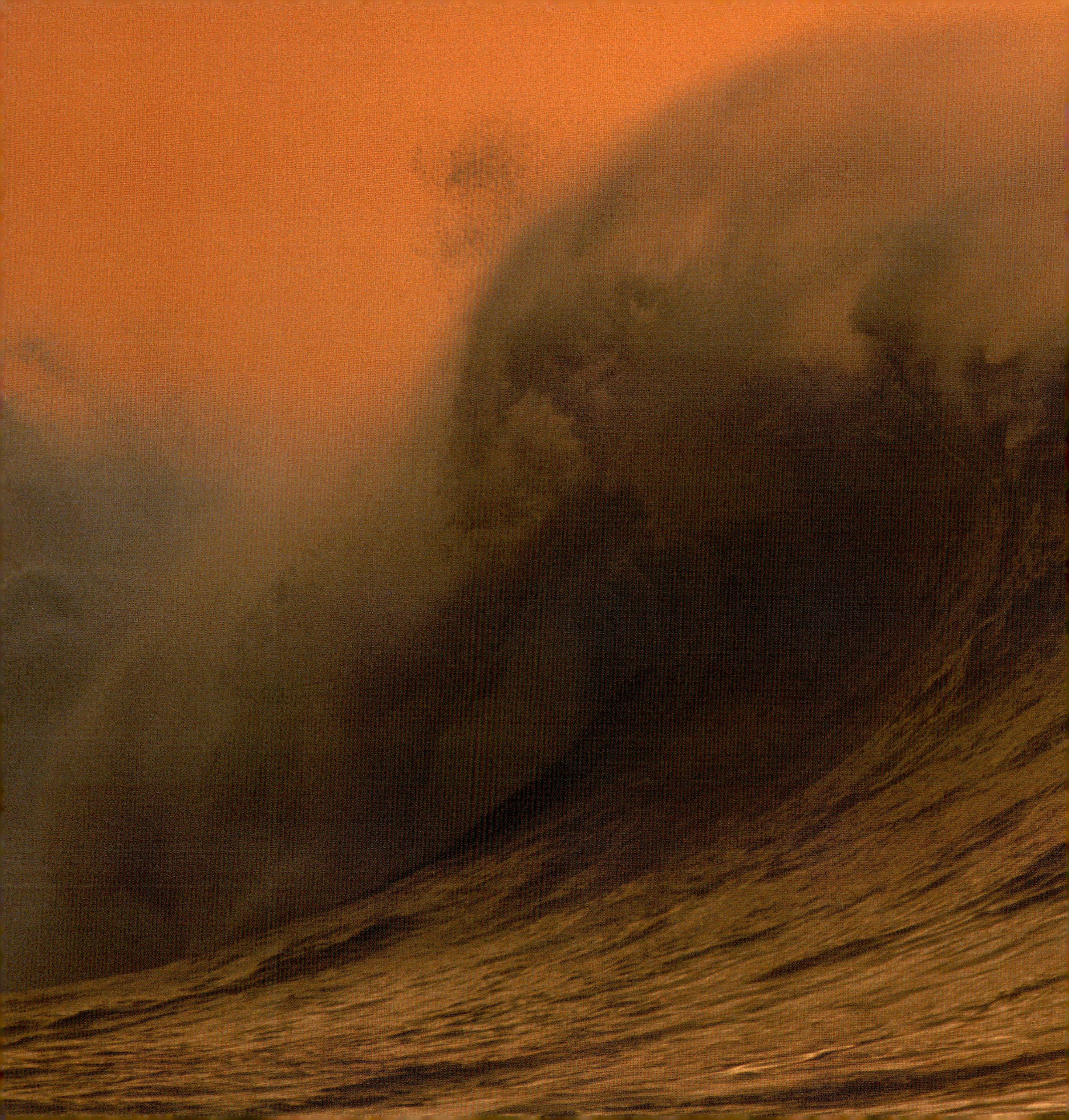

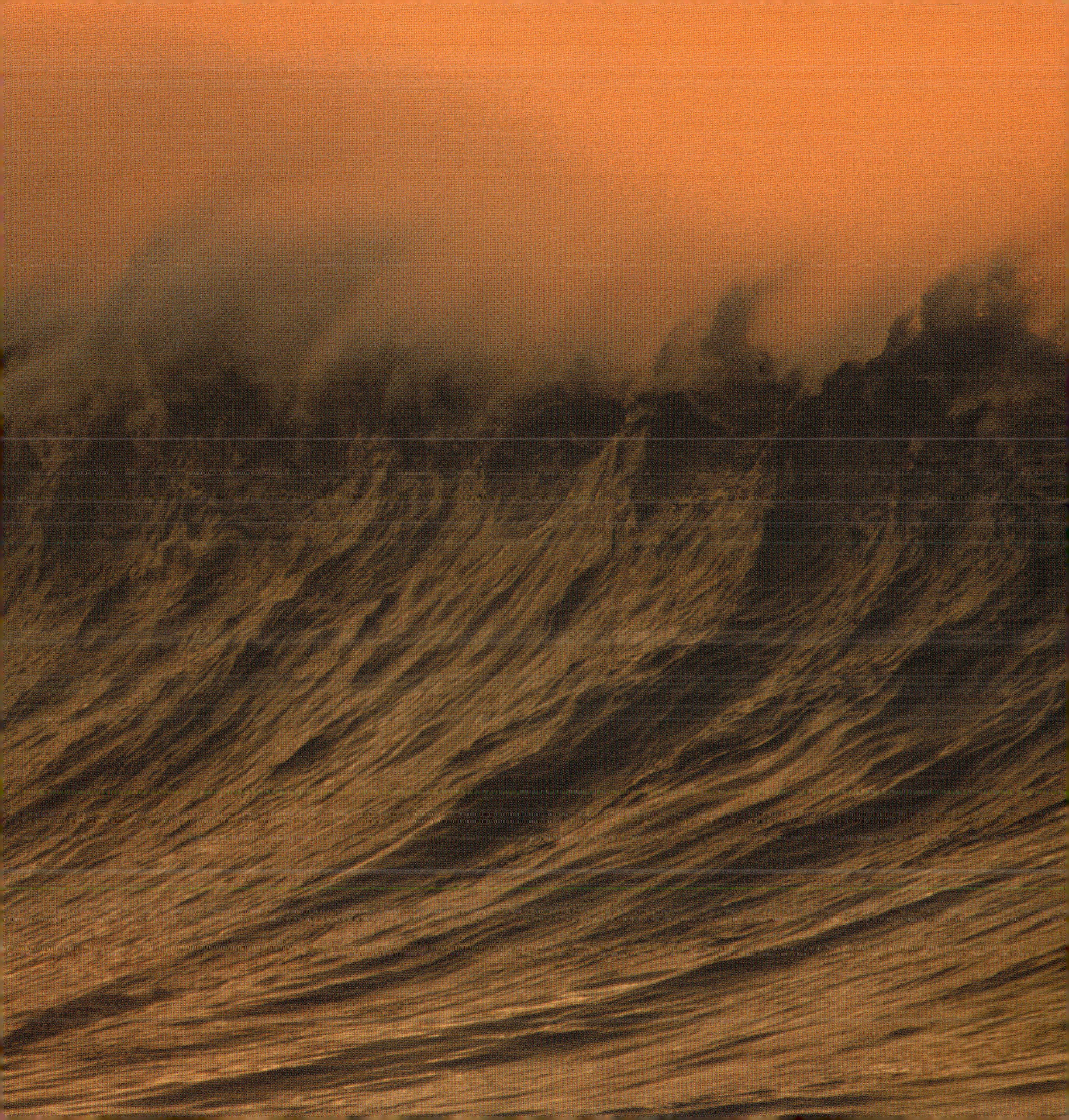

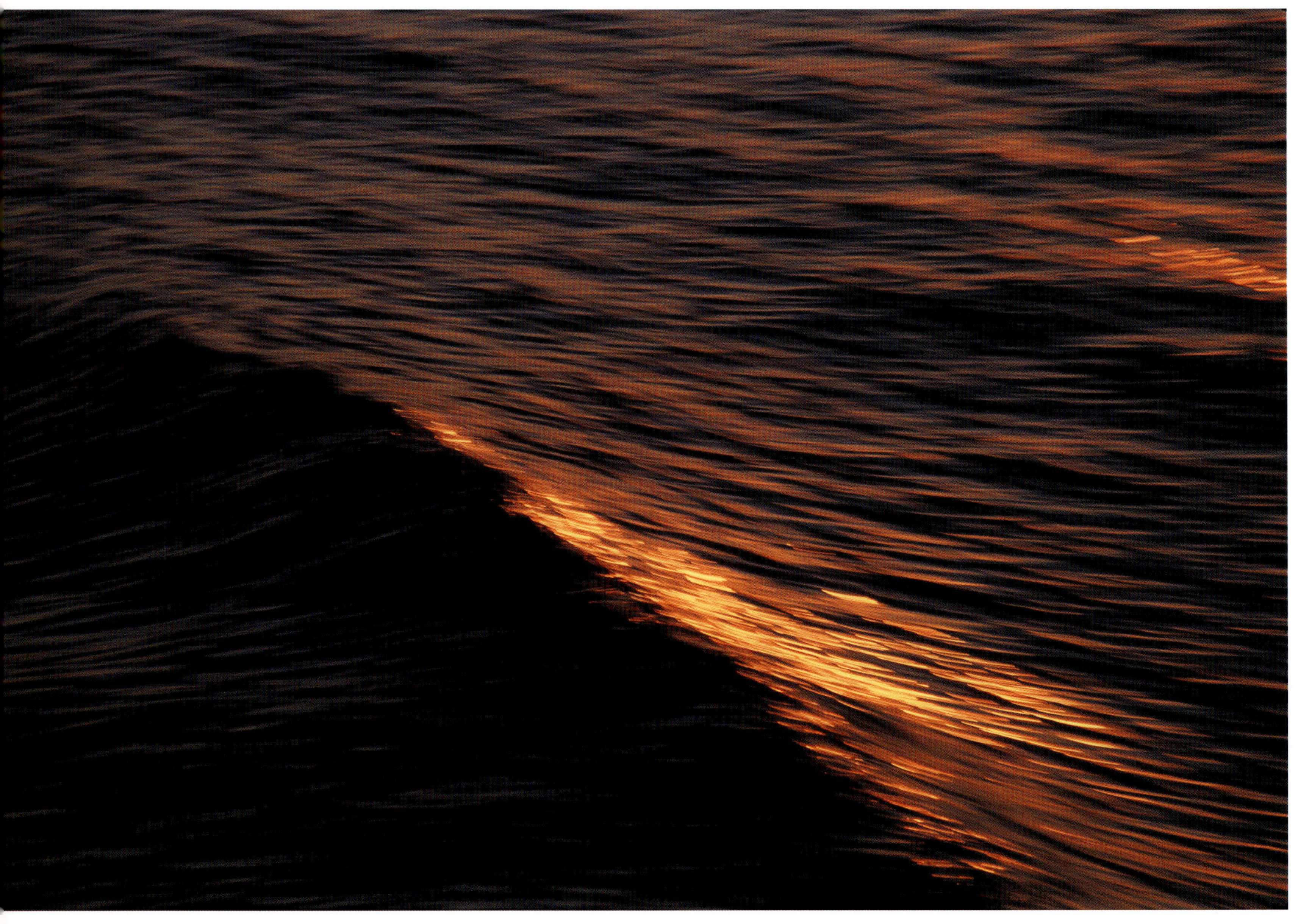

Evening Brushstrokes on the Ocean's Canvas
Subtle, silent movements across a canvas that covers the largest
expanse of nautical miles in the world. The Pacific Ocean.

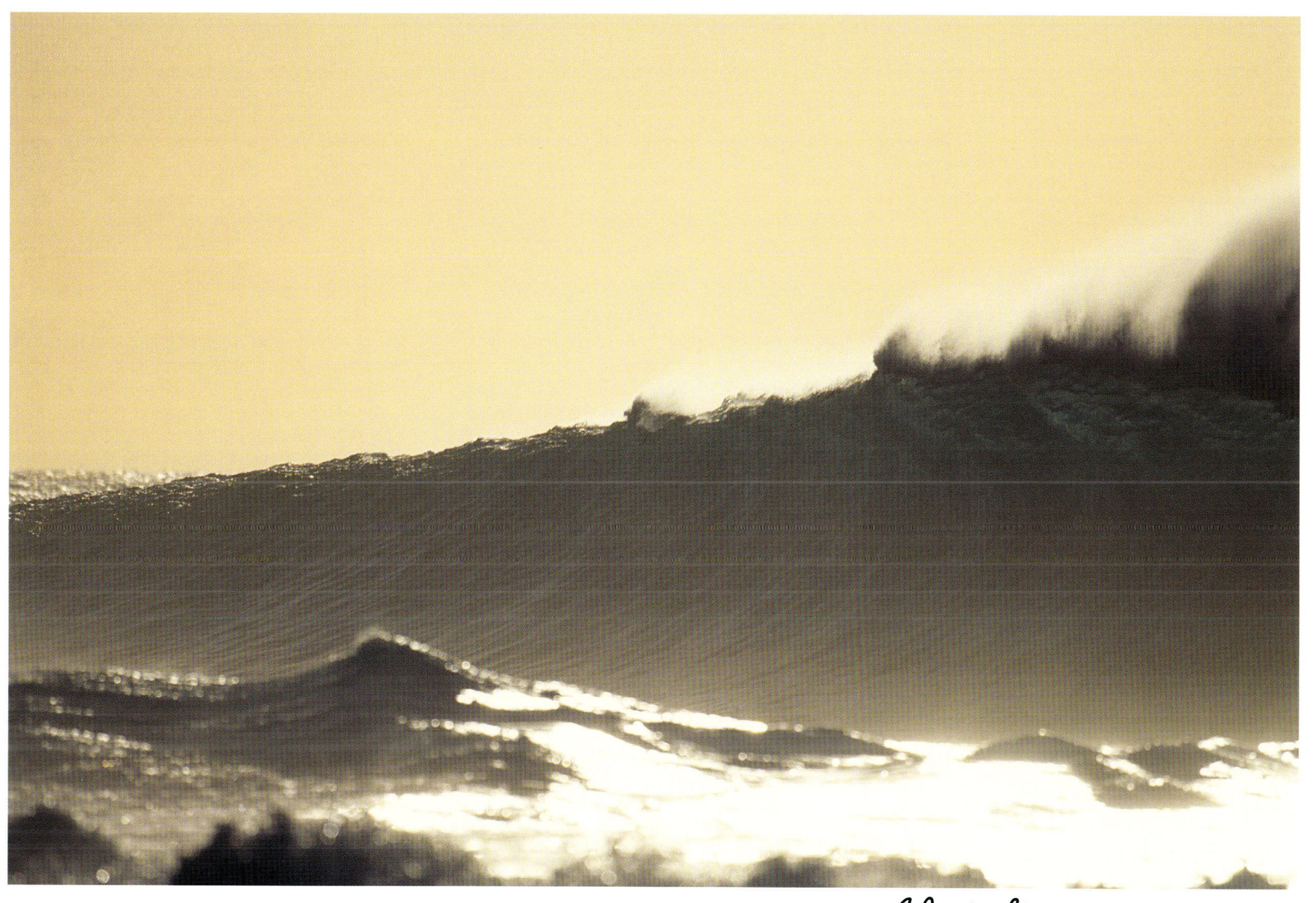

A Precise Line

that defines the edge of a wave. The mist of saltwater
that powders this wall is an afterthought due to the
agility of such a 'Freight Train.'

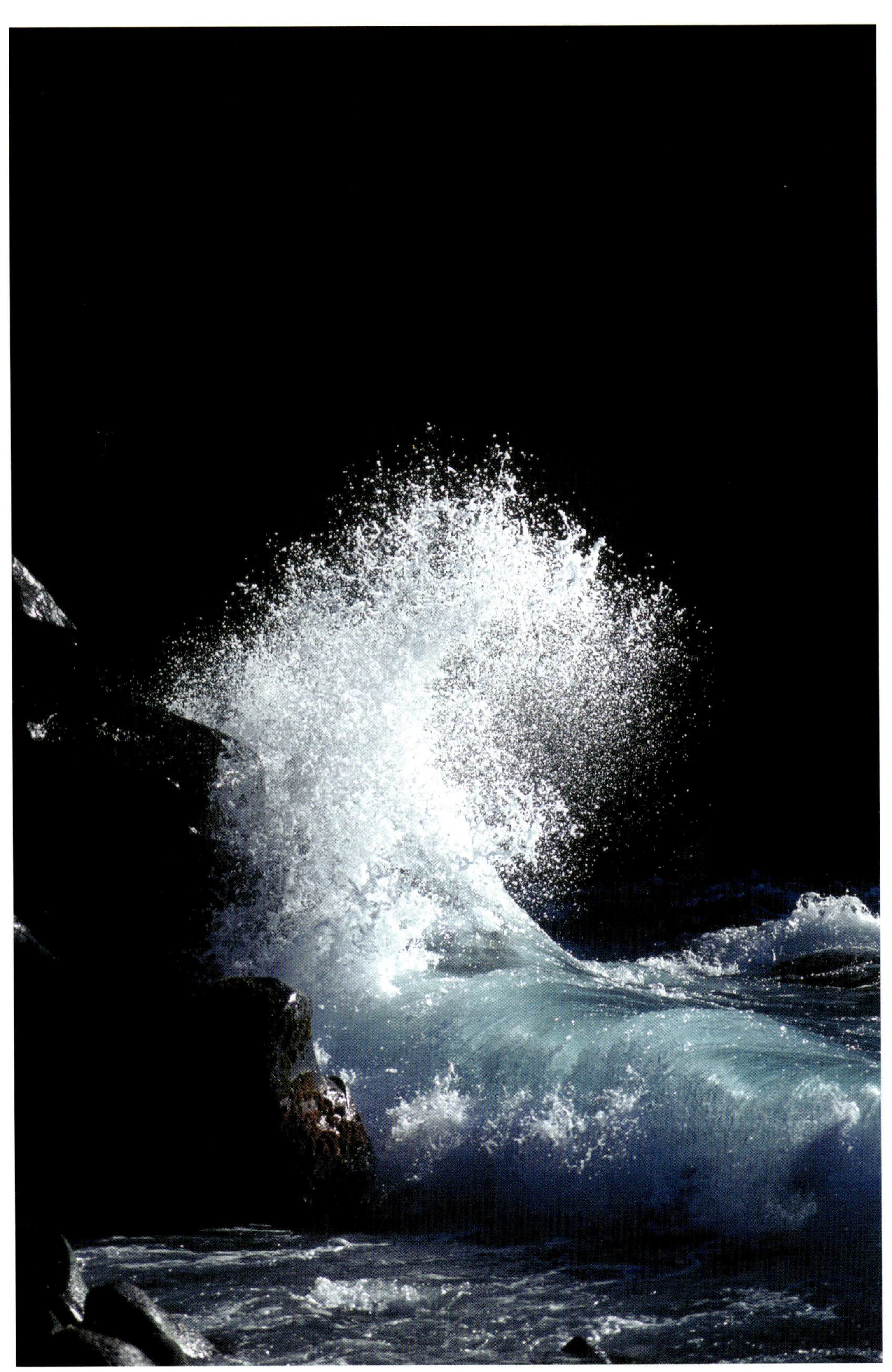

A Crash of the cymbals, the thunder of the tympani, and the mellowness of the french horn—Orchestral movements in the South Atlantic Ocean.

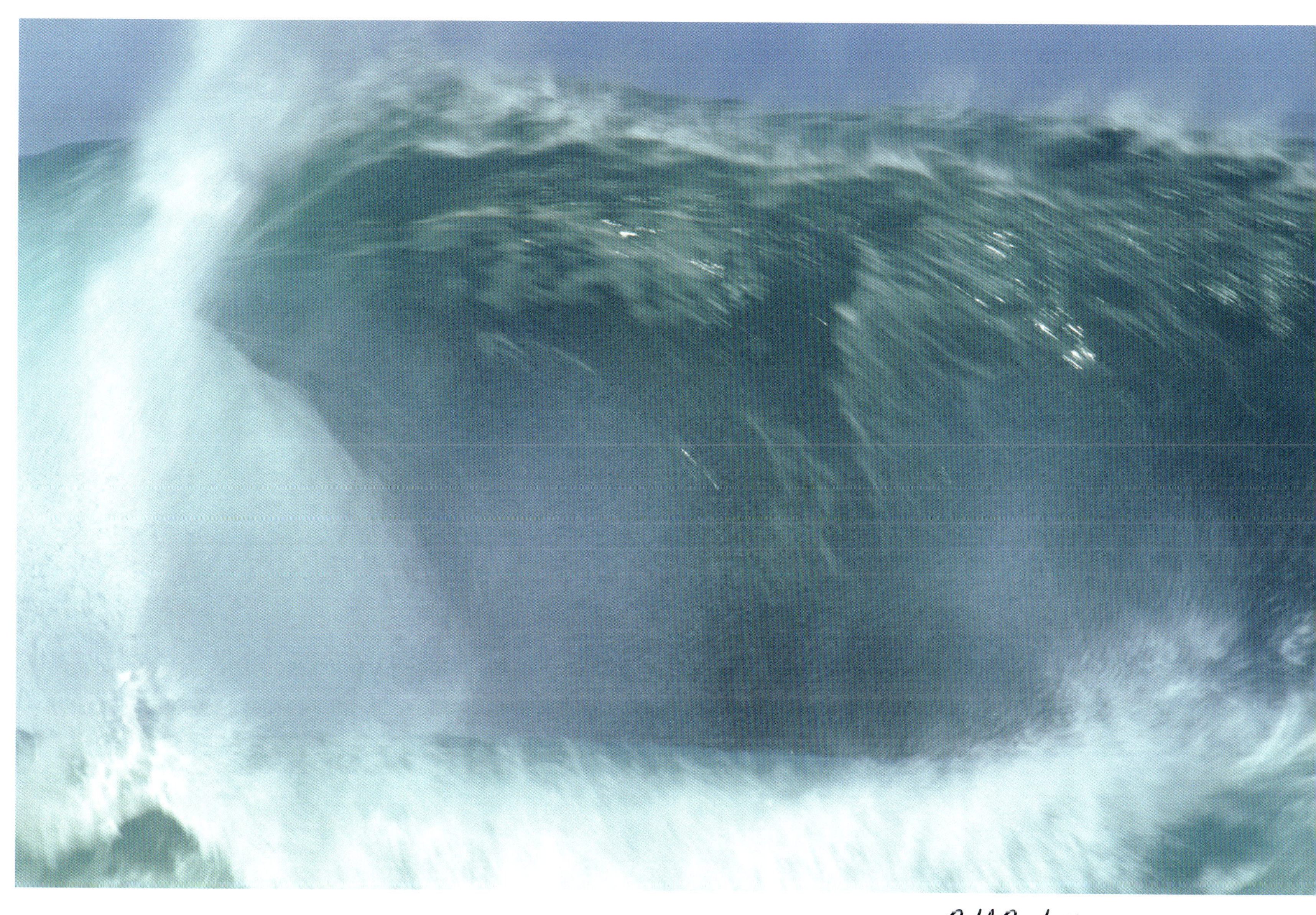

Cold Confusion
and a roar from within an aquatic beast.

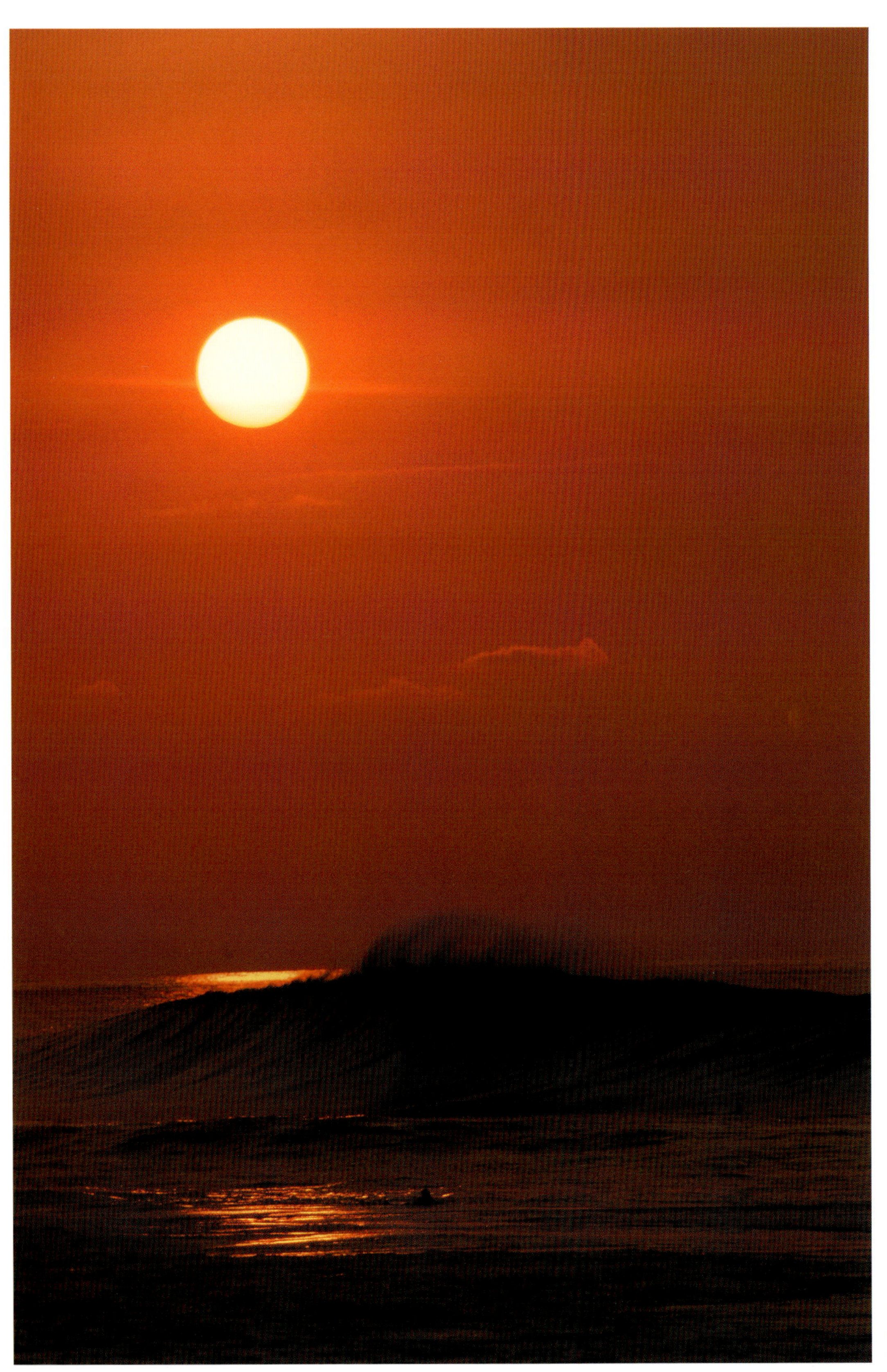

White Ball
in the Sky that overlooks an evening in red.
North Pacific Ocean.

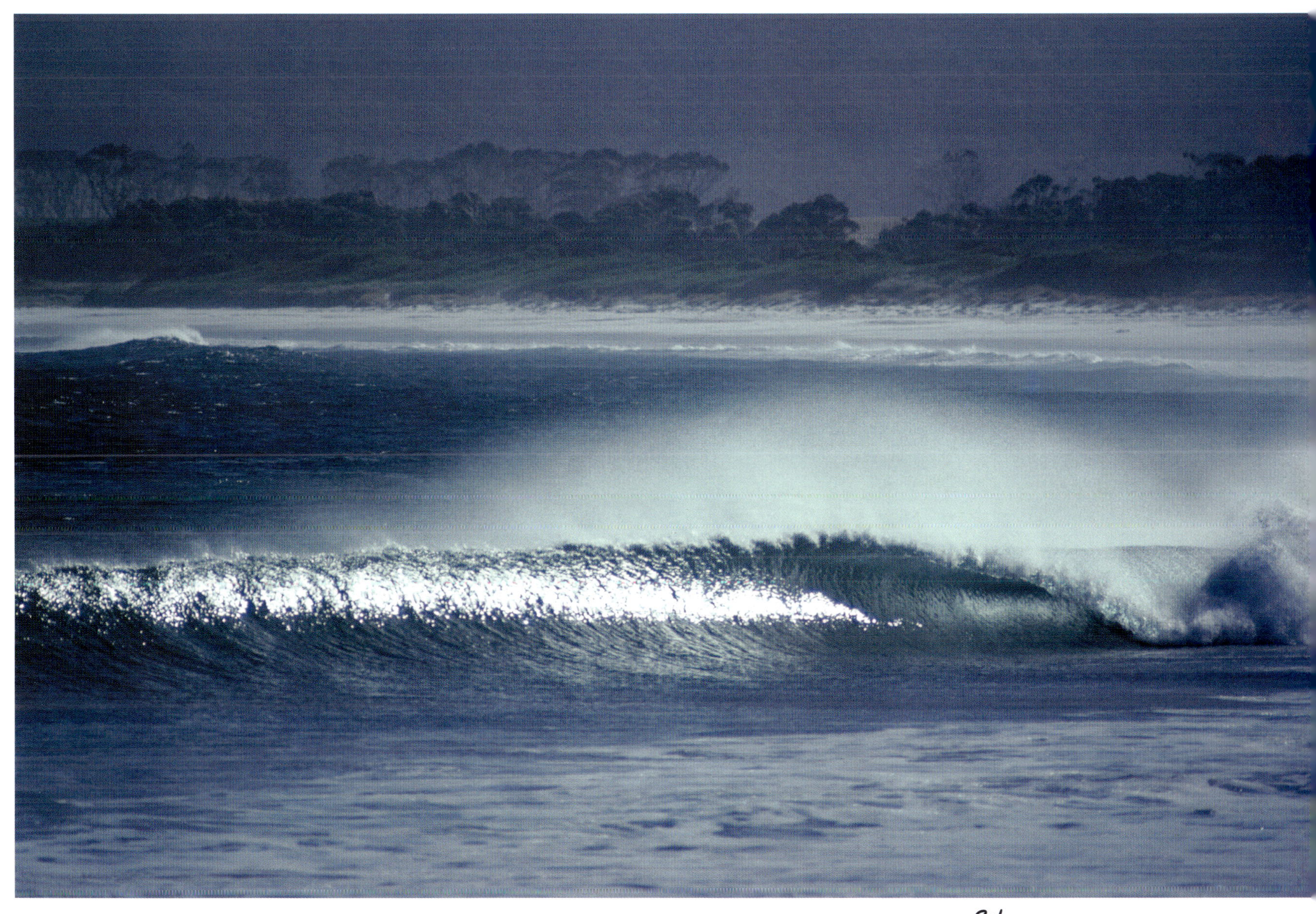

Silver,
Hot Streak on the beaches of Mexico.

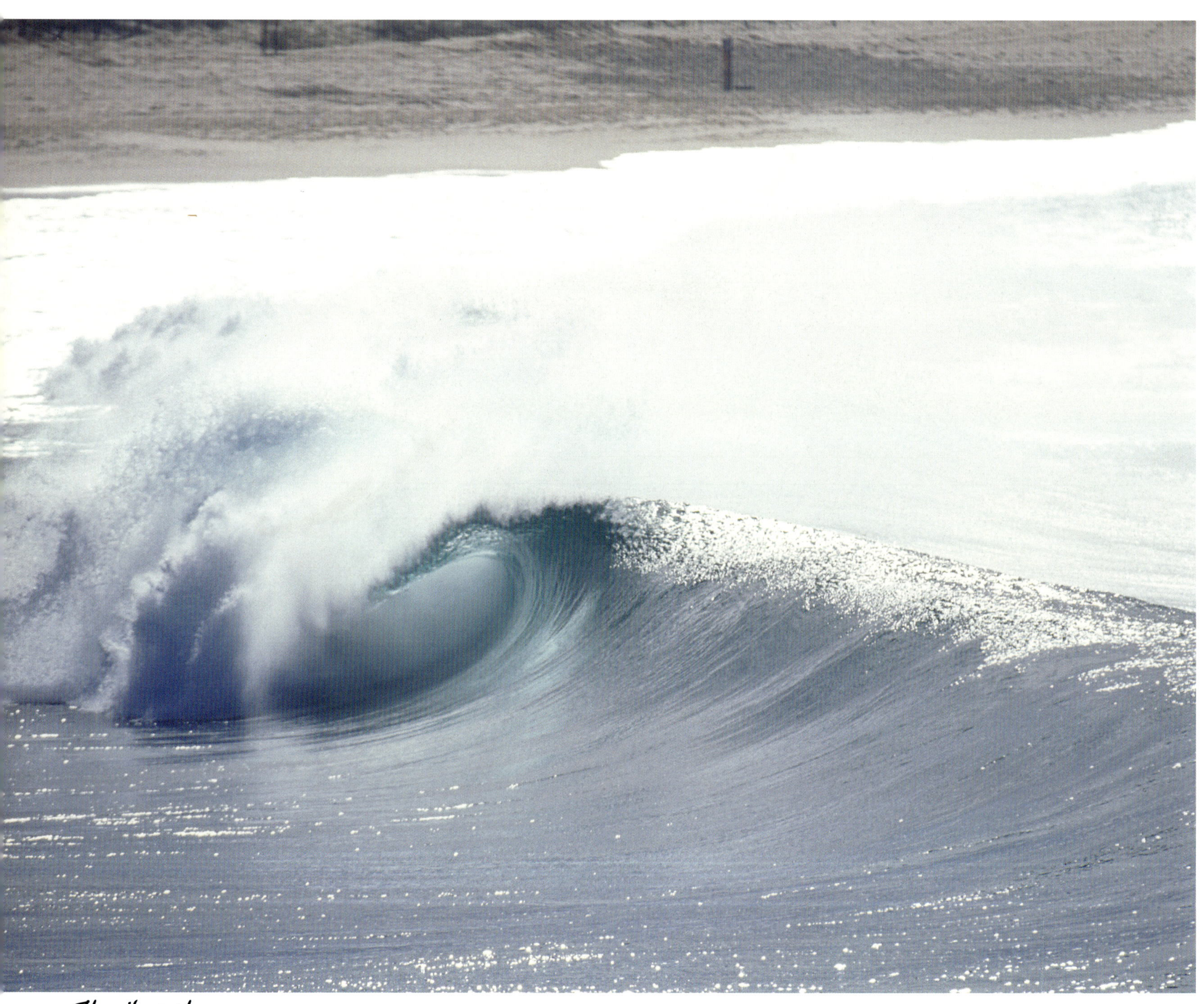

The Horseshoe
of a Desert in Africa.

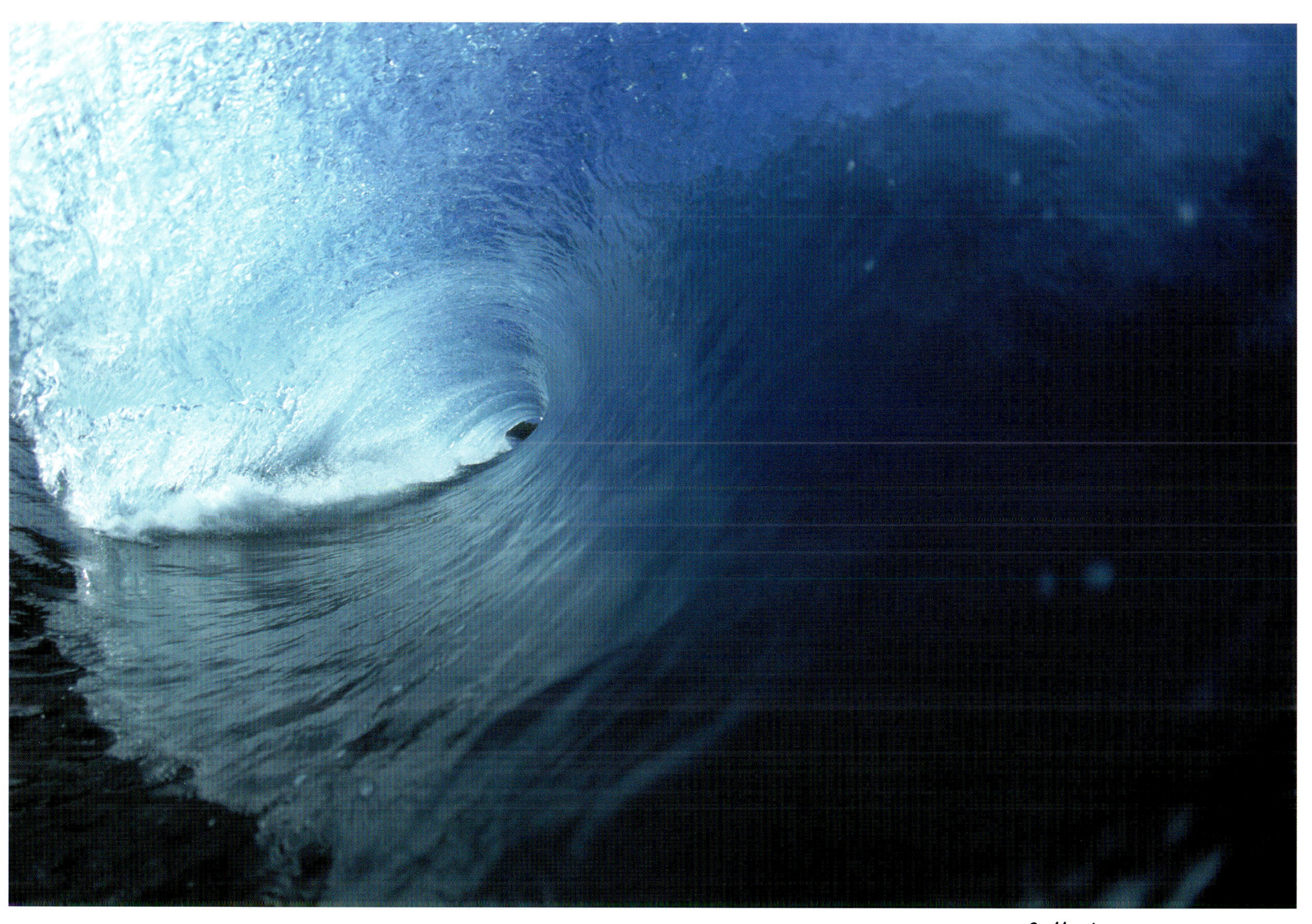

Reflection.
on Itself in different shades of Blue

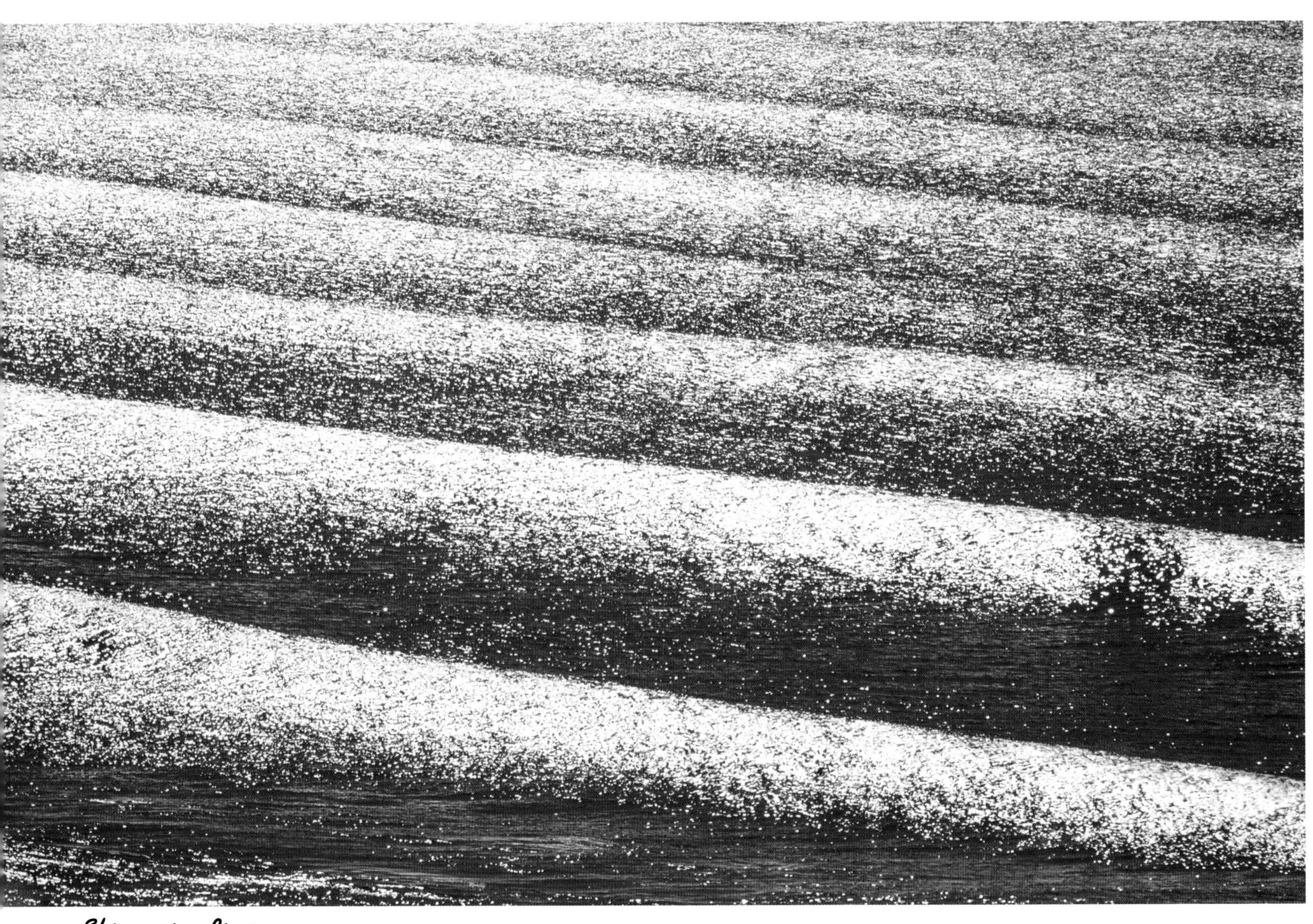

Shimmering Lines
of the mid-day sky.

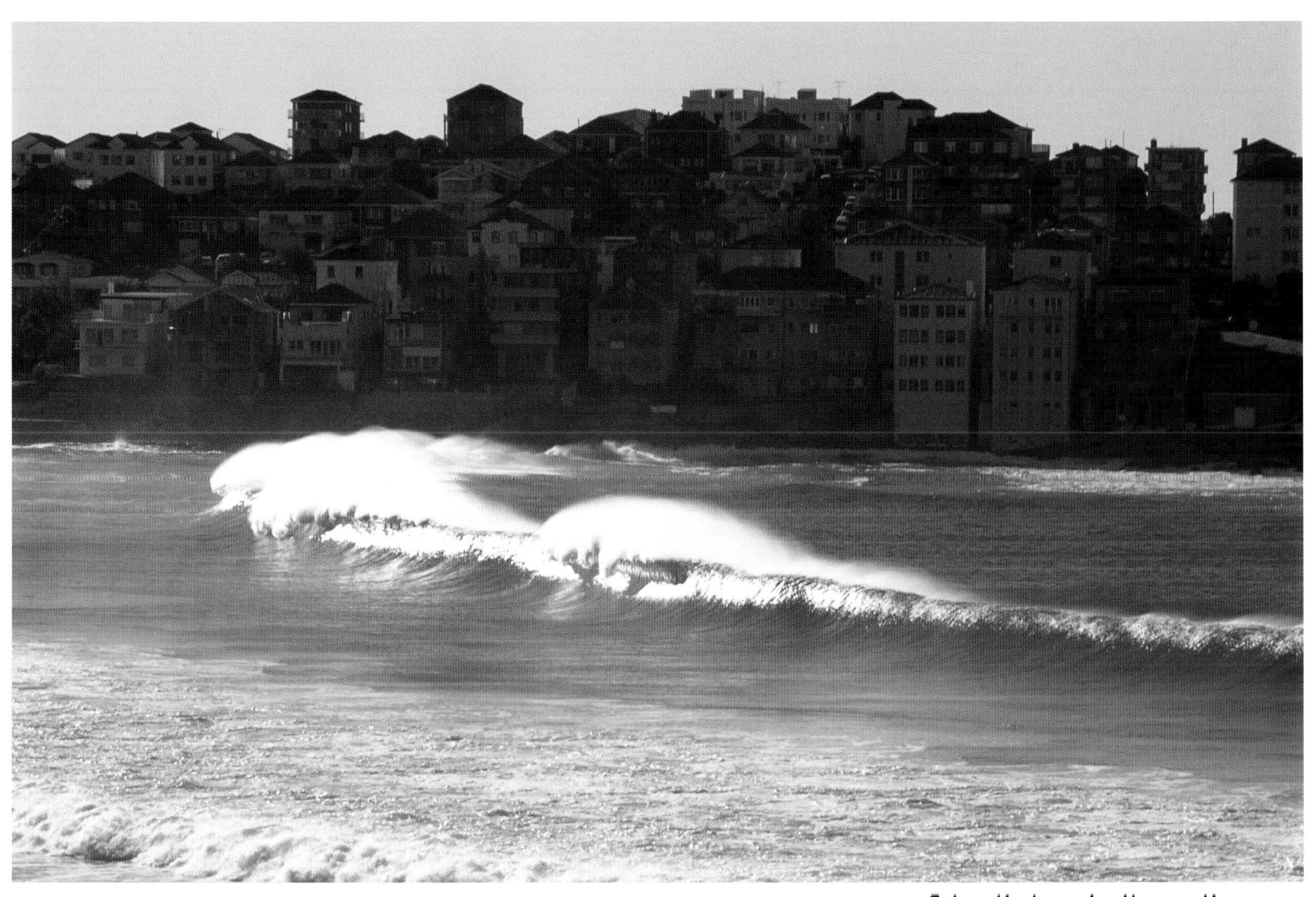

Cities that are built near the ocean are in constant threat from storms, erosion, and large surf. But in our longing to be near the waves of the ocean, we disregard that completely as viewed here on a beach in France.

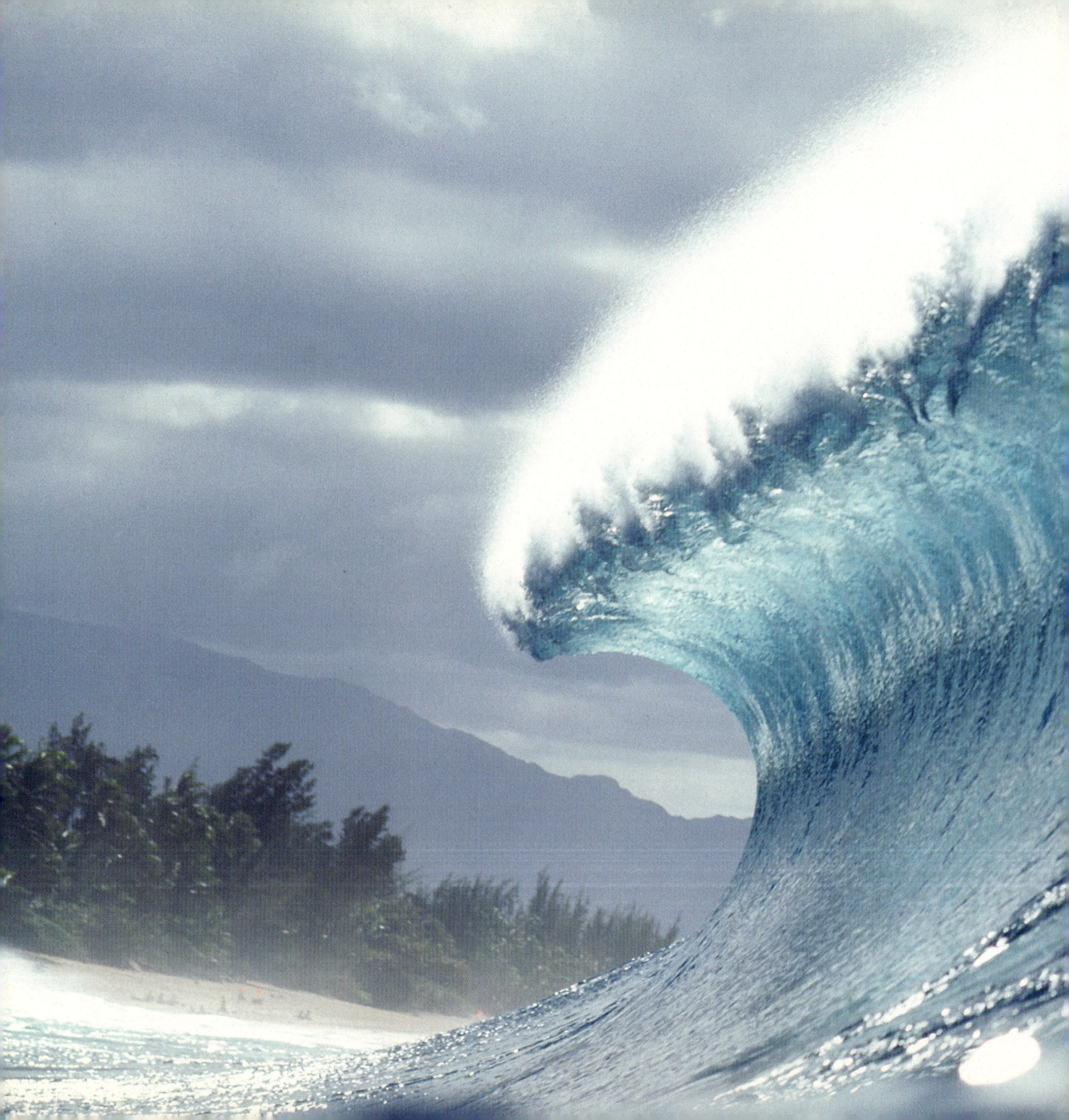

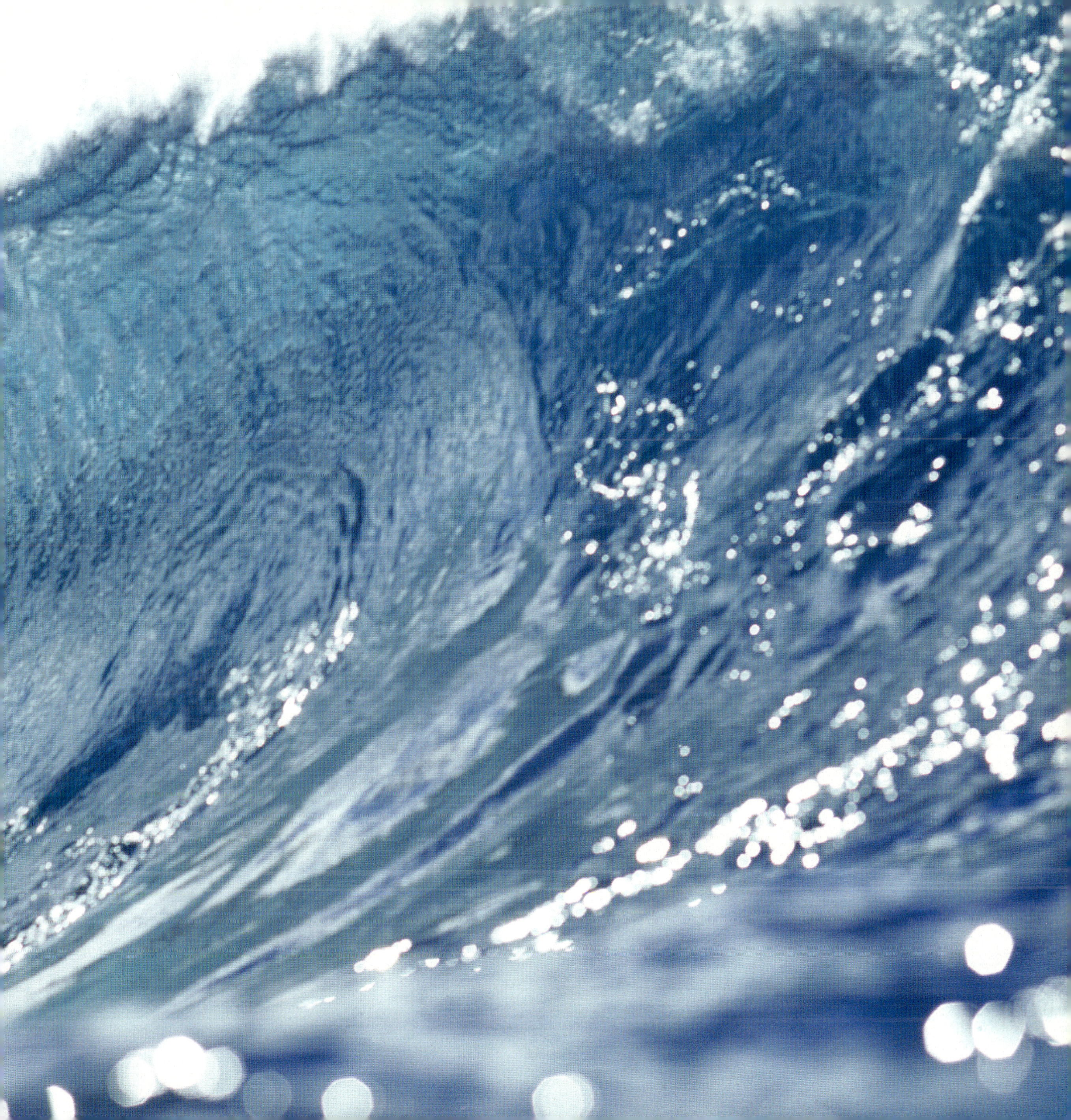

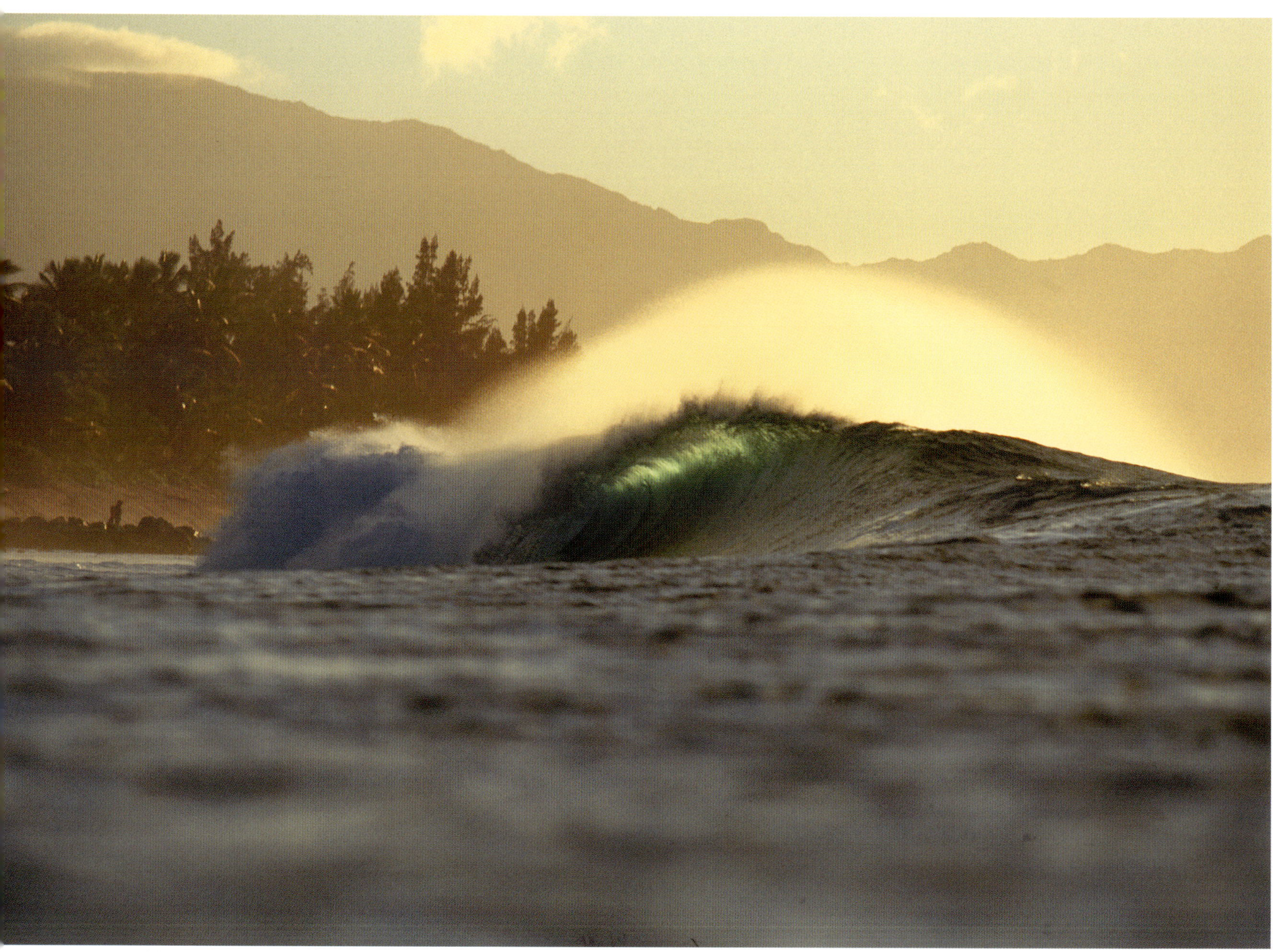

Emerald Eye

of a wave on the North Shore of Oahu.
The dusk during the day backlights the way.

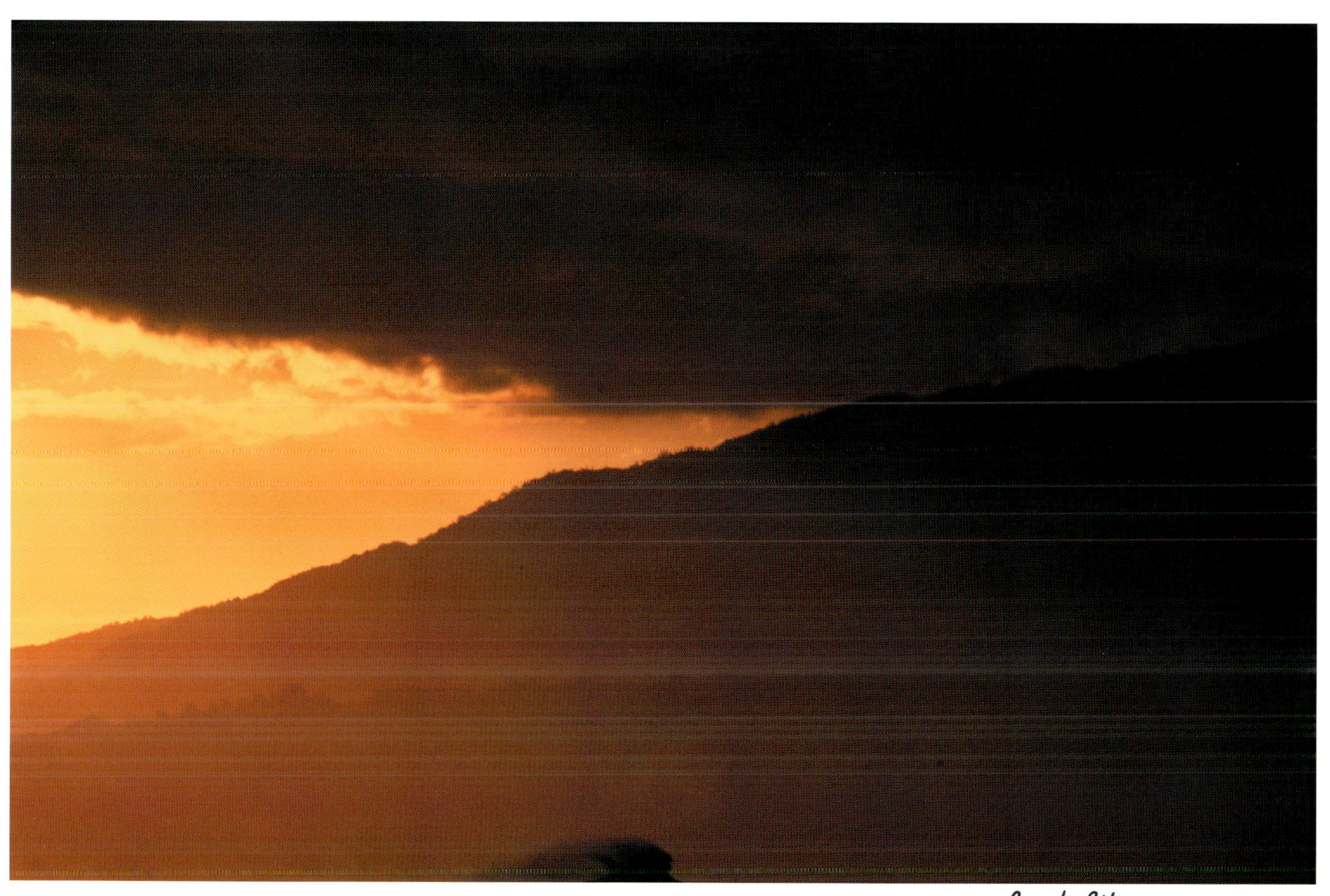

Lonely Wisp
of the crest on a wave that trolls through
a North Pacific Ocean sunset.

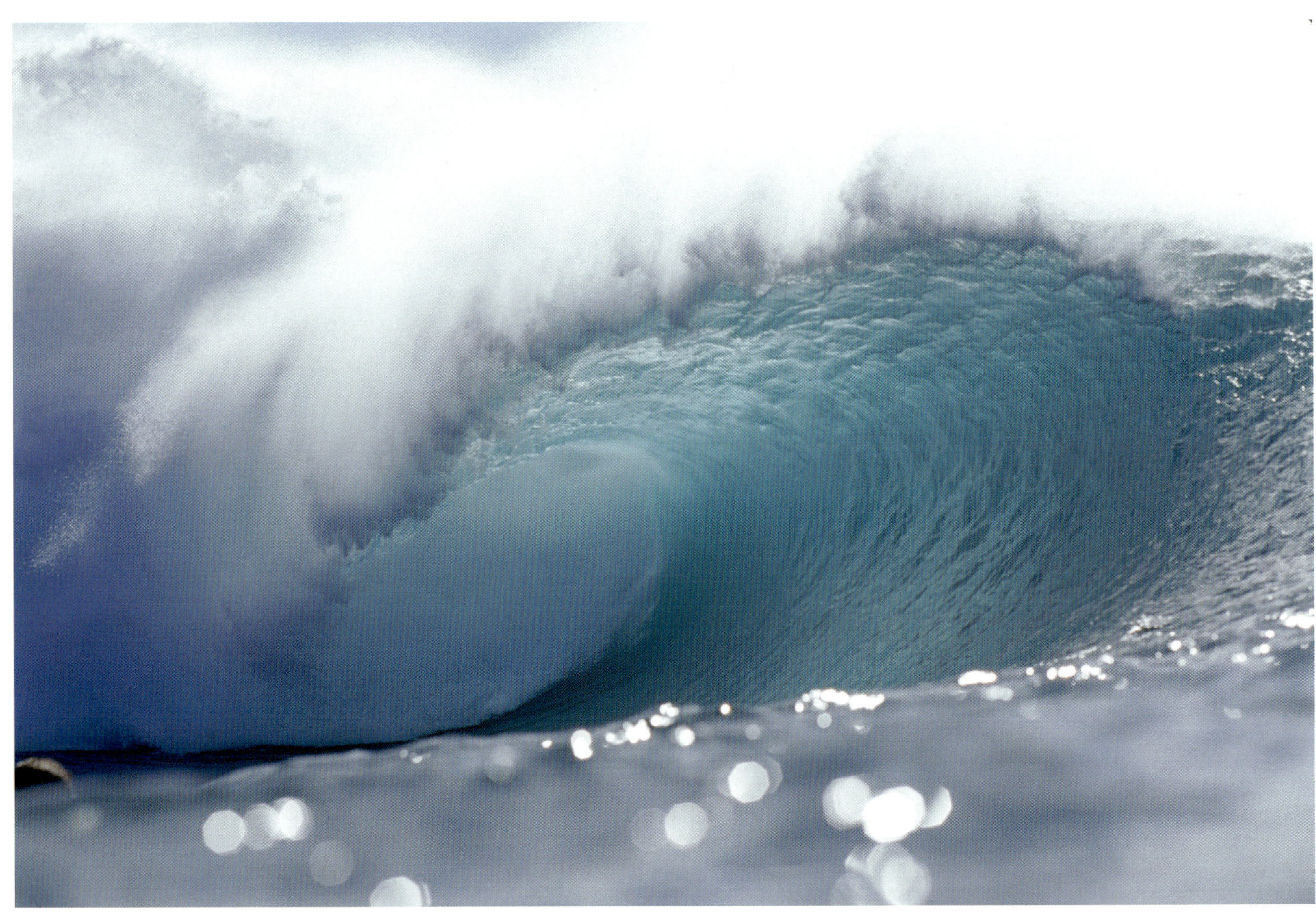

A Roar from the gladiator pit

A whip crack. A canon burst. A shotgun fires.
All of those sounds from the inside of this South
Pacific Ocean wave.

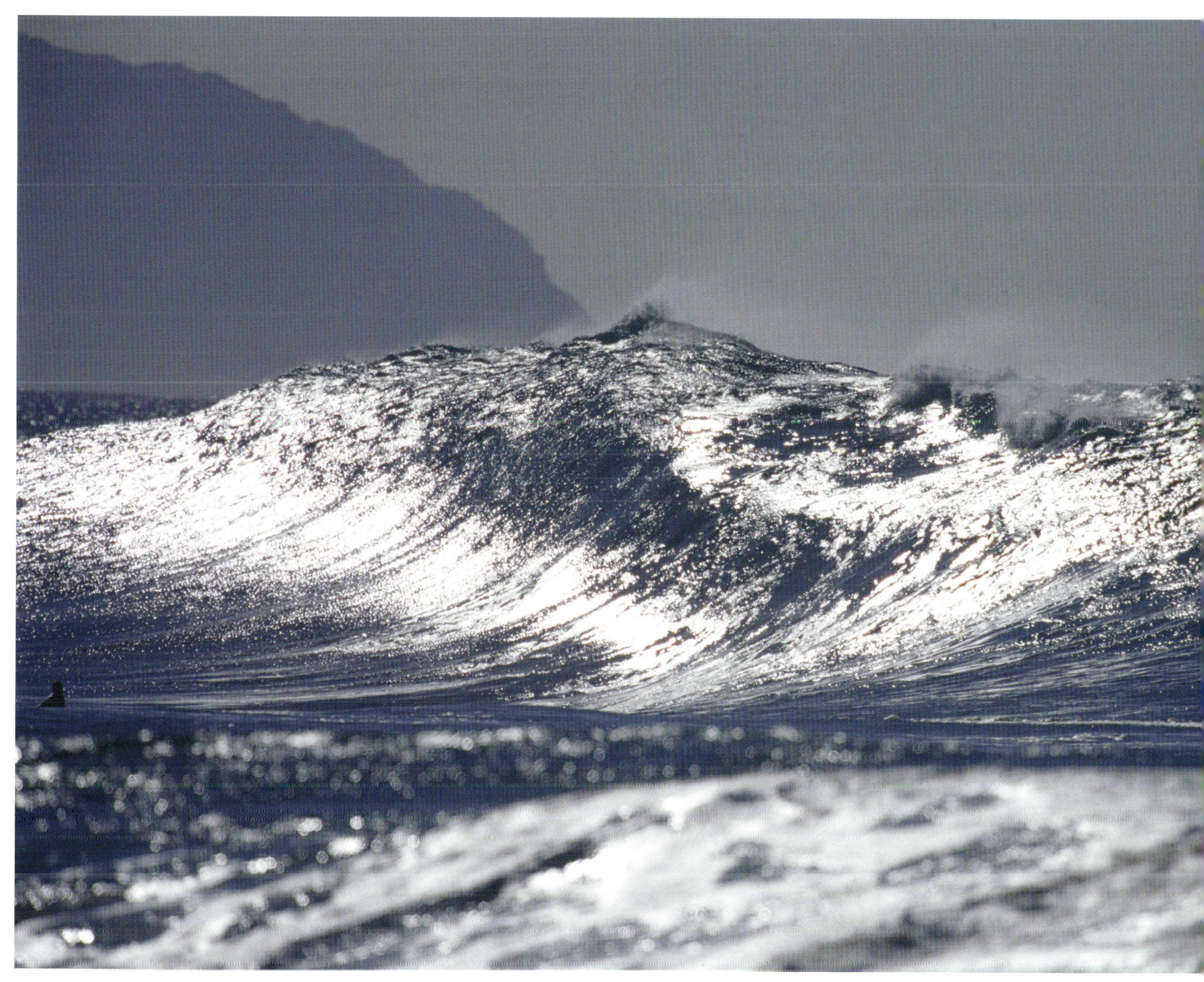

The Mound

of unsculptured clay becoming a design
as it reaches land near Tasmania.

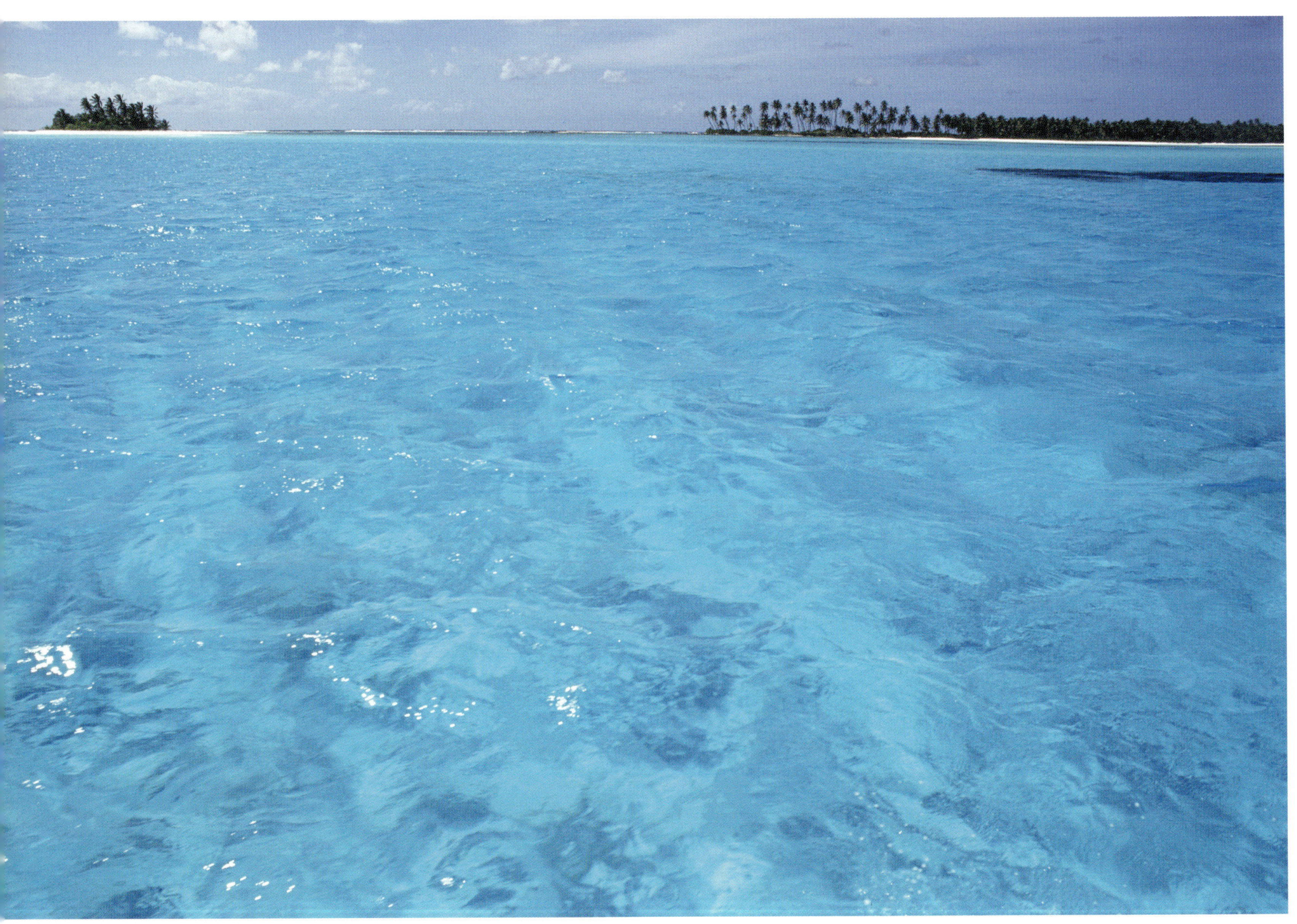

The Clear piece
of Island that is undoubtably peaceful.

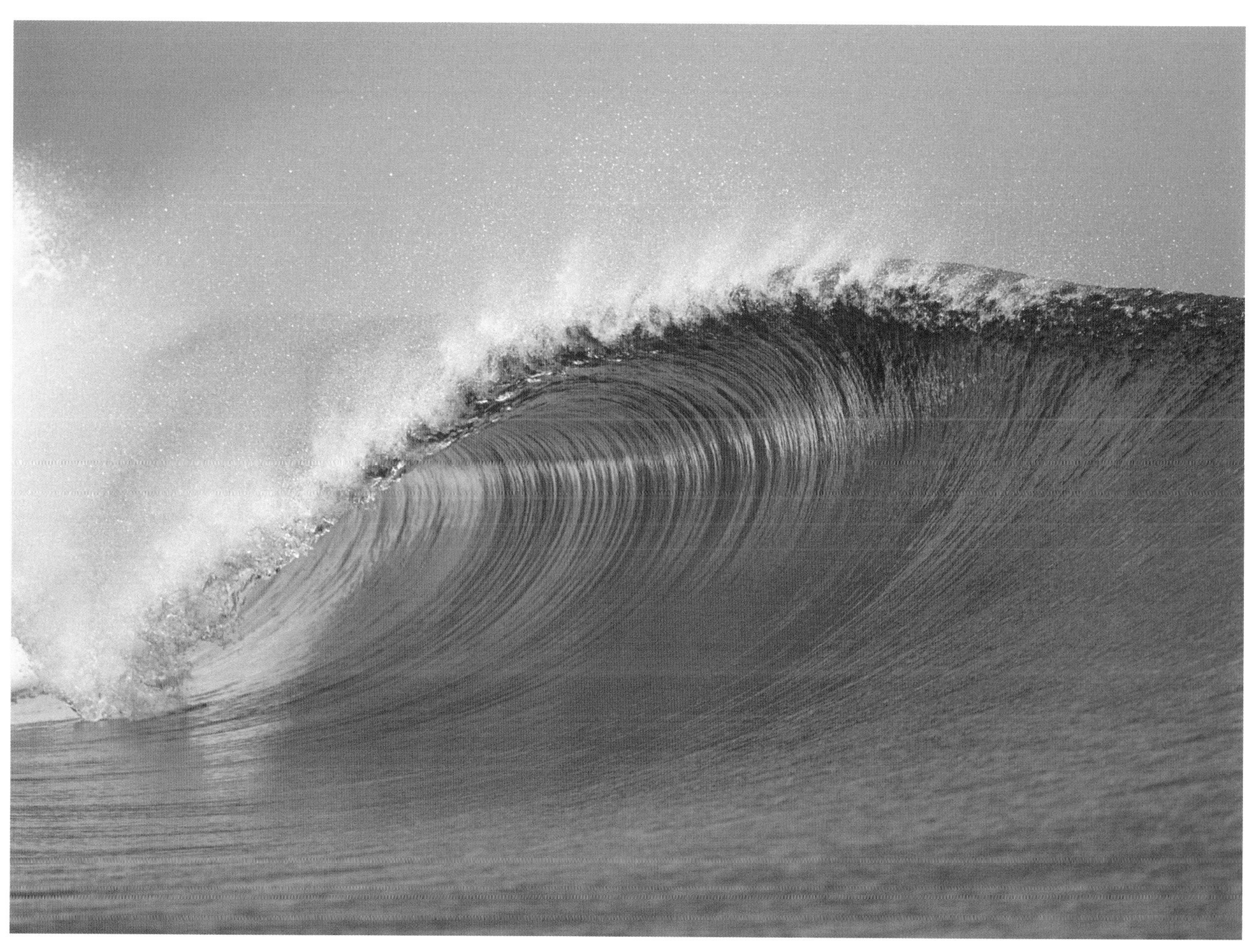

Stripes
of the Blue Screw in Tahiti.

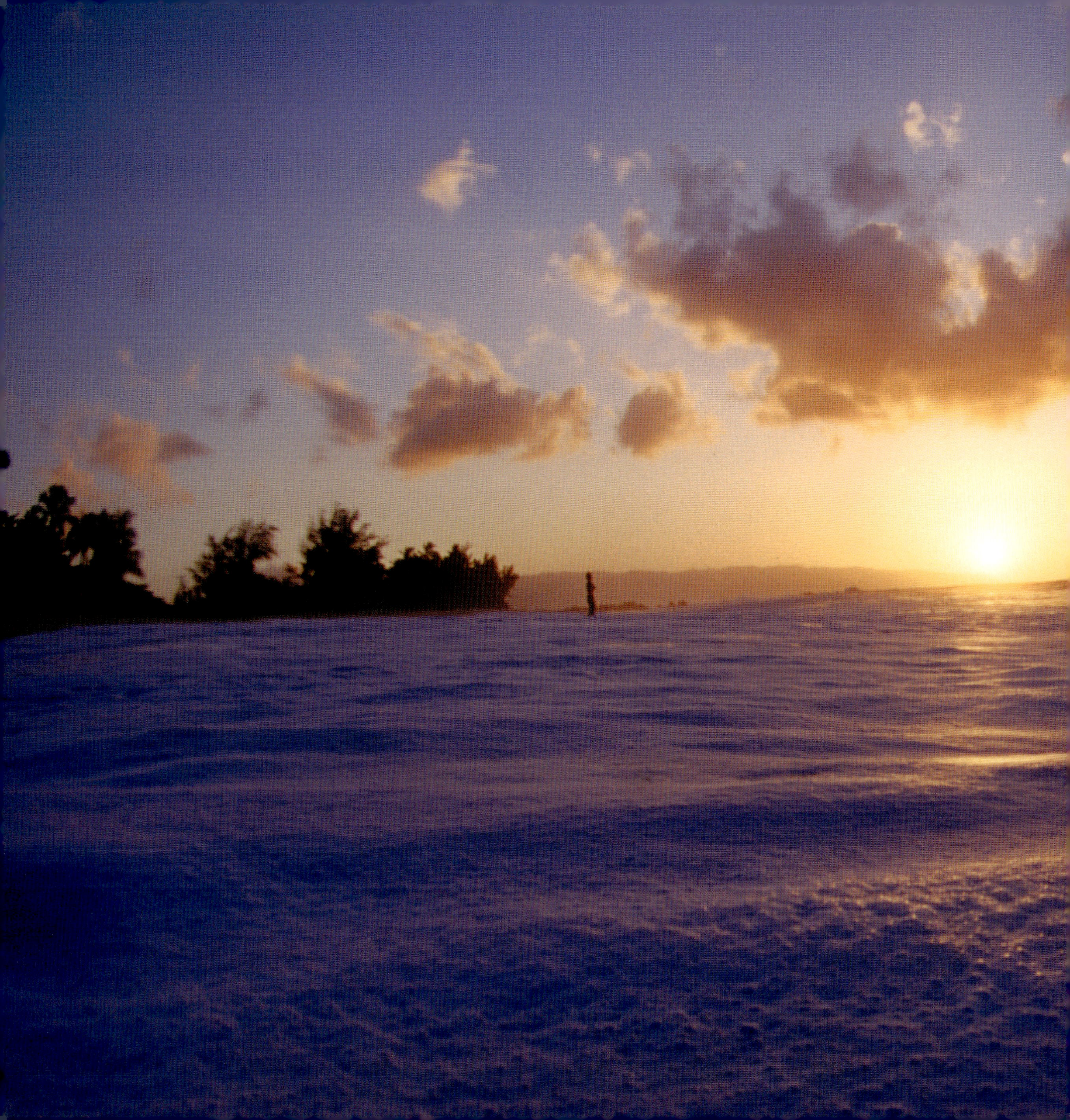

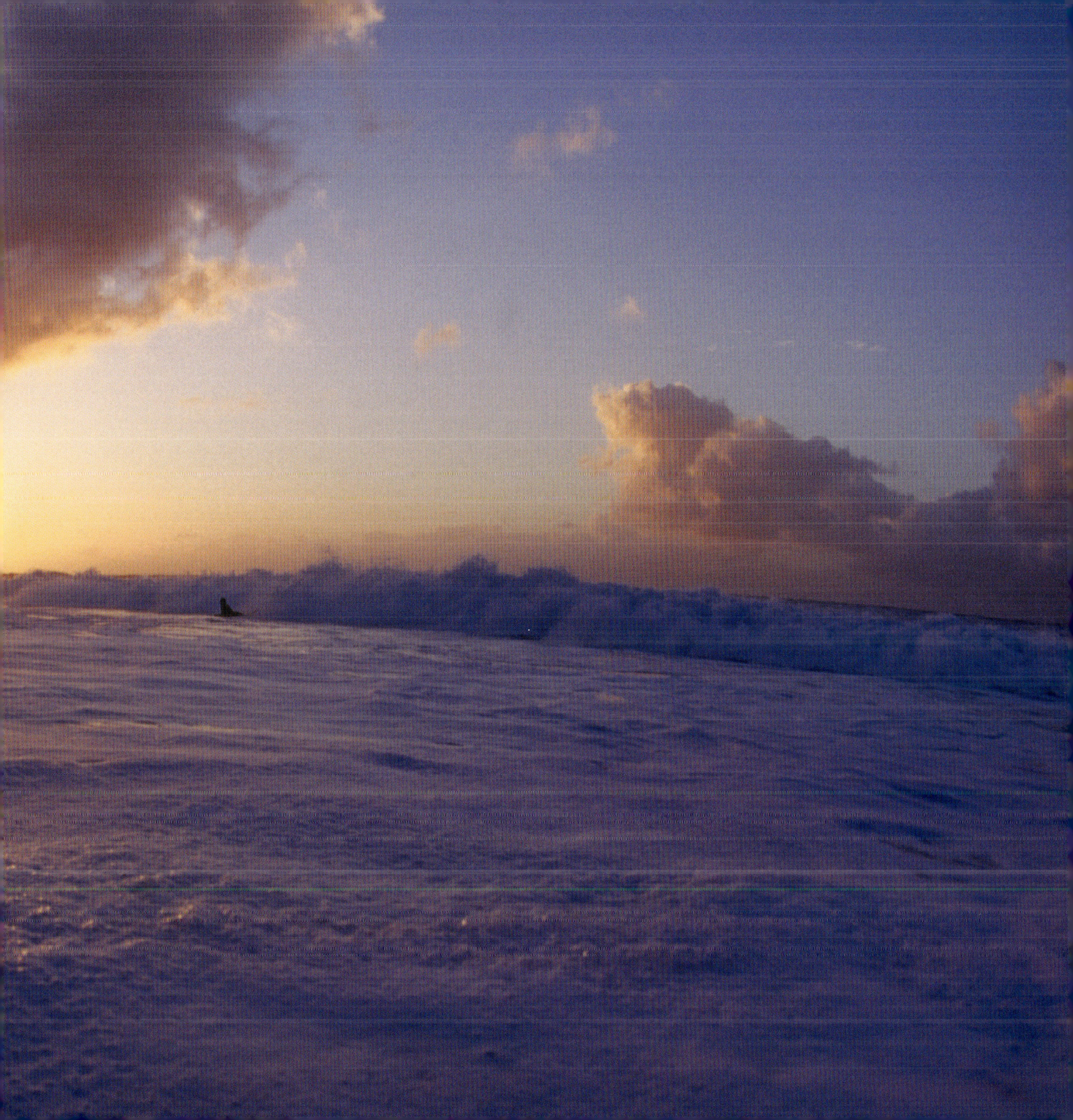

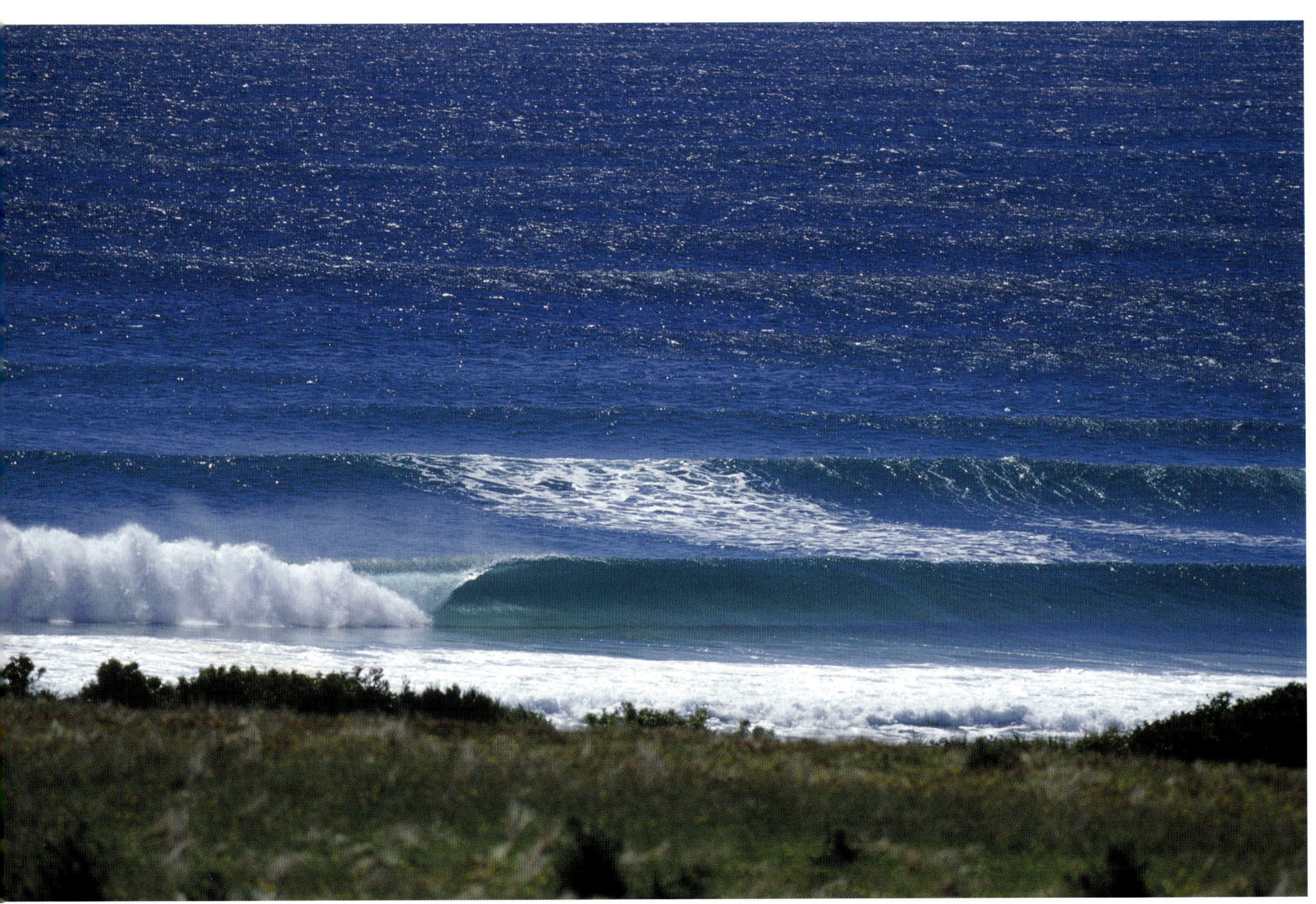

Found in the rugged Western Coast of Australia.

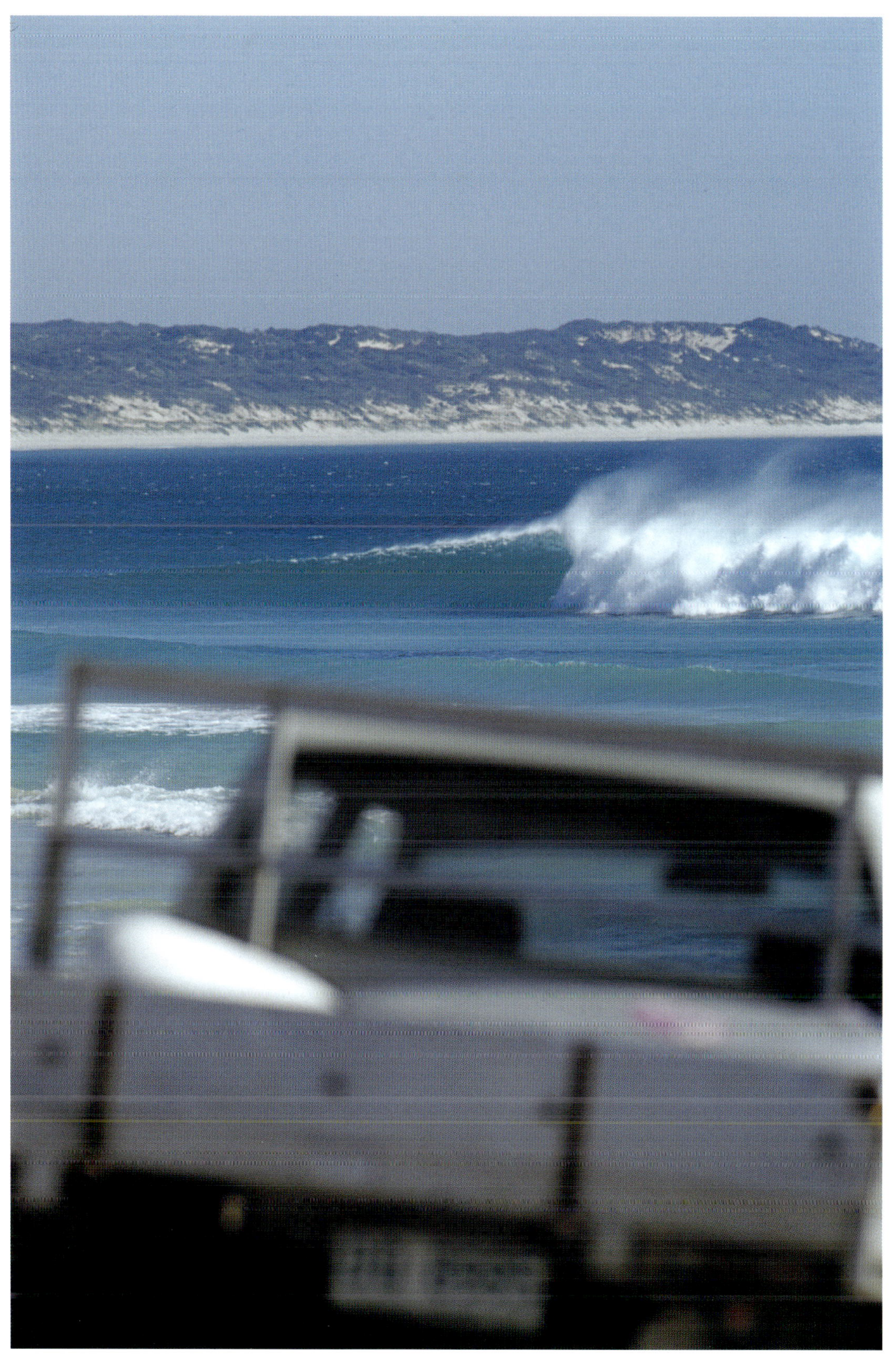

The Lure and Hook
of the Ocean drives someone to remote
places just to be near excellent waves.

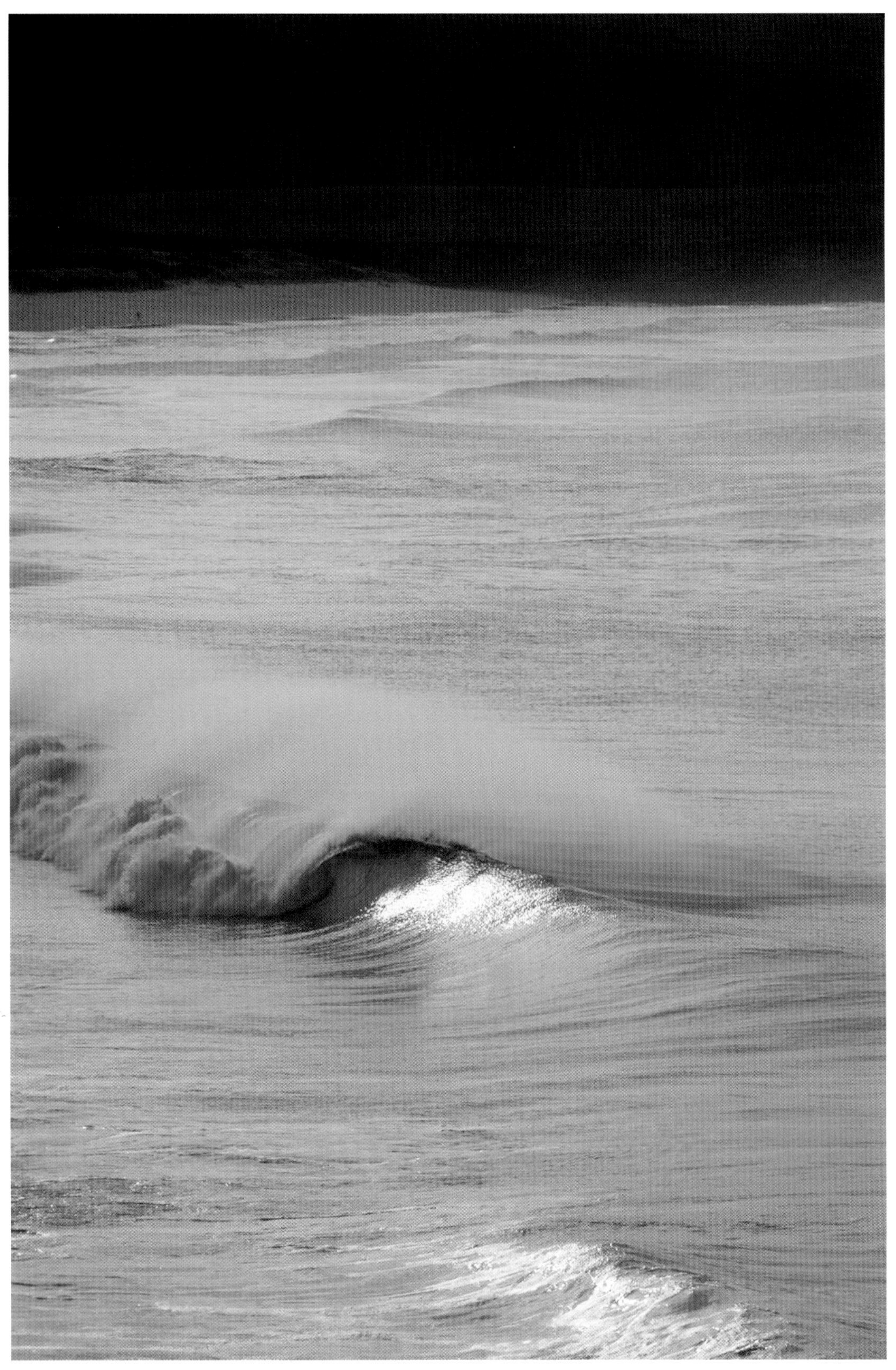

Gray
and Unappreciated on an early morning.

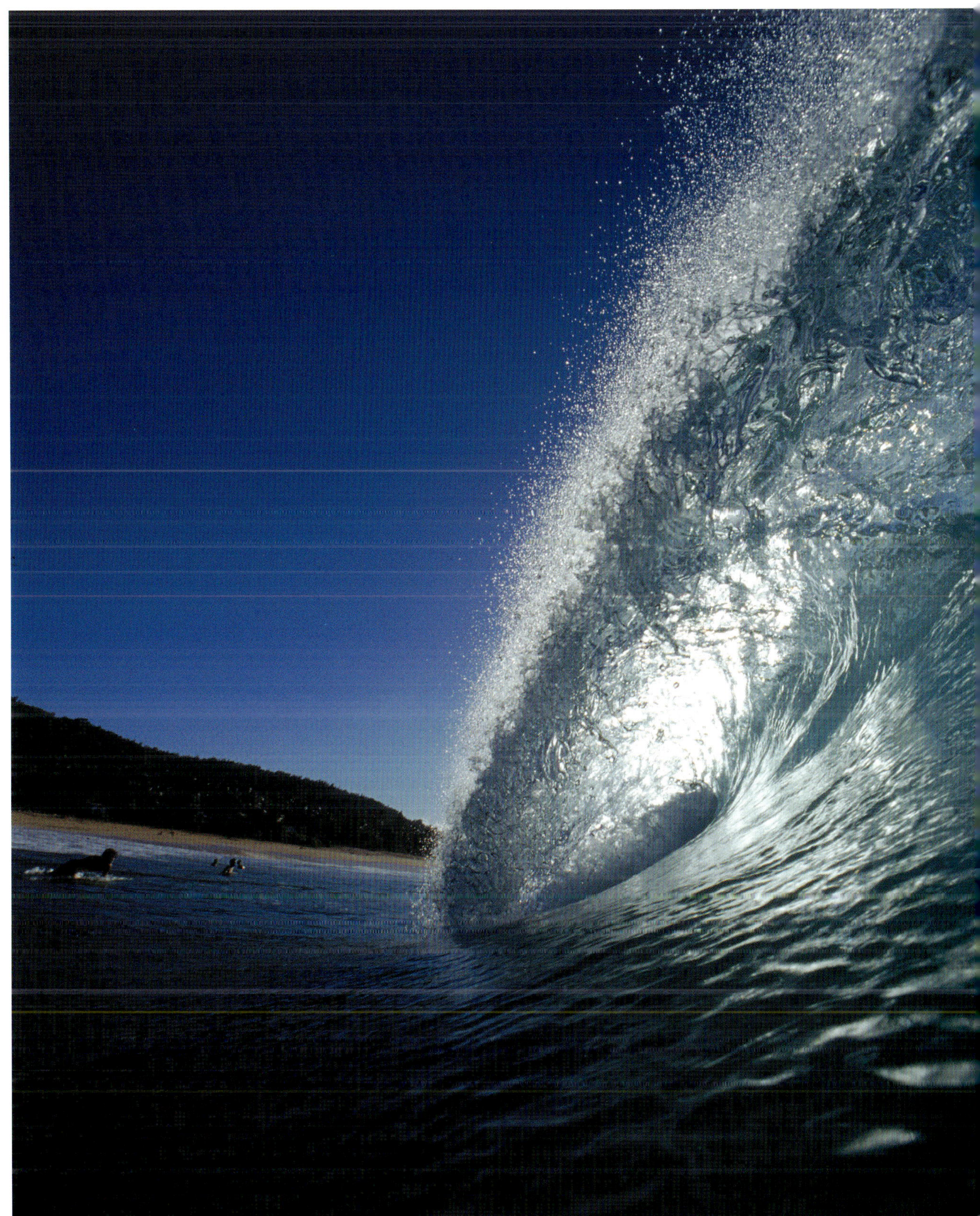

Slope
of what appears to be falling
ice is nothing more than the
gentleness of a Hawaiian Wave.

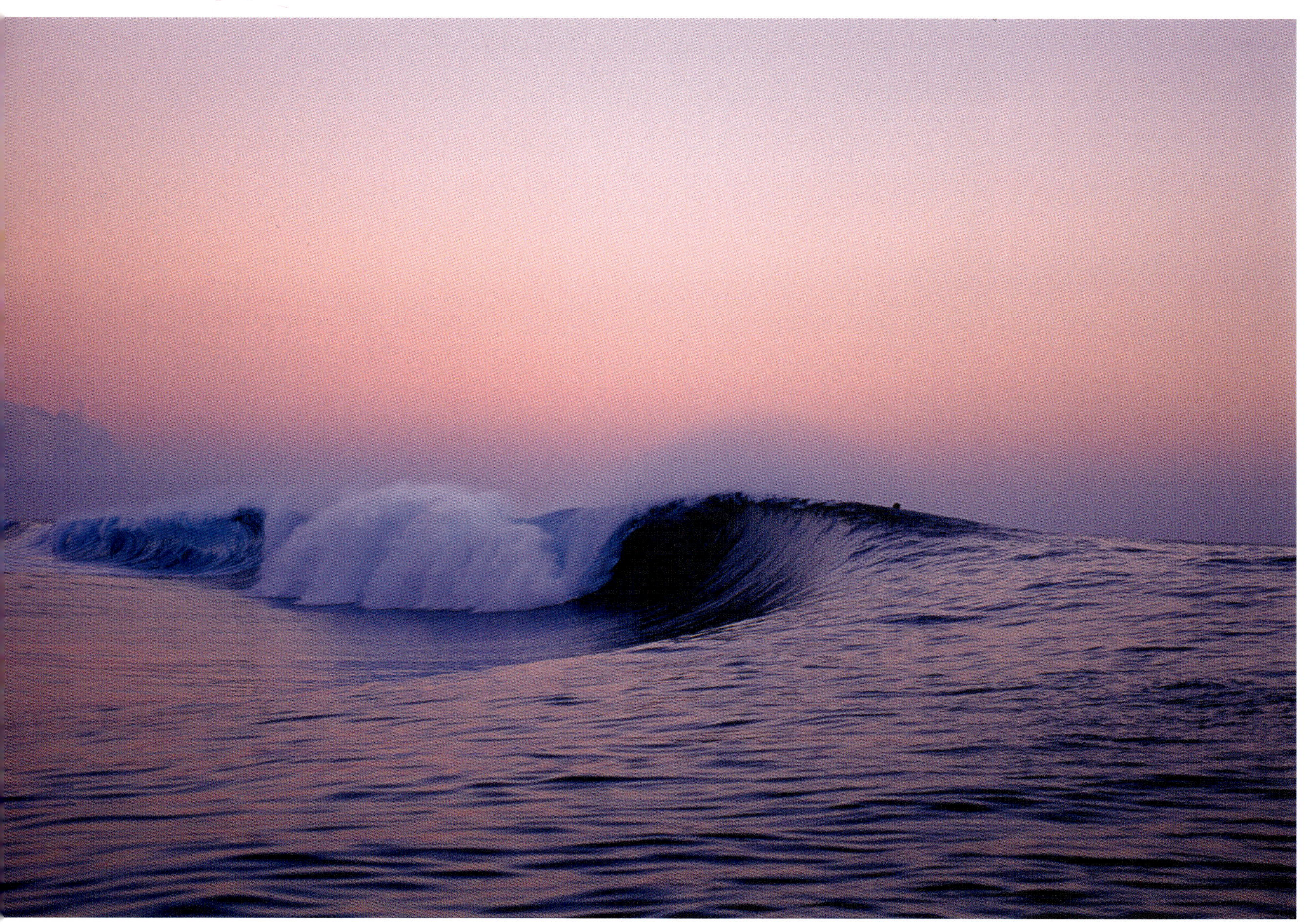

Violet Violence

in different tones. The sun has gone down, but the waves still rise.

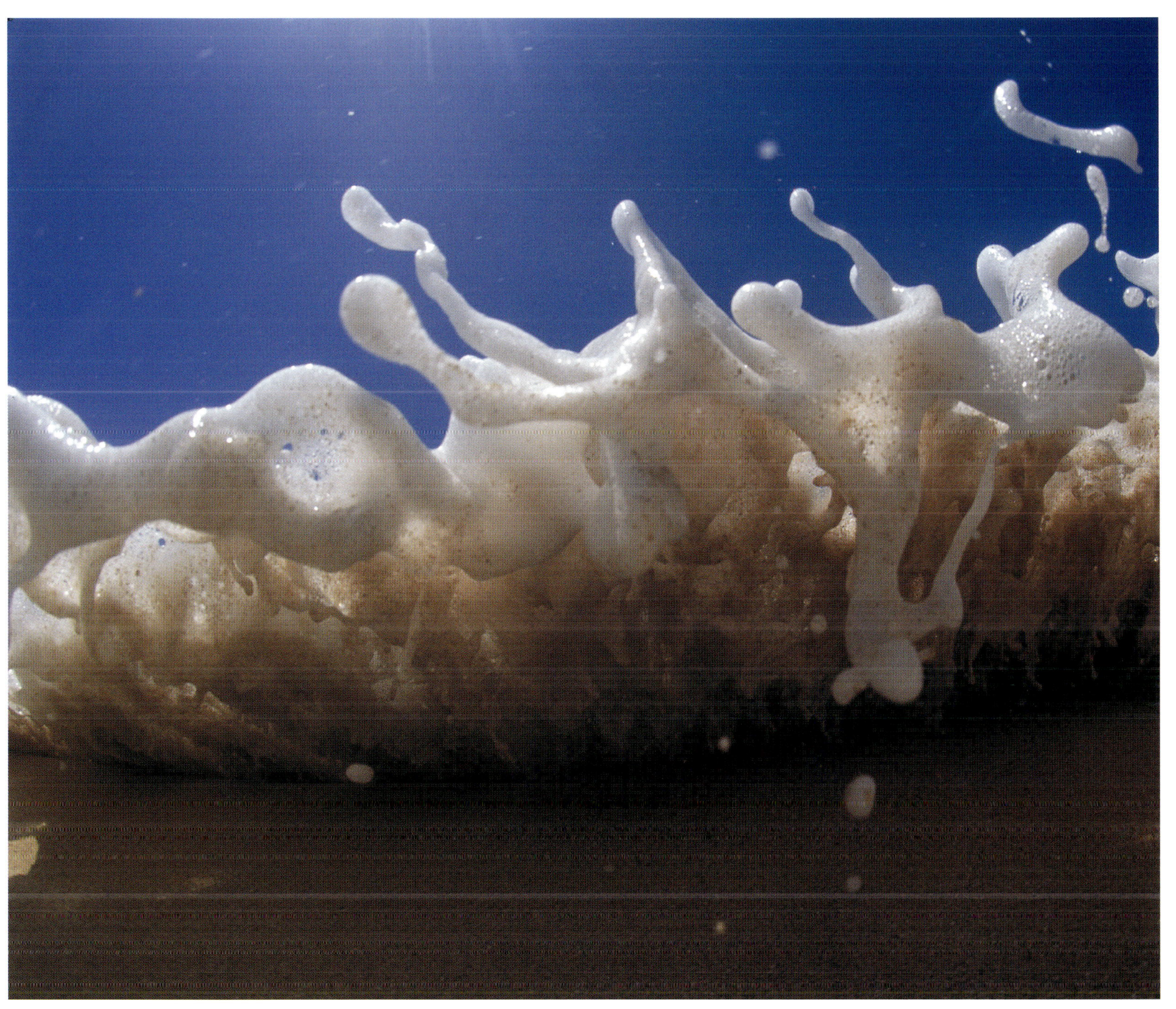

Spilled Milk
This photograph was taken just as saltwater washed
into a slope of sand and then burst vertically.

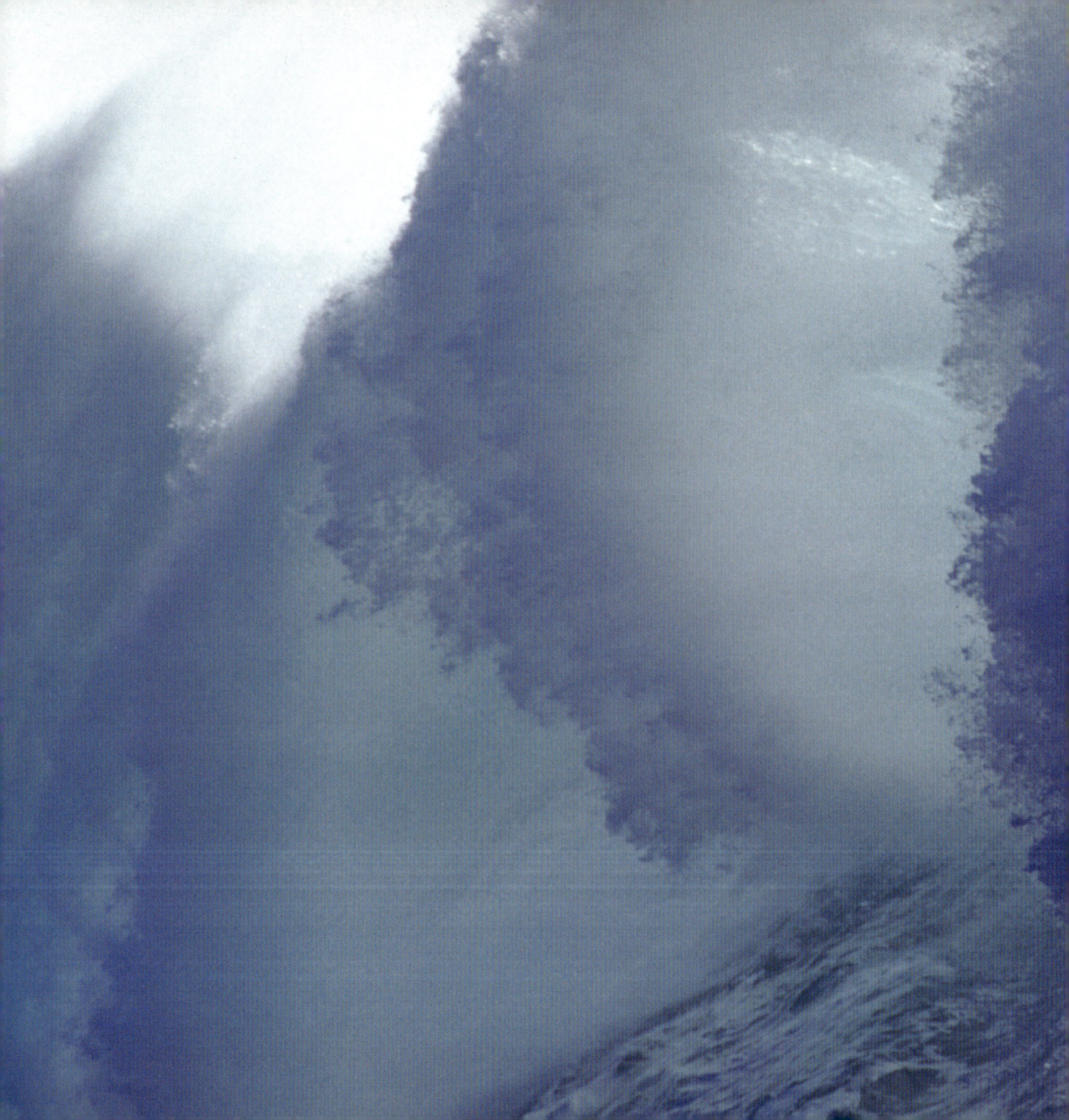

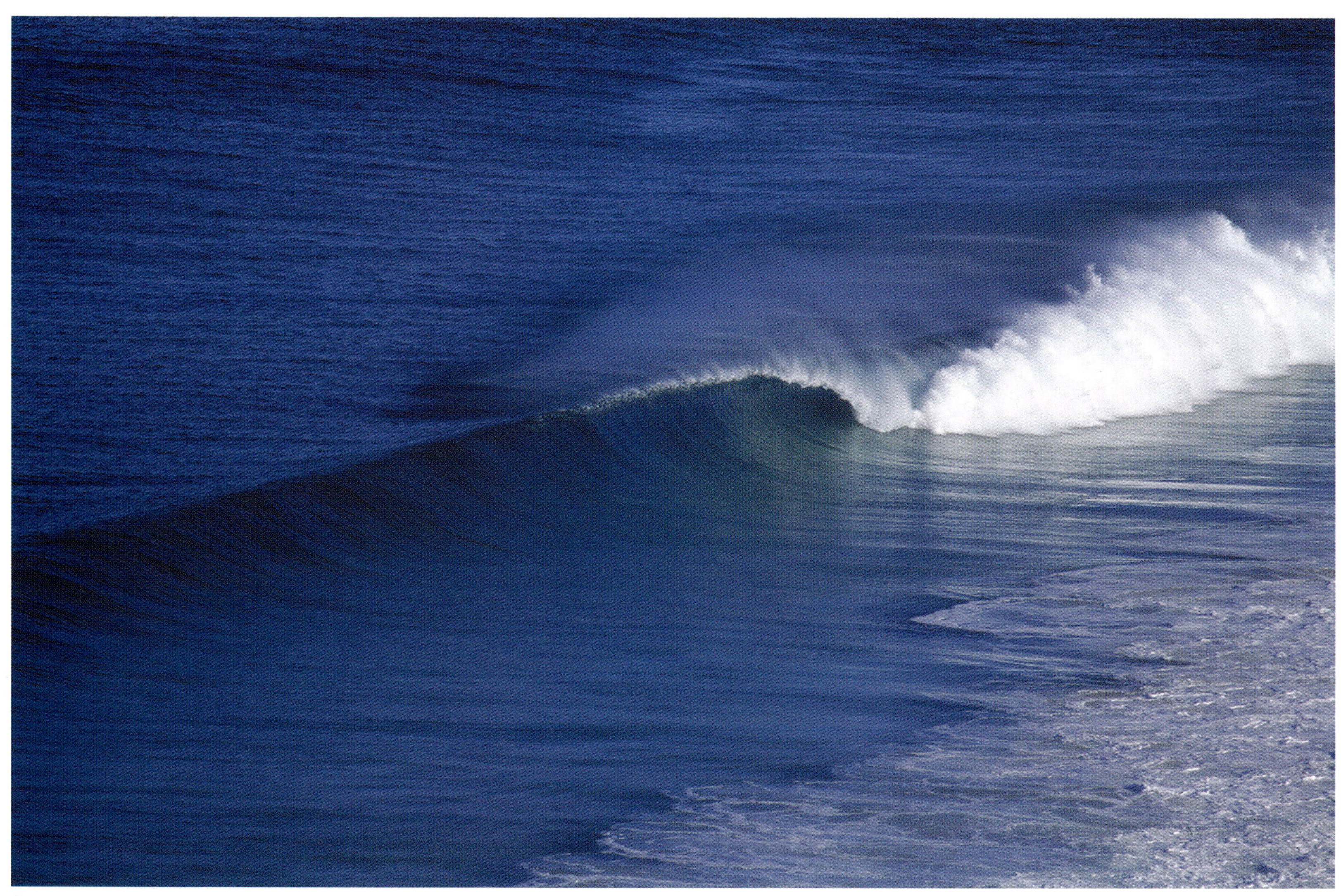

Feeling Blue
and lonely on the coast of New Zealand.

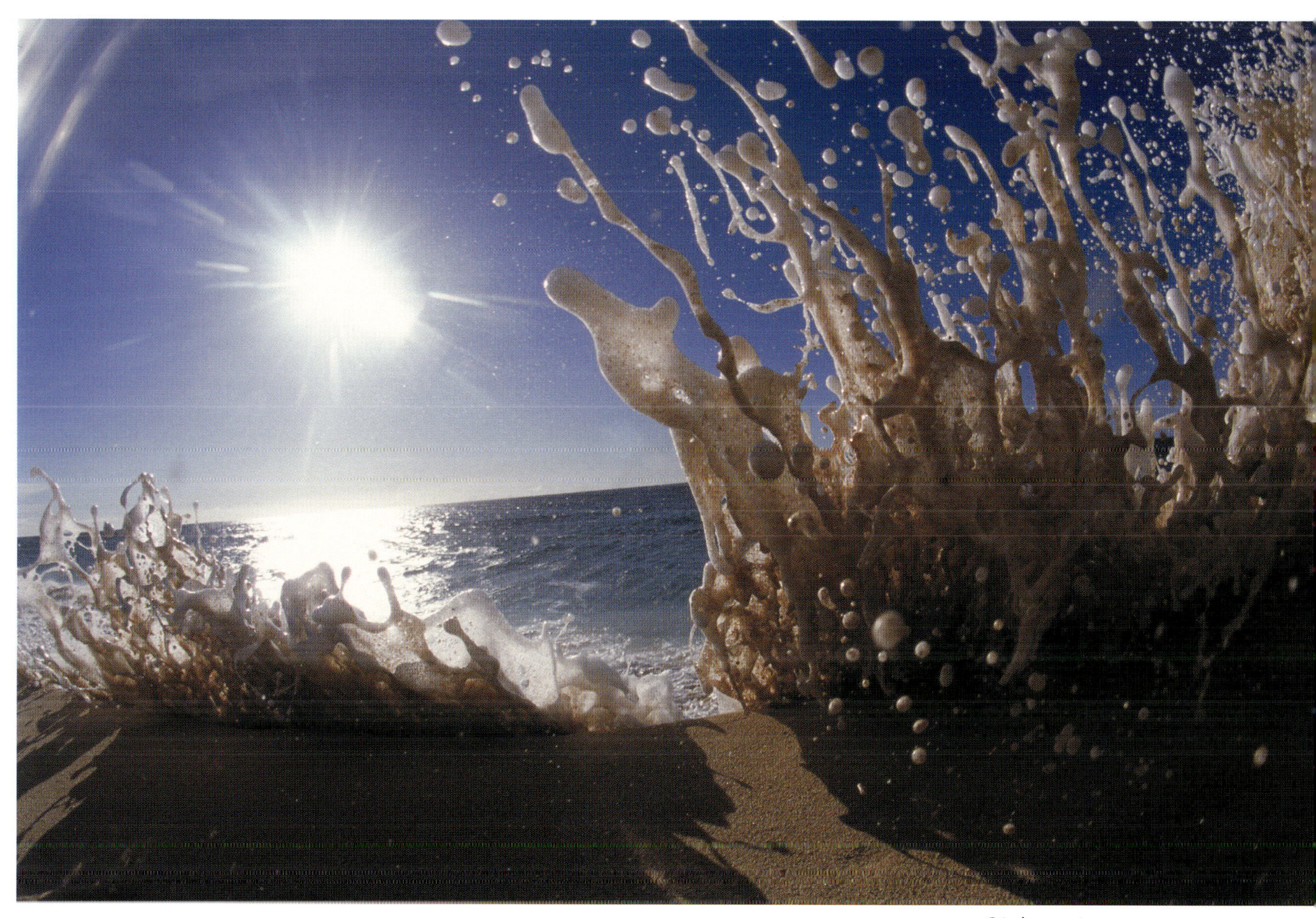

Stalagmites
Saltwater is stopped in the lens of
the camera as it juts towards the sky.

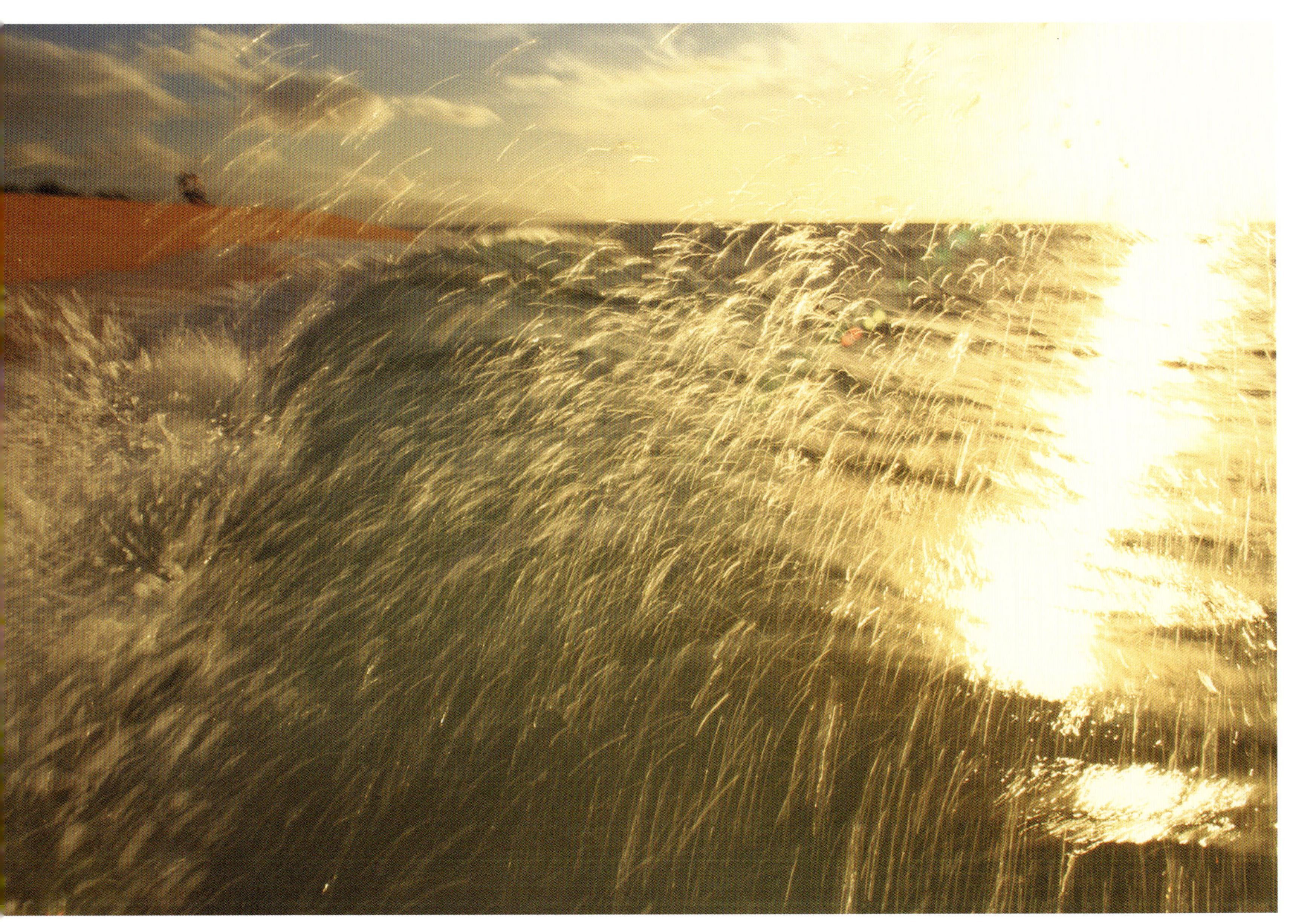

Pounding
on the Shoreline and a lasersline of sunlight pierces a wave as it lands on shore.

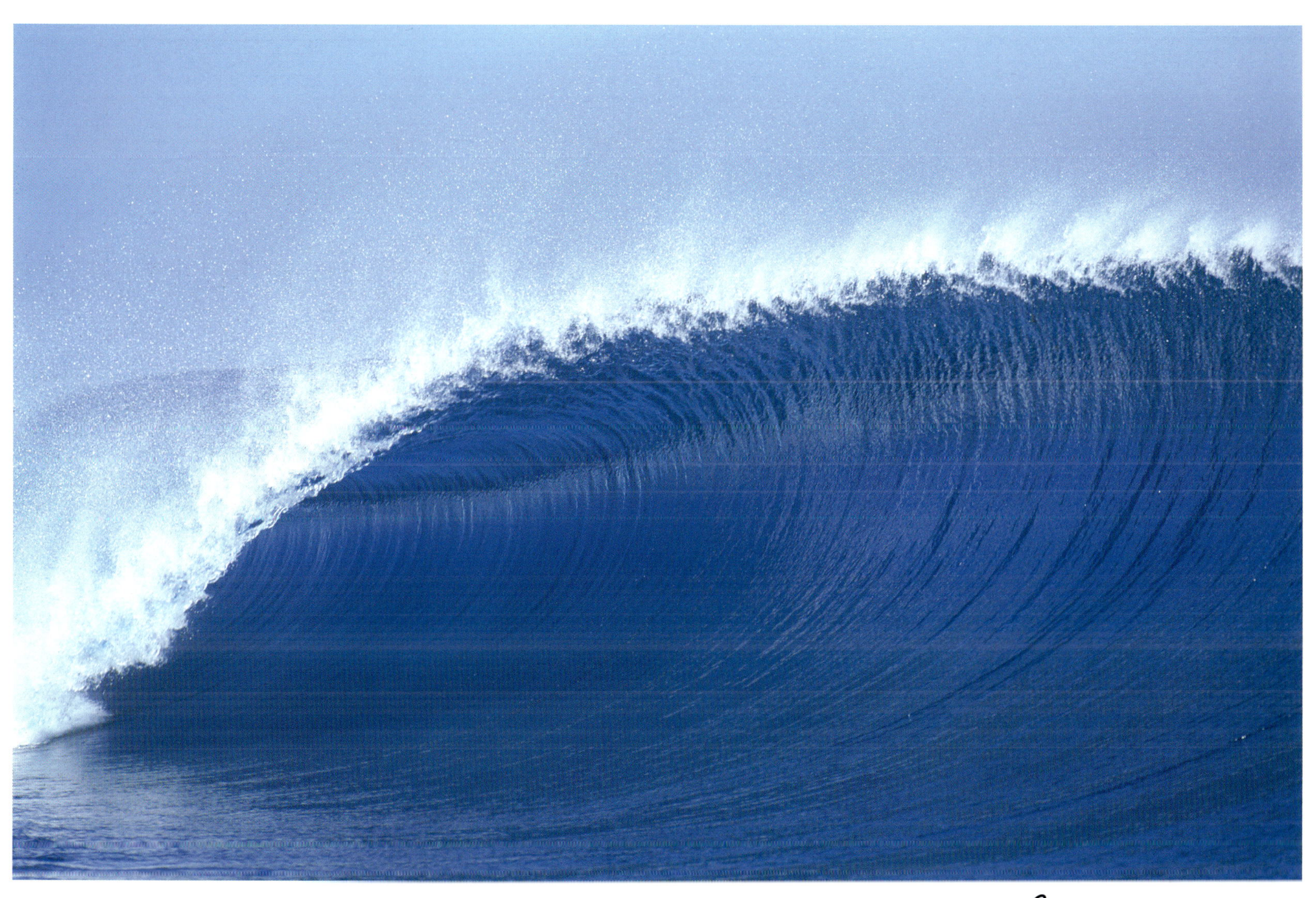

Crisp,
White Line is drawn down a falling
wave in the South Pacific Ocean.

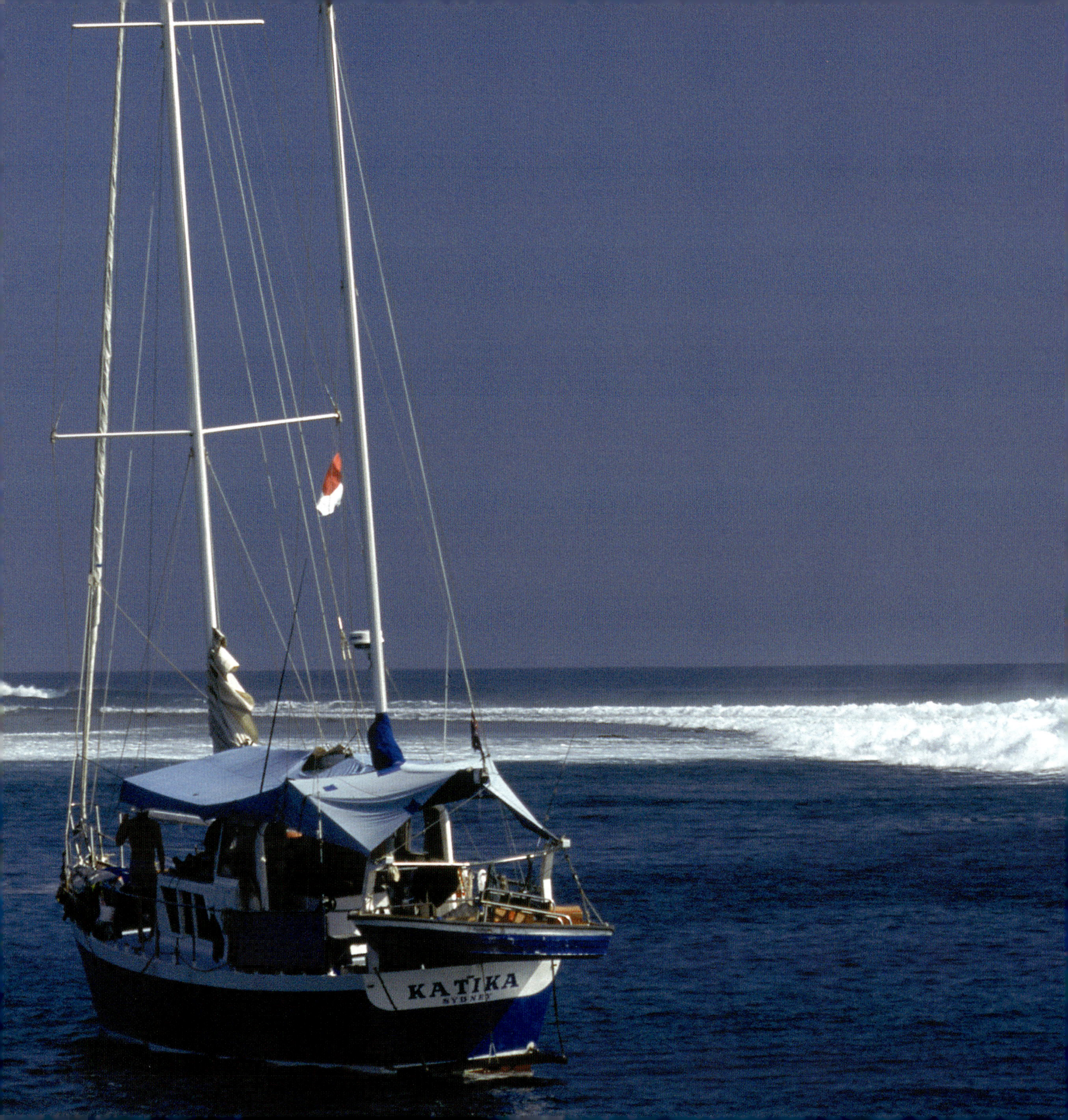

KATIKA
SYDNEY

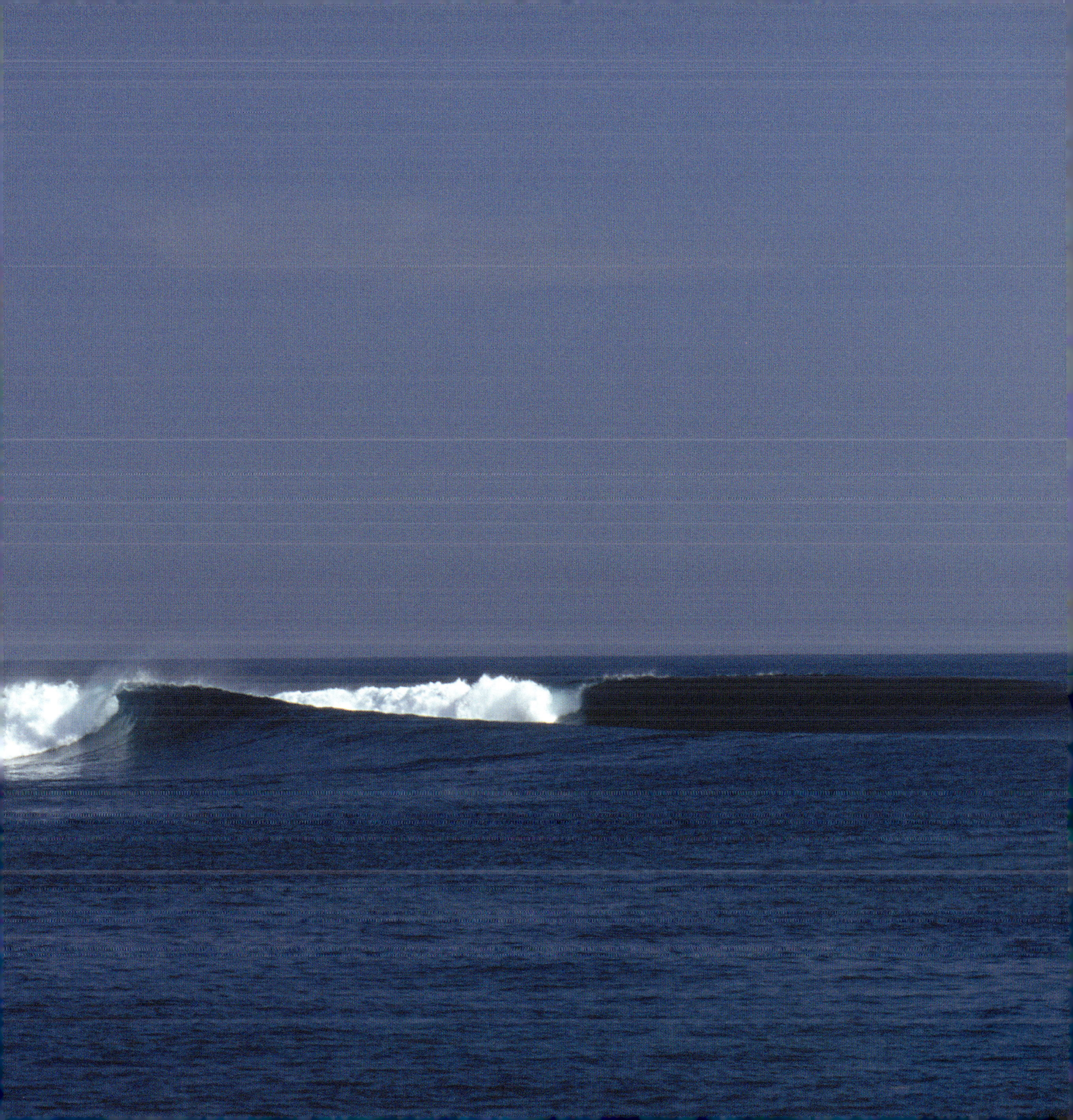

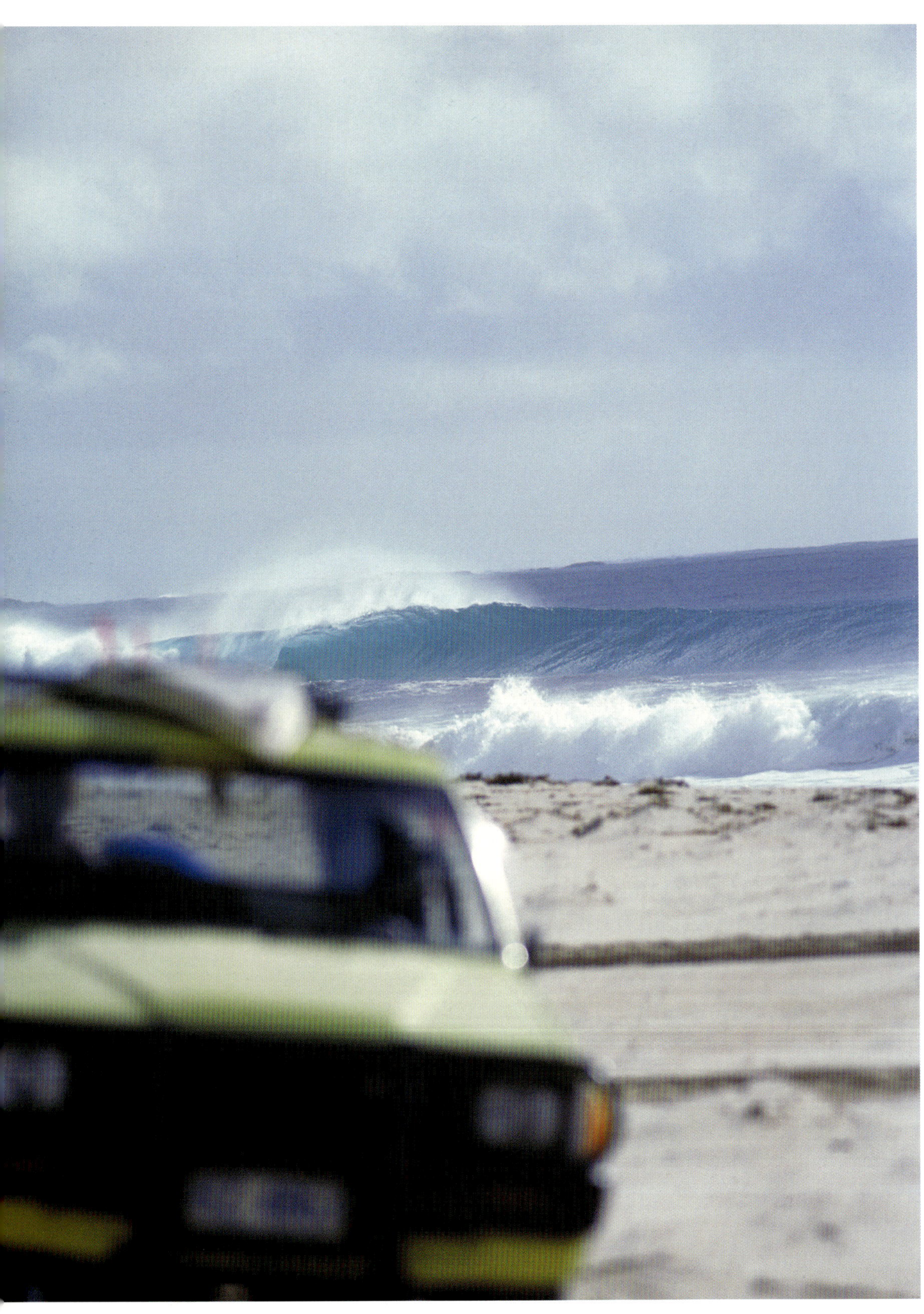

Intrusion of Machine
on a beach. Watermen have no
other choice for access sometimes.

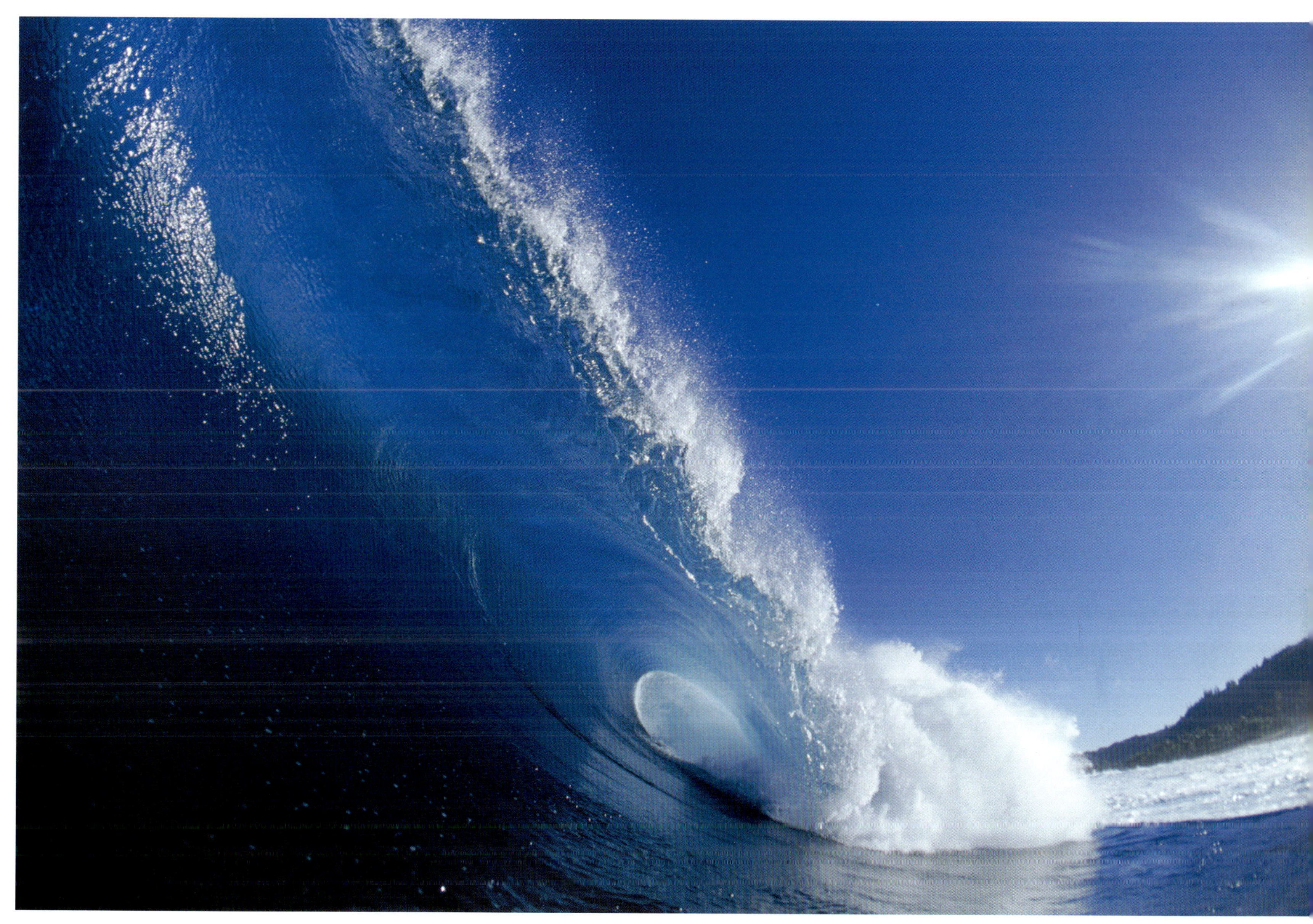

Cascade of Blues
in the Hawaiian Morning.

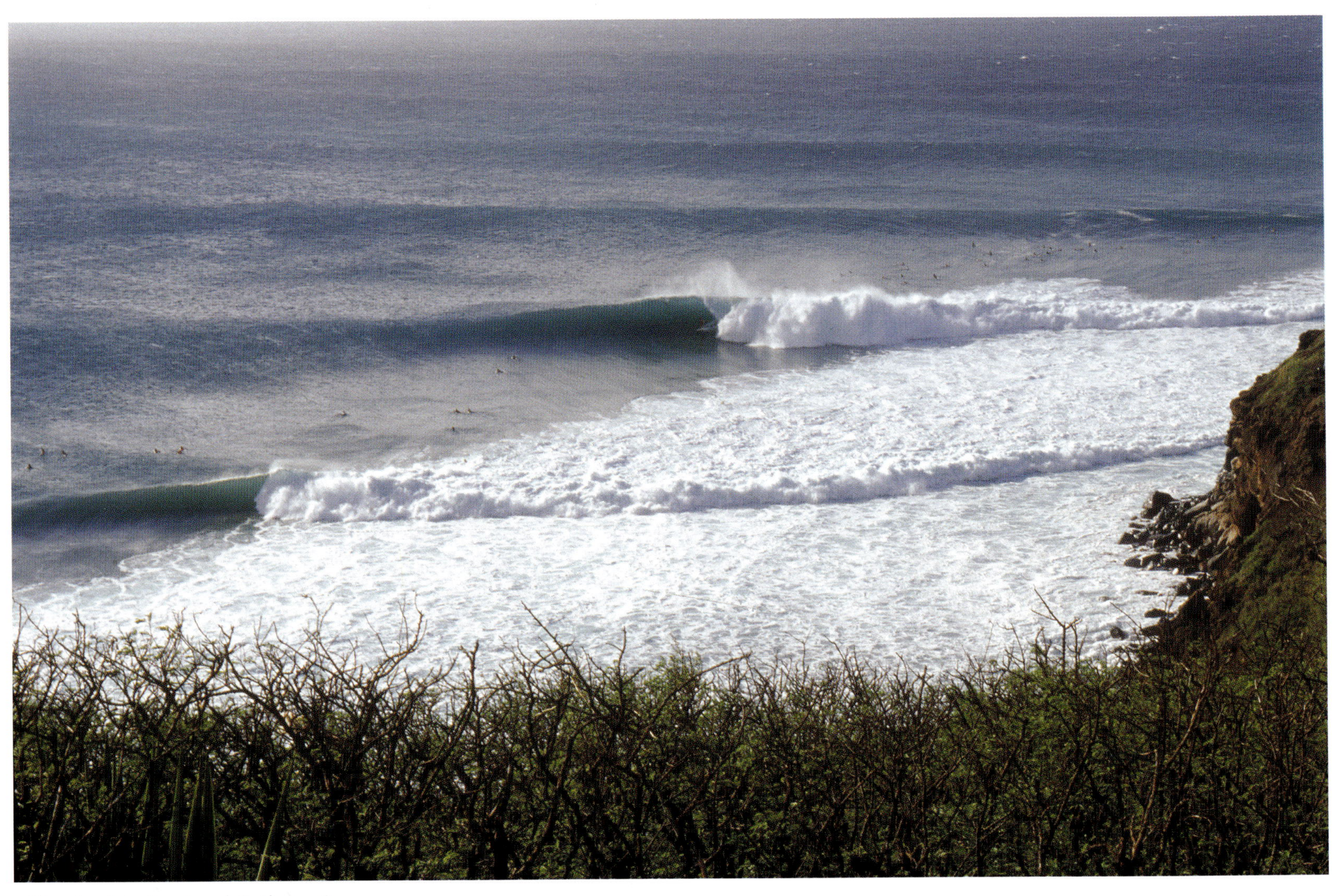

The Right Angle of White Foam

To a surfer this is considered 'the lineup.' 'Lineup' refers to how that waves are breaking and where. This is a very good 'lineup.'

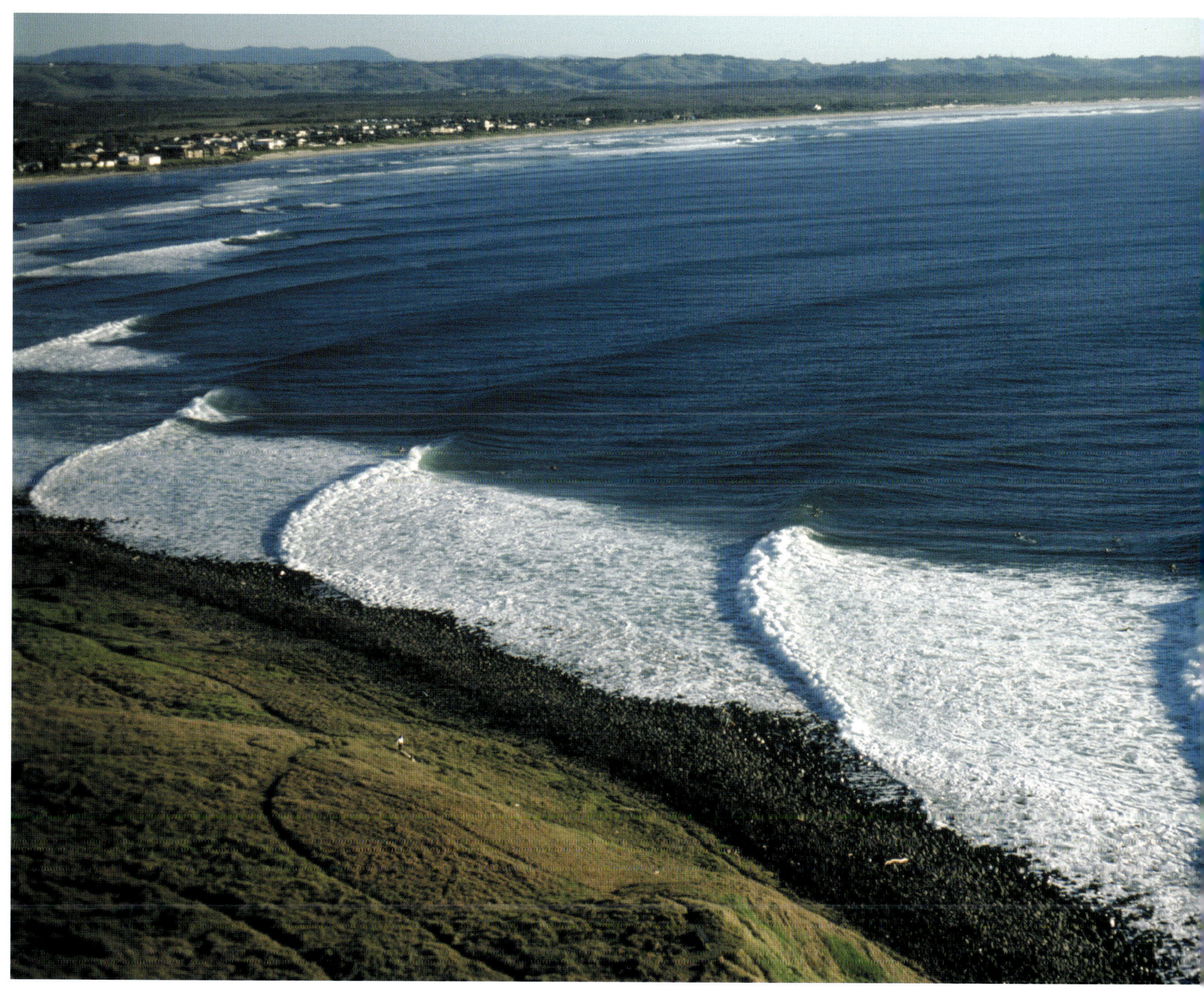

Approaching Waves
to a Local Village in Australia.

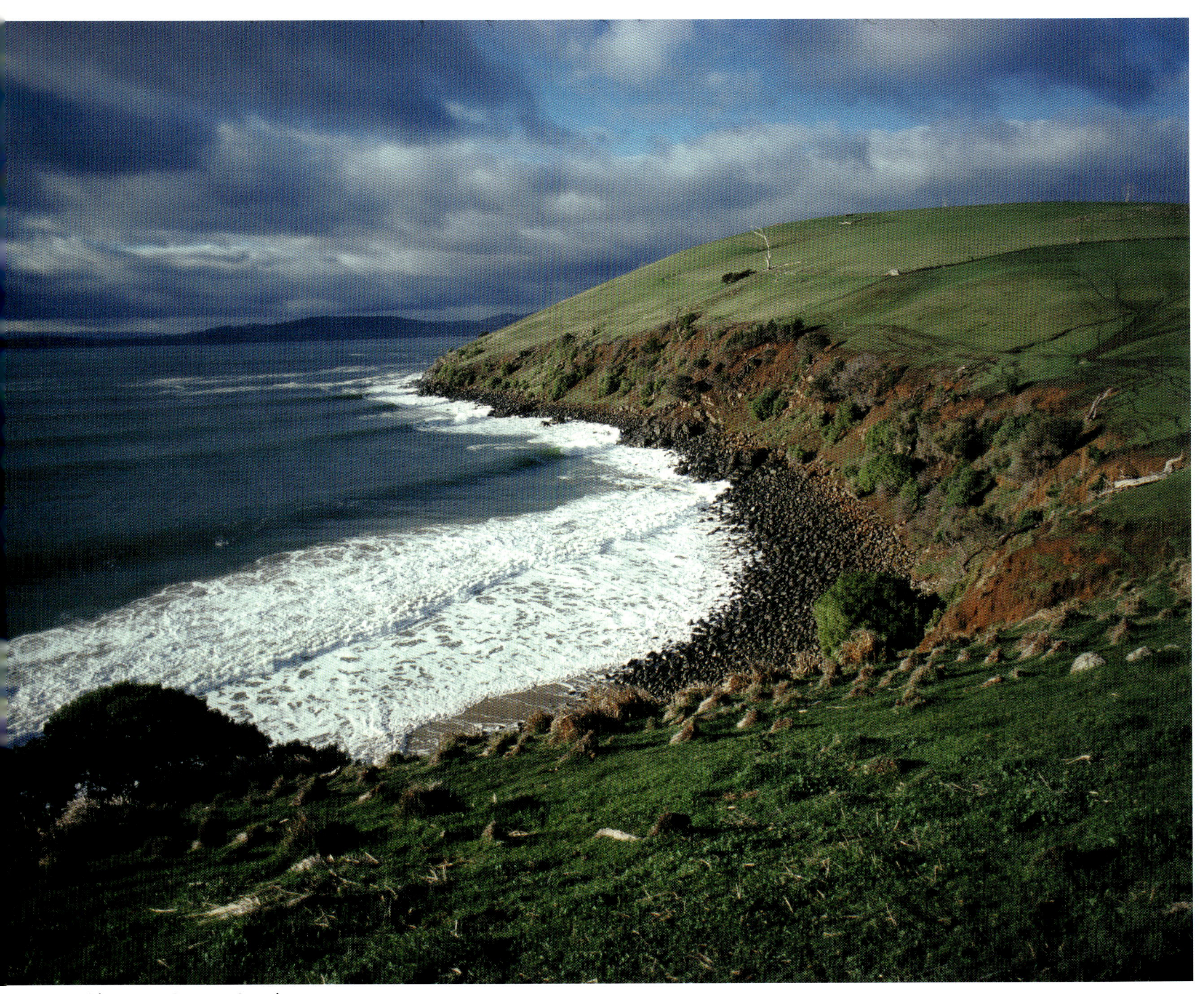

Abrasive Green Landscape
against a Harsh Sky. Notice how the point of land
makes a 'curl' much similar to that of a breaking wave.

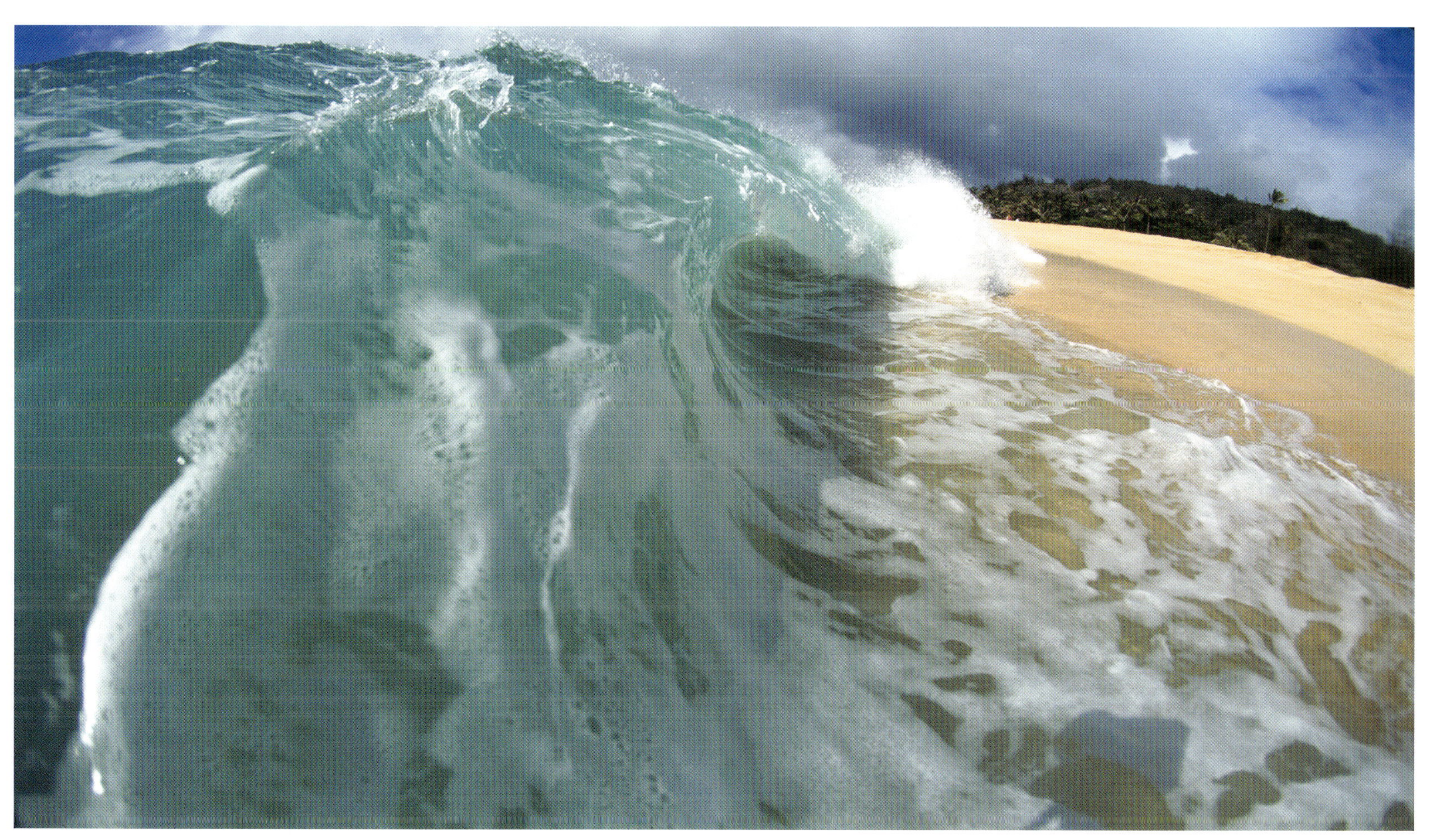

Surge onto the Sand

Shorebreak such as this is responsible for the movement of sand and an intense surge of saltwater onto beaches.

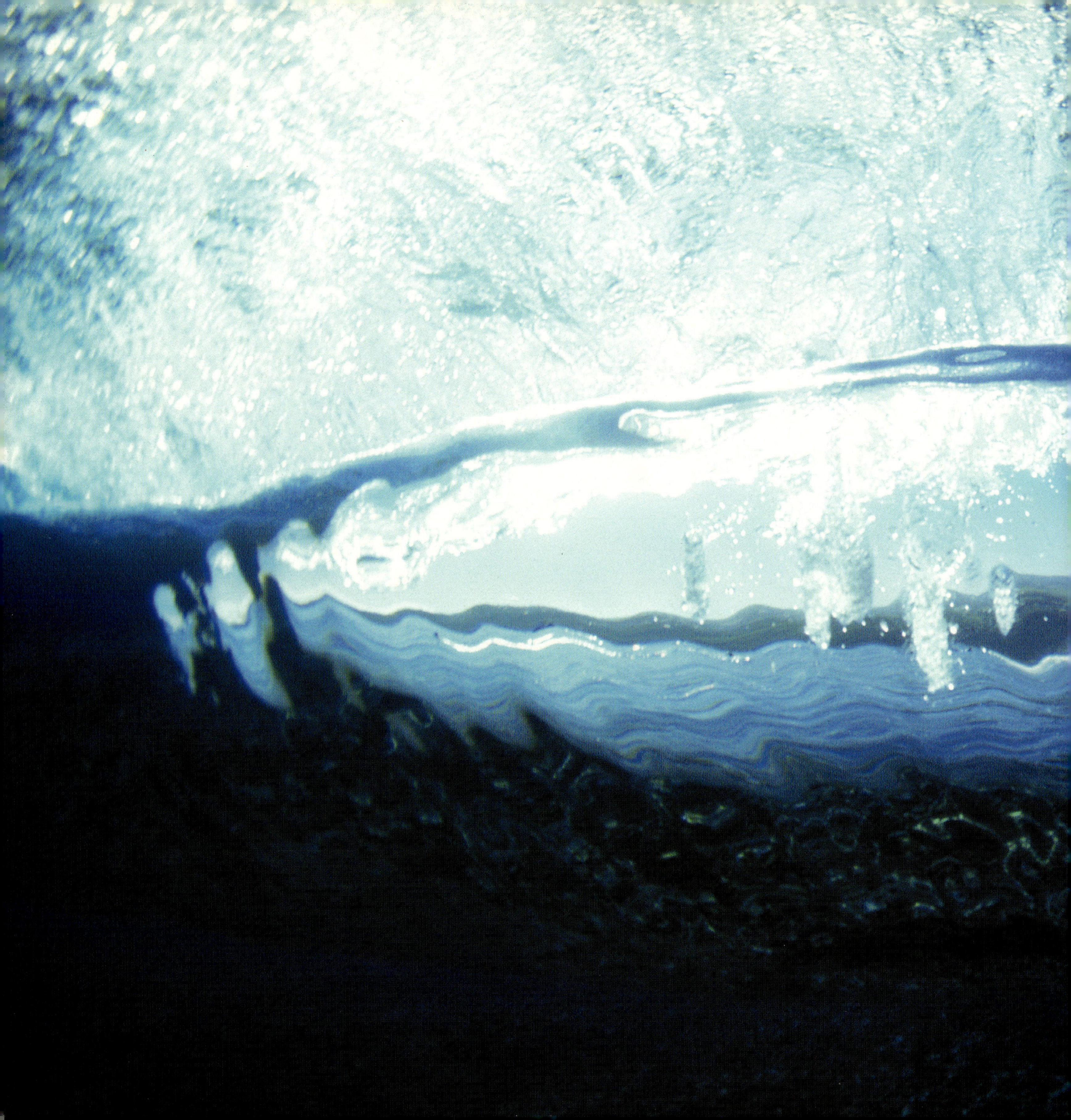

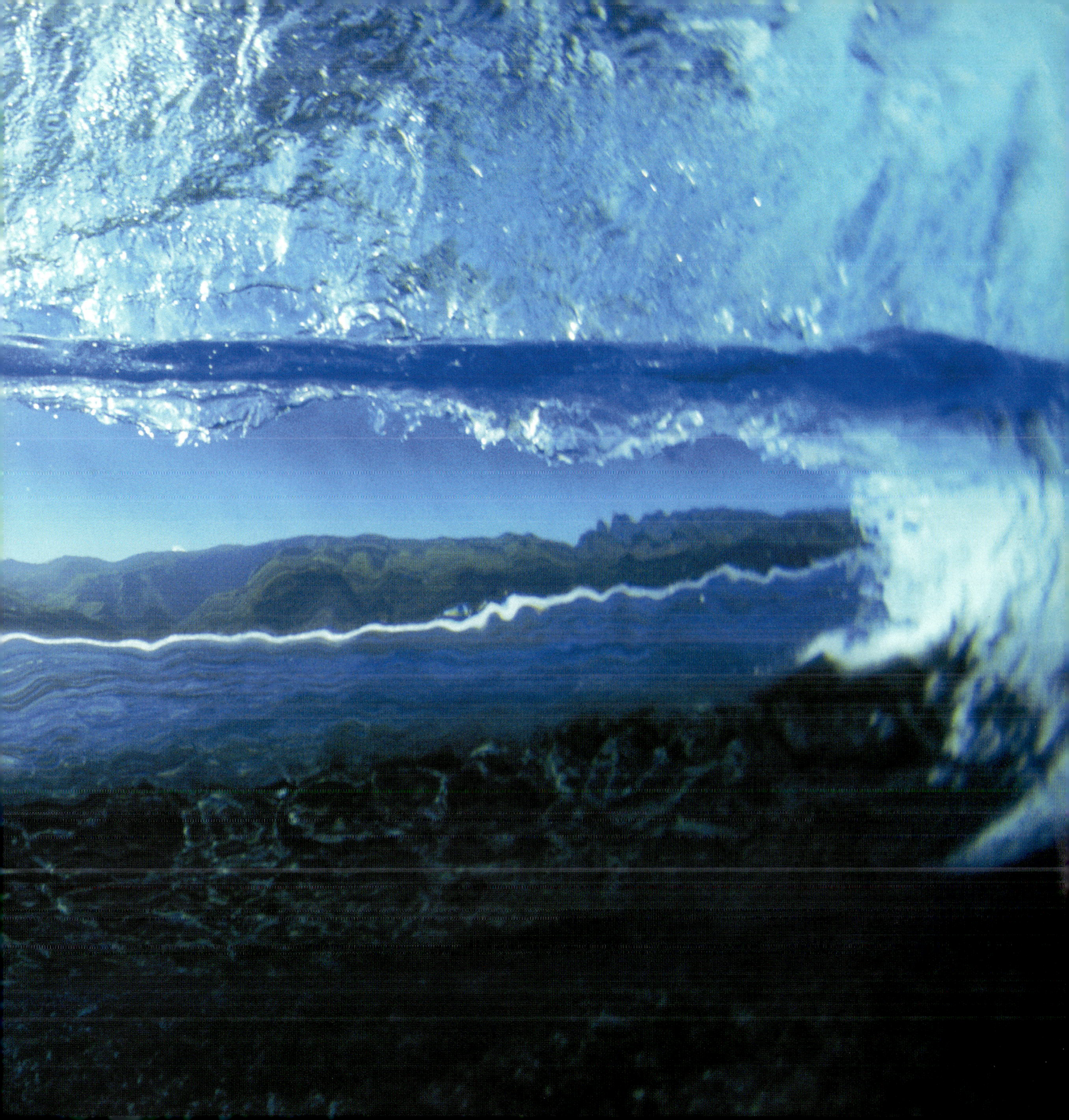

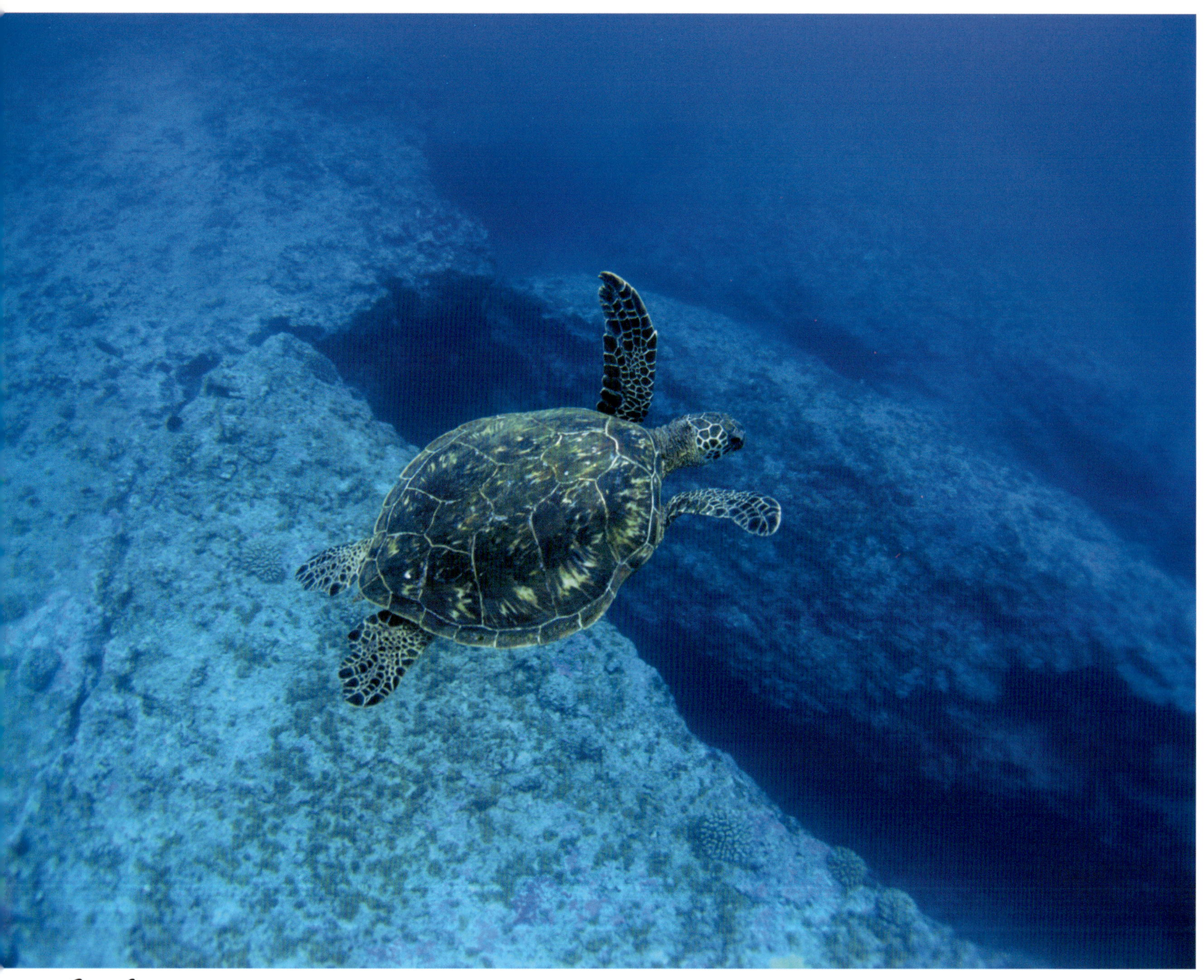

Free Aqueous
Flight of the Turtle.

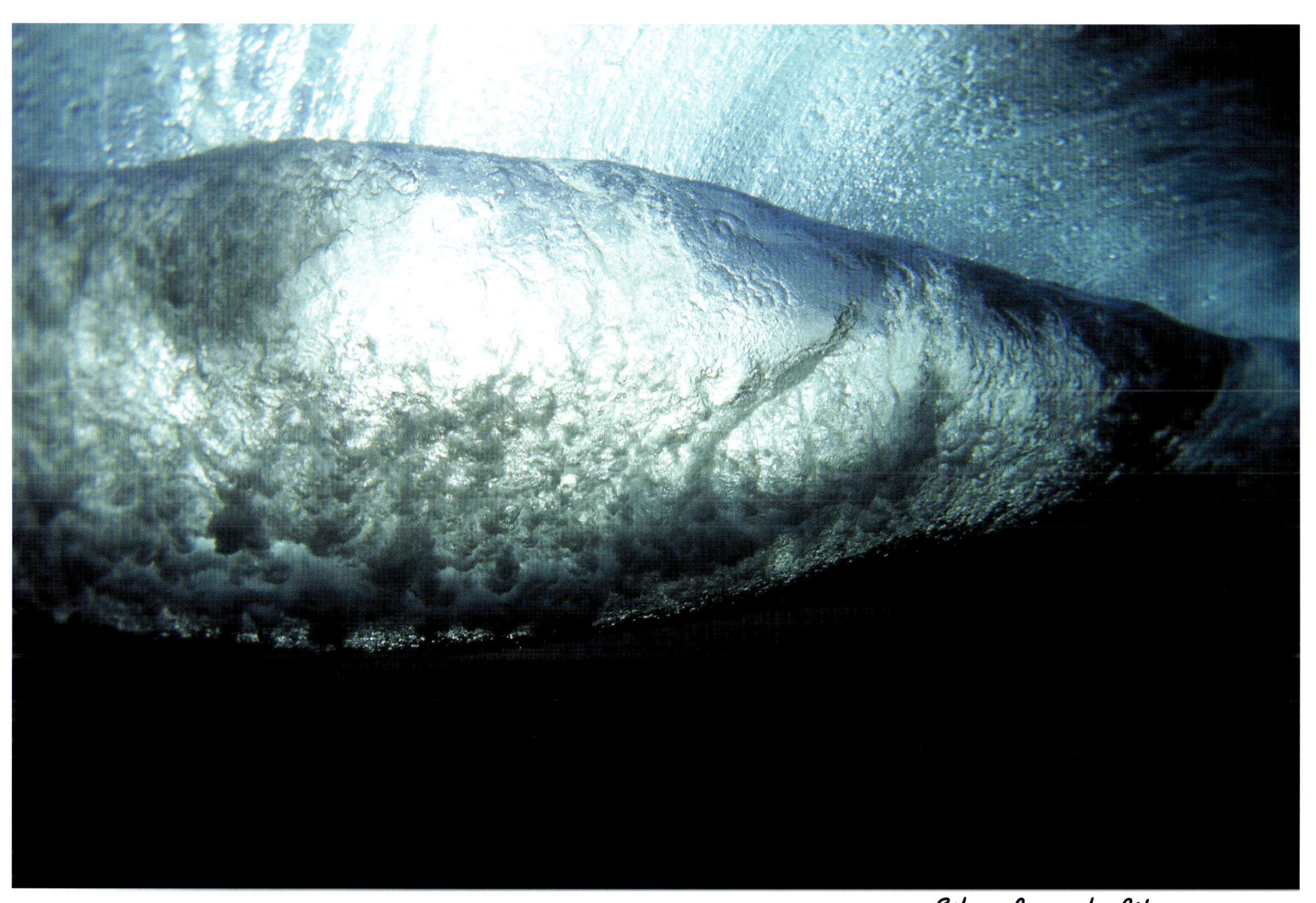

Silver Lung of a Wave

If a wave were a living creature this would be its respiratory system. South Pacific Ocean, Tahiti.

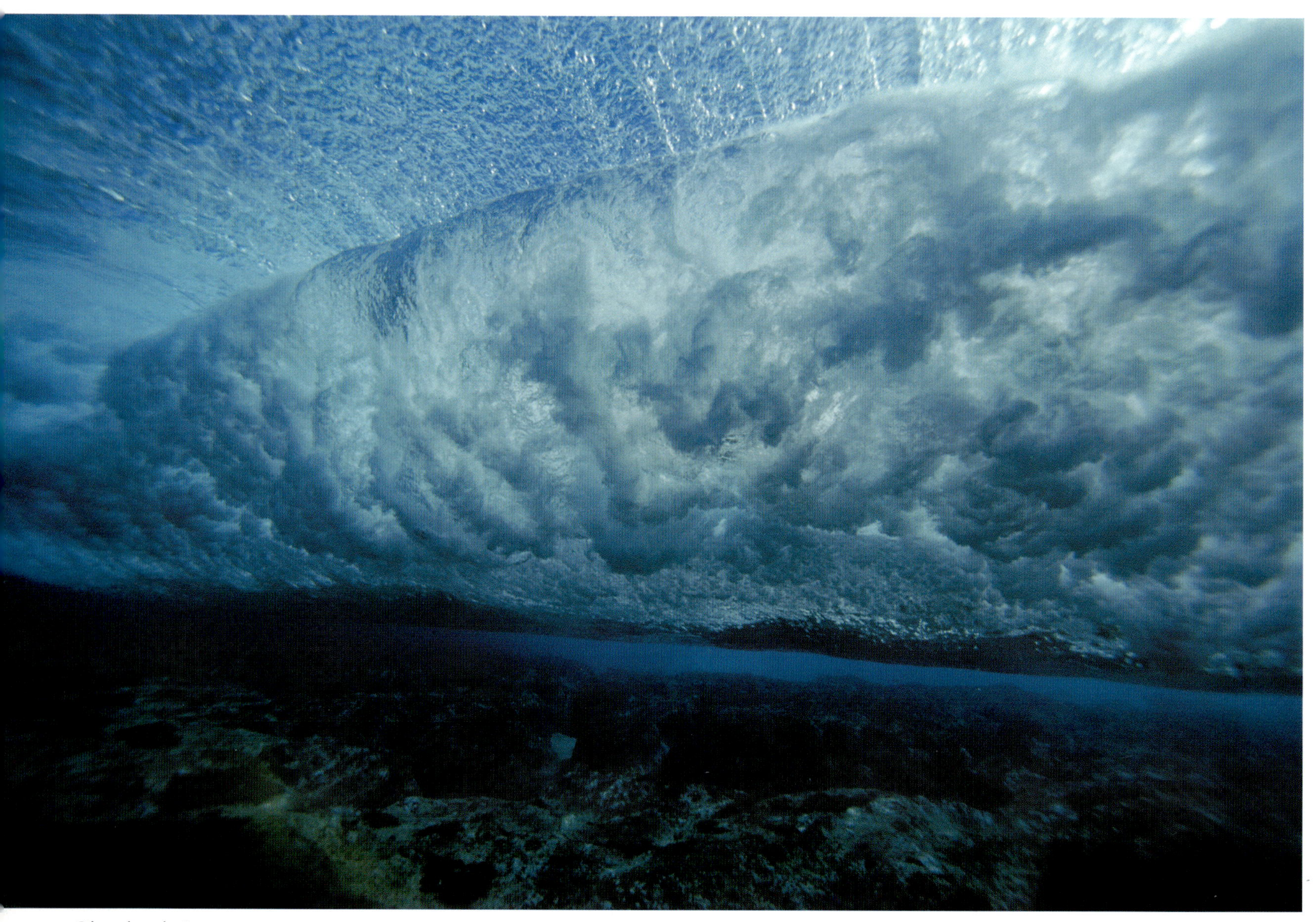

Clouds of Foam
from Underwater with precise lines of a passing wave.

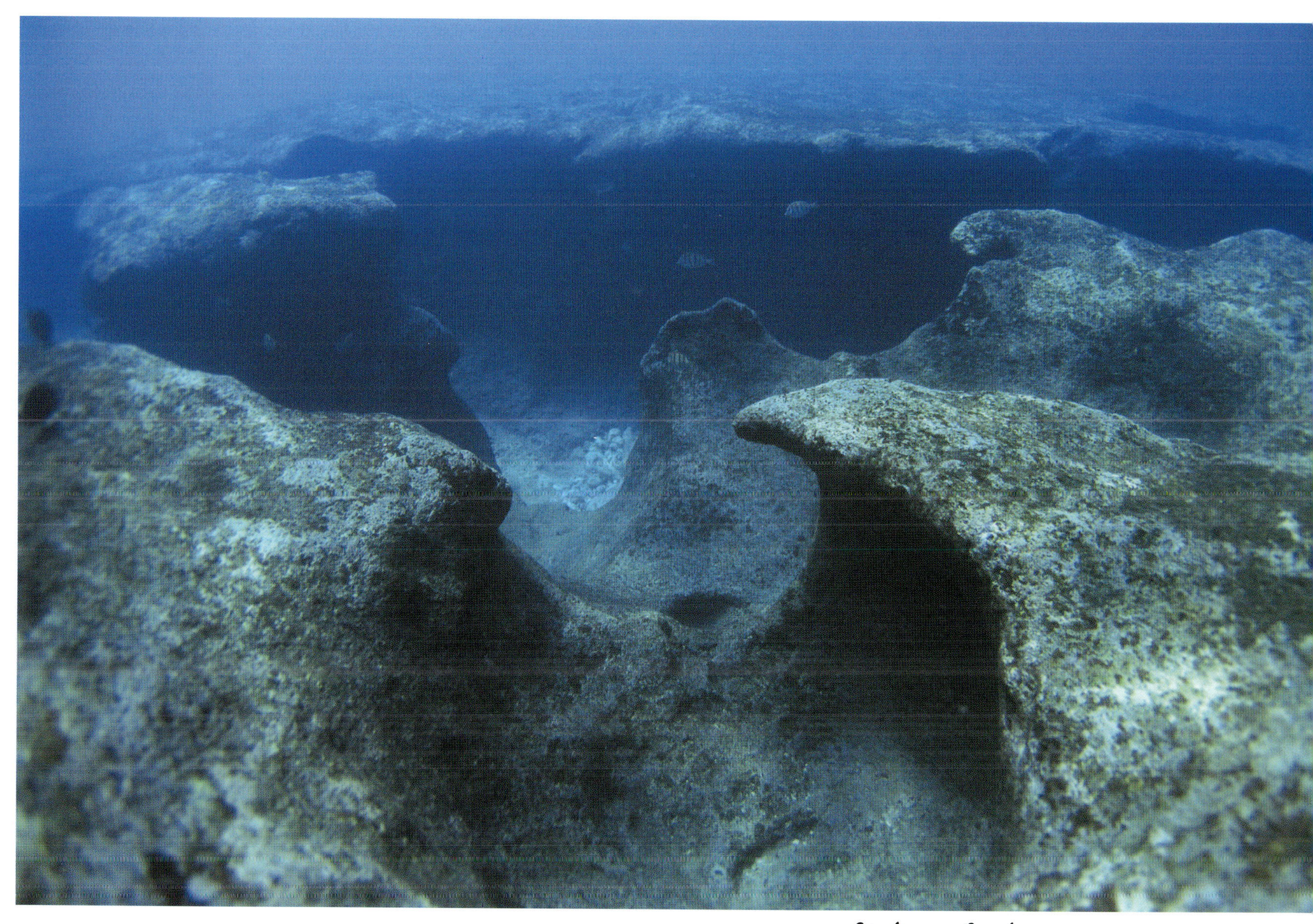

Undersea Landscape,
more like a mountain range. To be accurate in the title
these should be the Peaks of Pipeline, Island of Oahu.

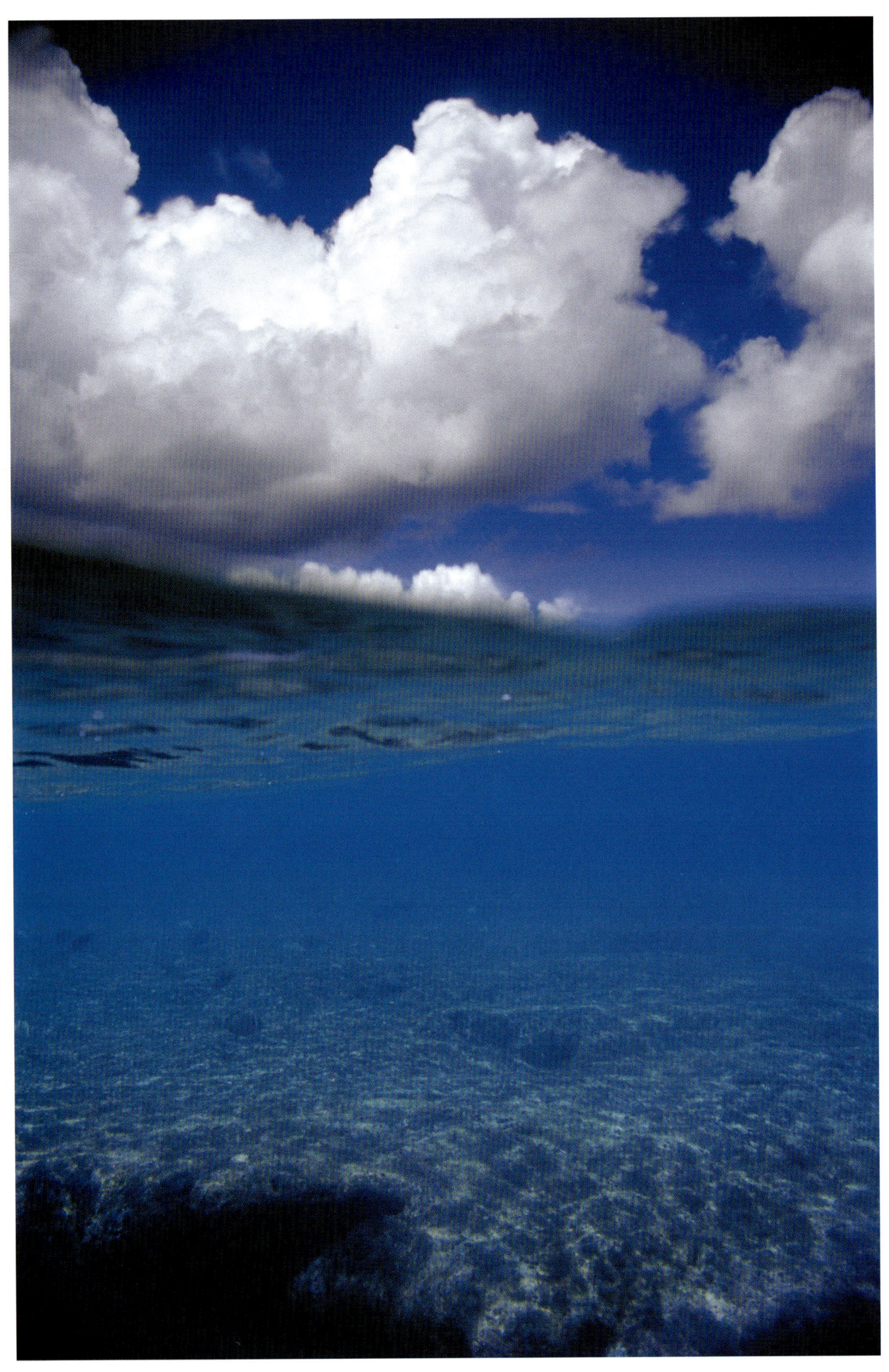

Deep and the High
The Deep: hydrogen with two oxygen molecules.
The High: primarily oxygen molecules.

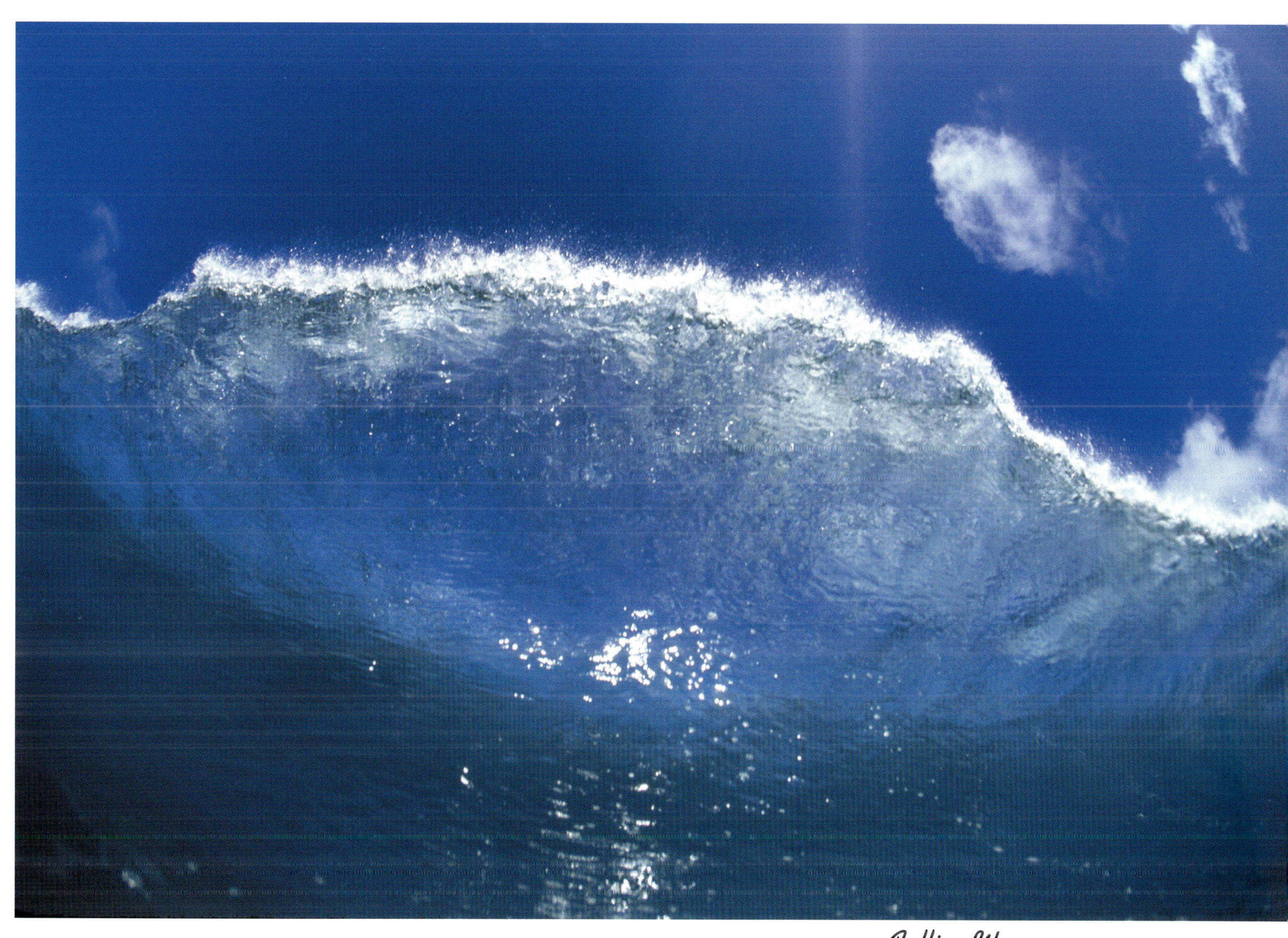

Falling Wave,
this one is coming down right onto the camera.

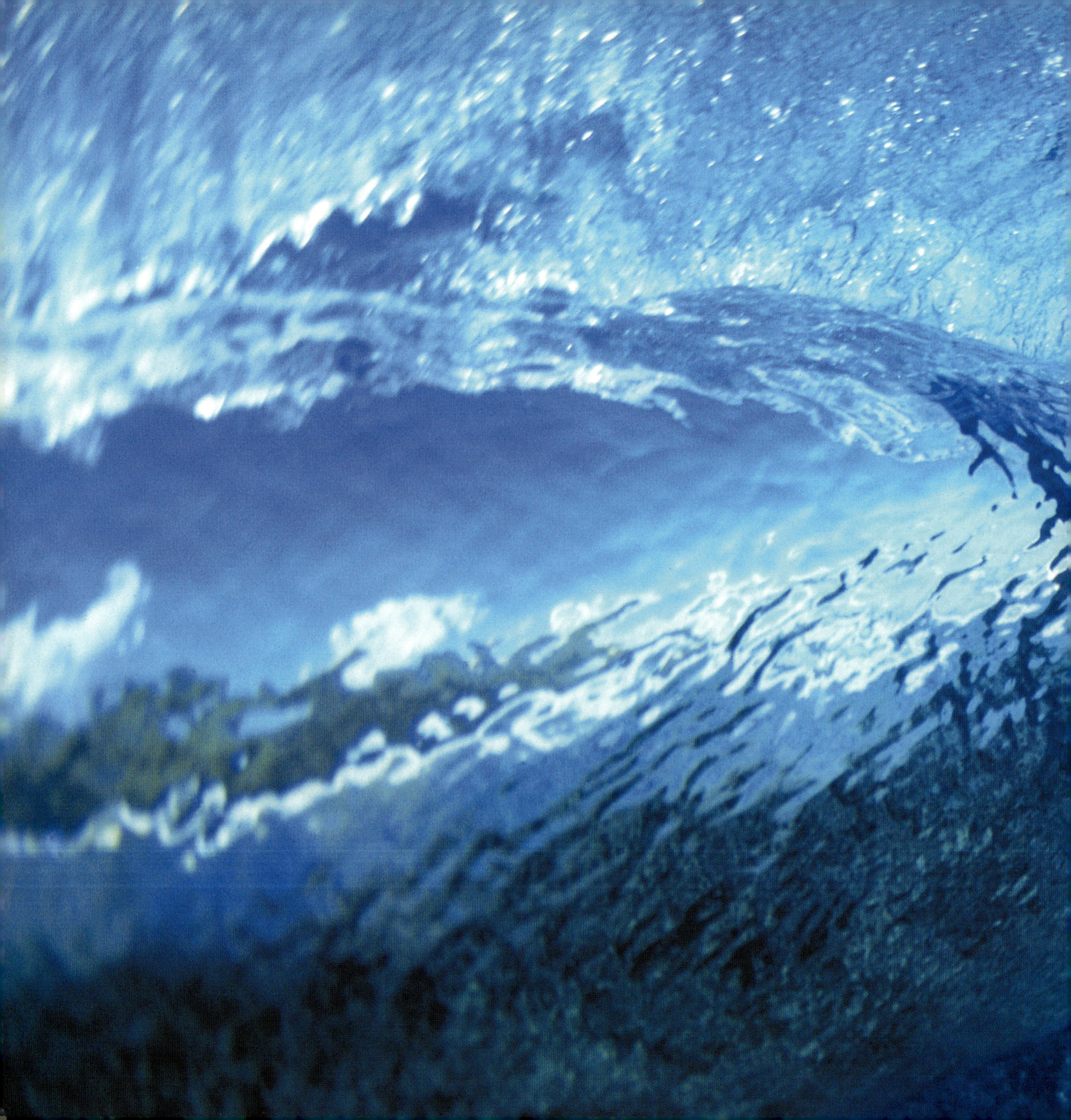

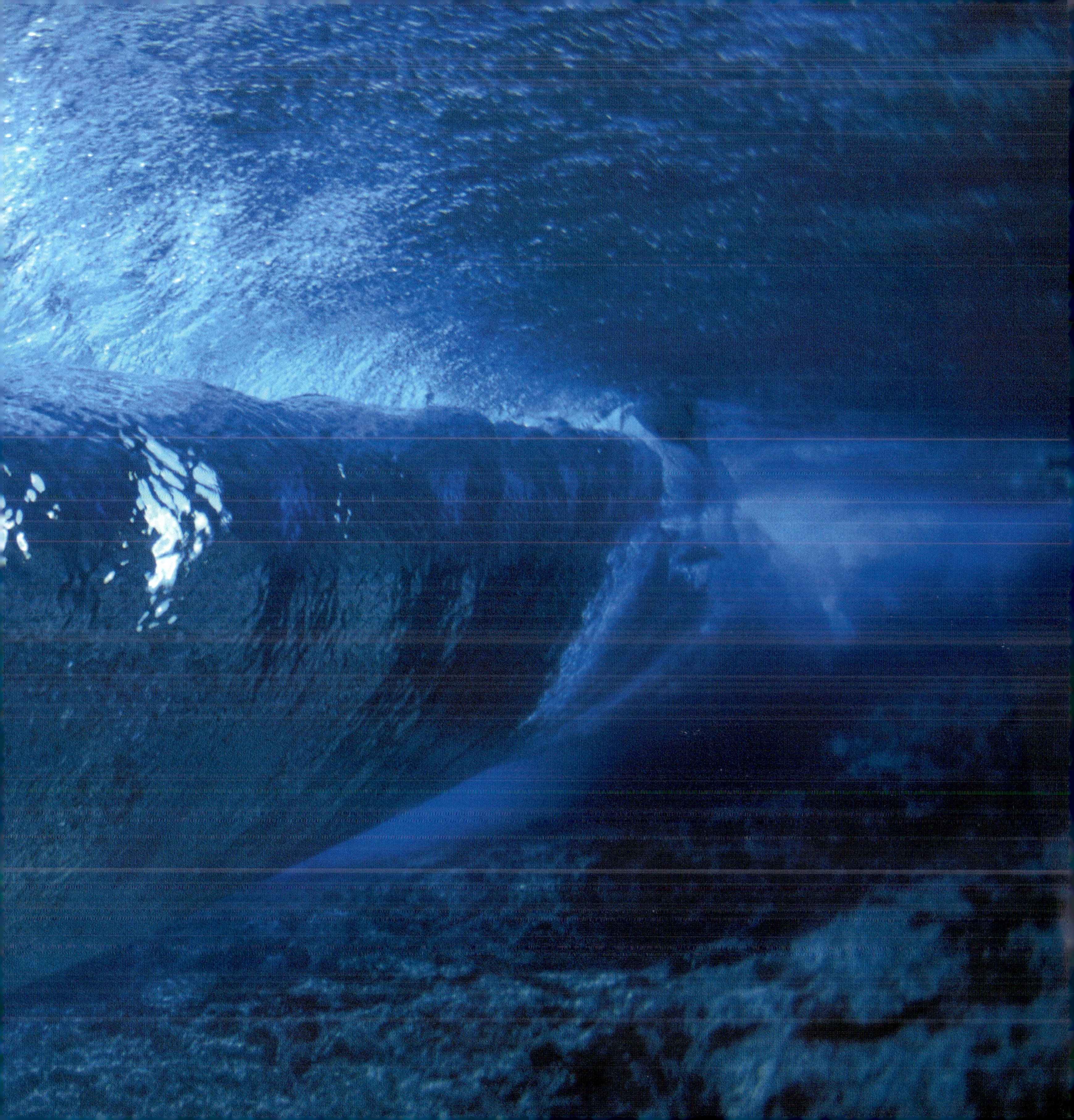

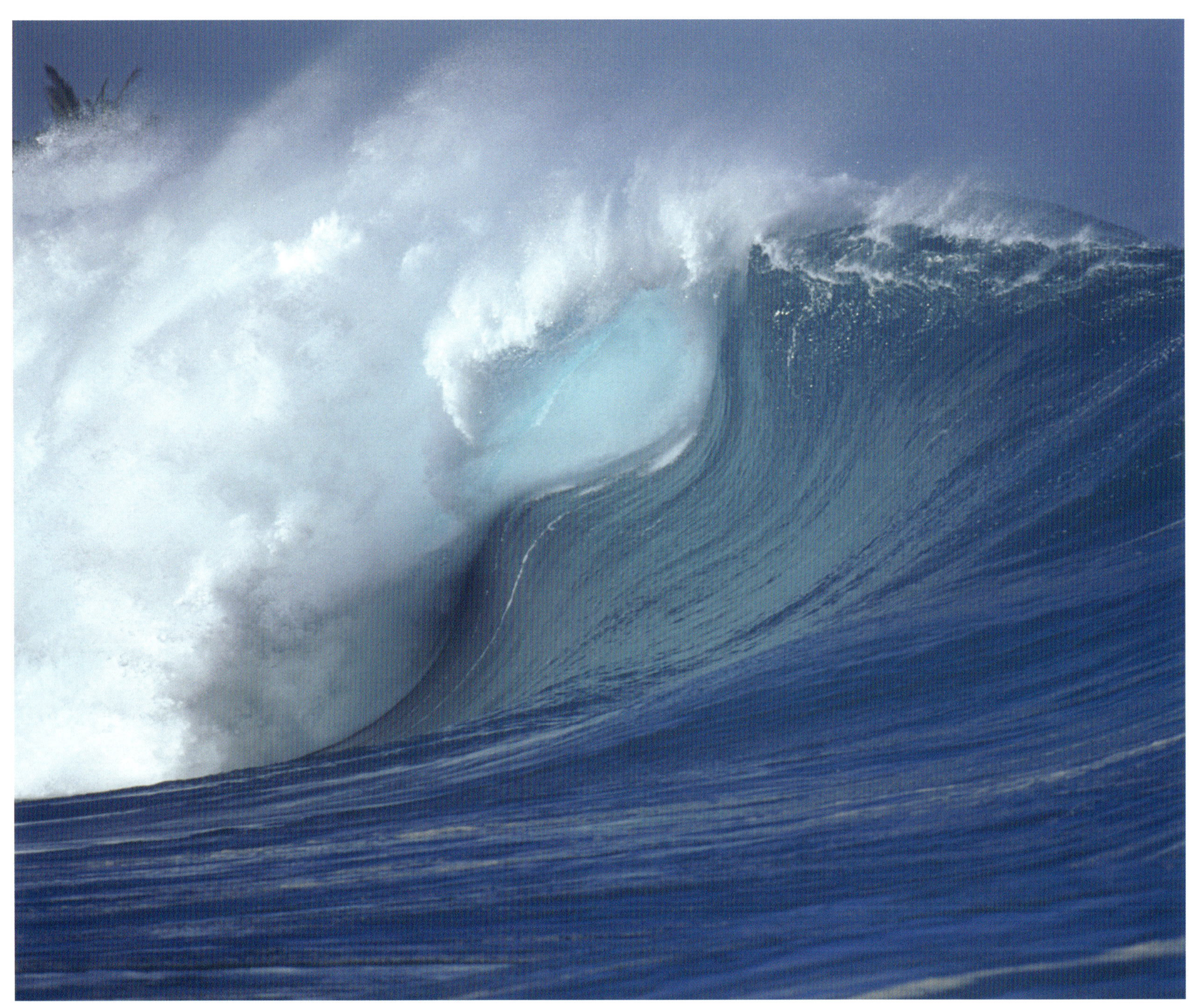

Waves caught amongst each other,
creating steps together. North Pacific Ocean.

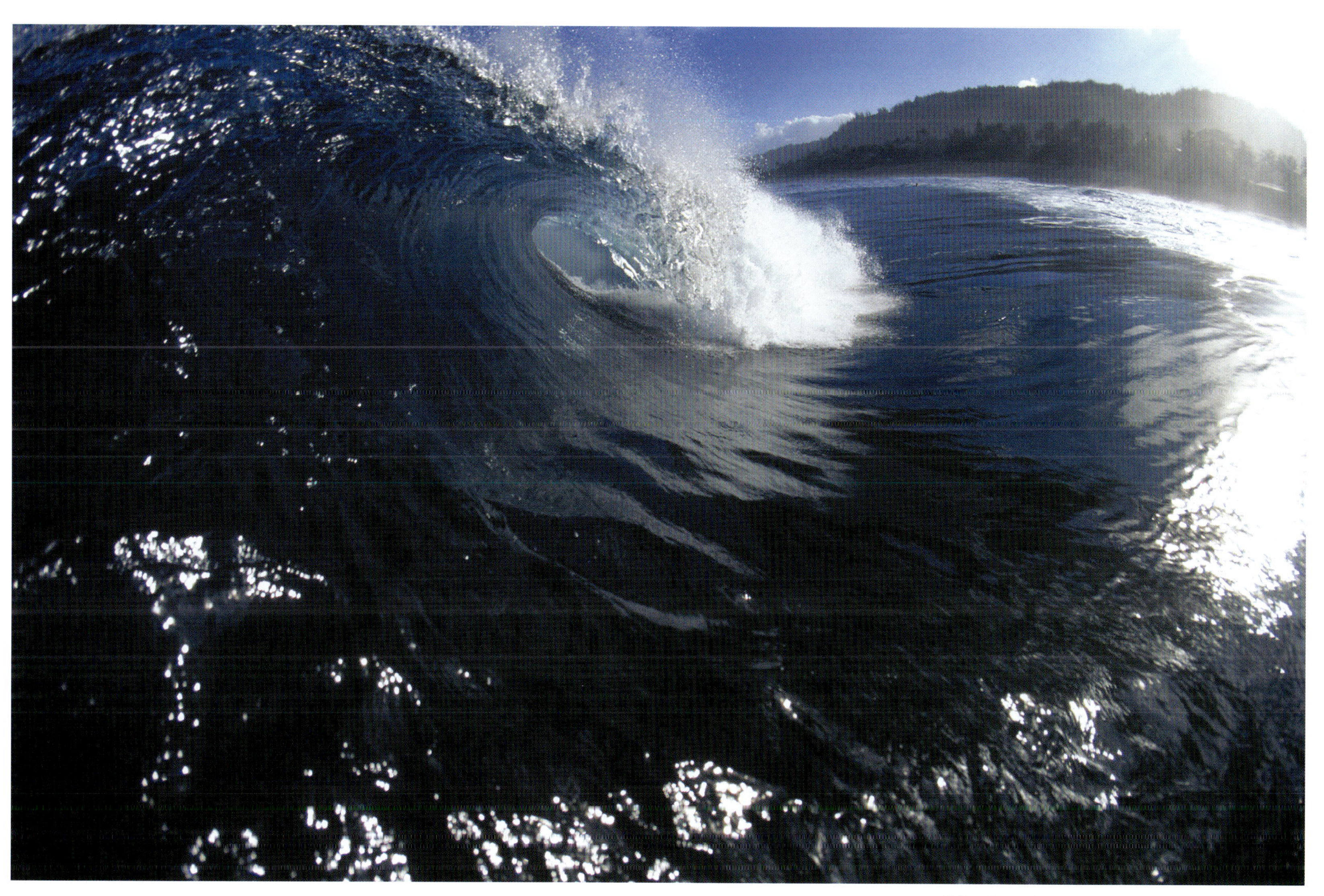

Blackwater
in the Morning with a line of shine from the sun.

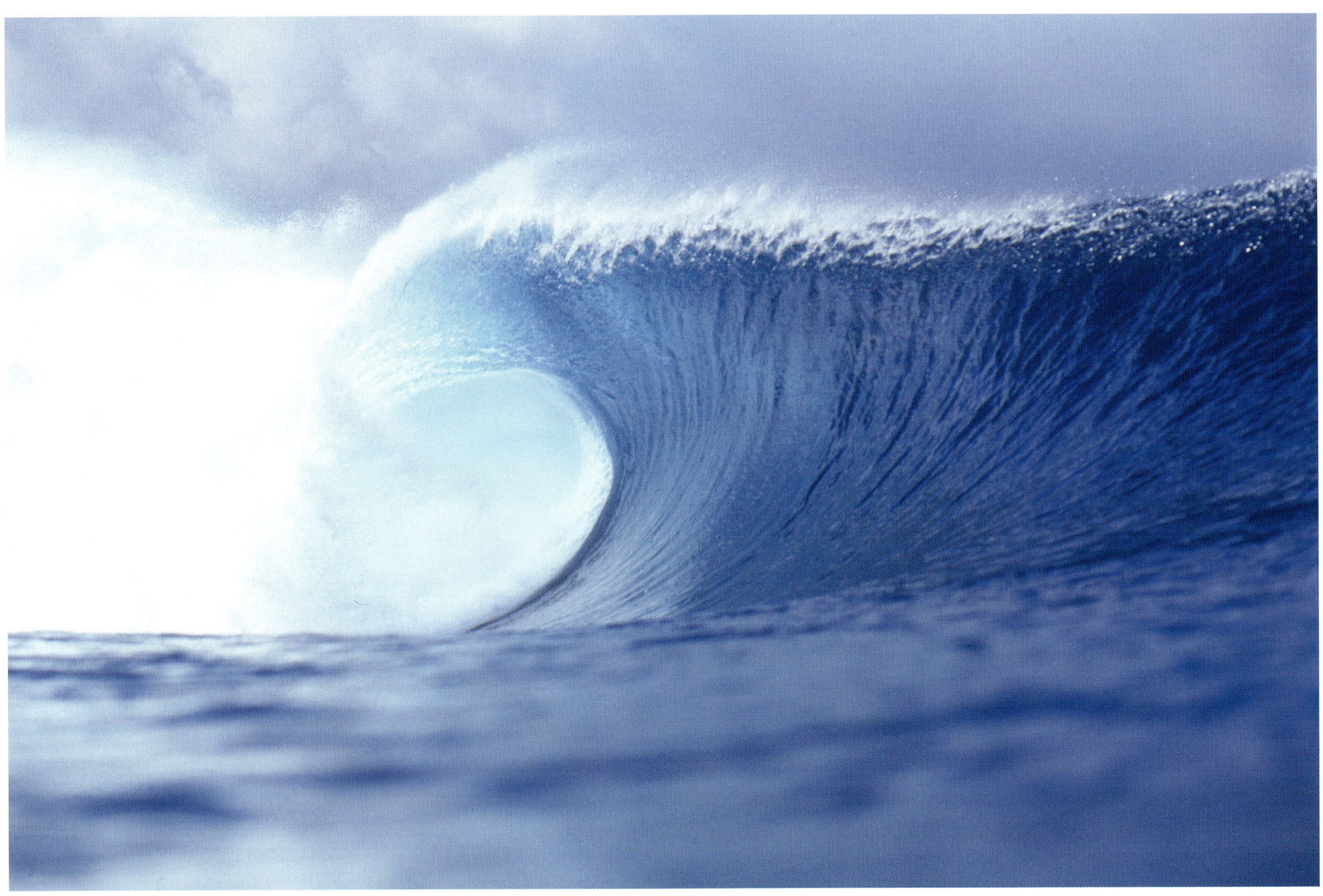

When a wave
such as this approaches land, it comes out of deep water,
then is abruptly grabbed by a shallow reef and the
wave rises up becoming a powerful expression of fury.

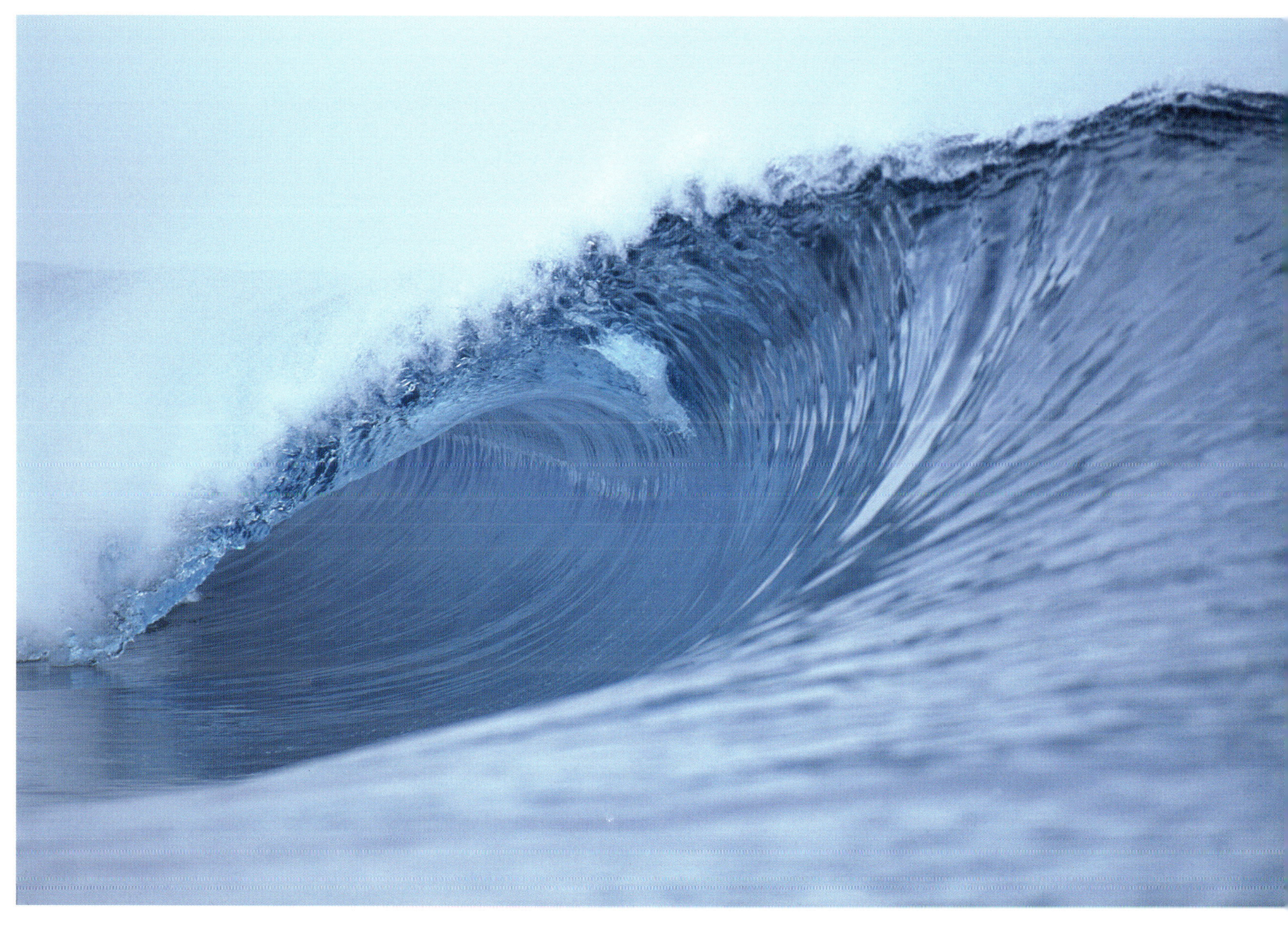

Inside the Cave

The wave is a cylinder. A pipe. South Atlantic Ocean.

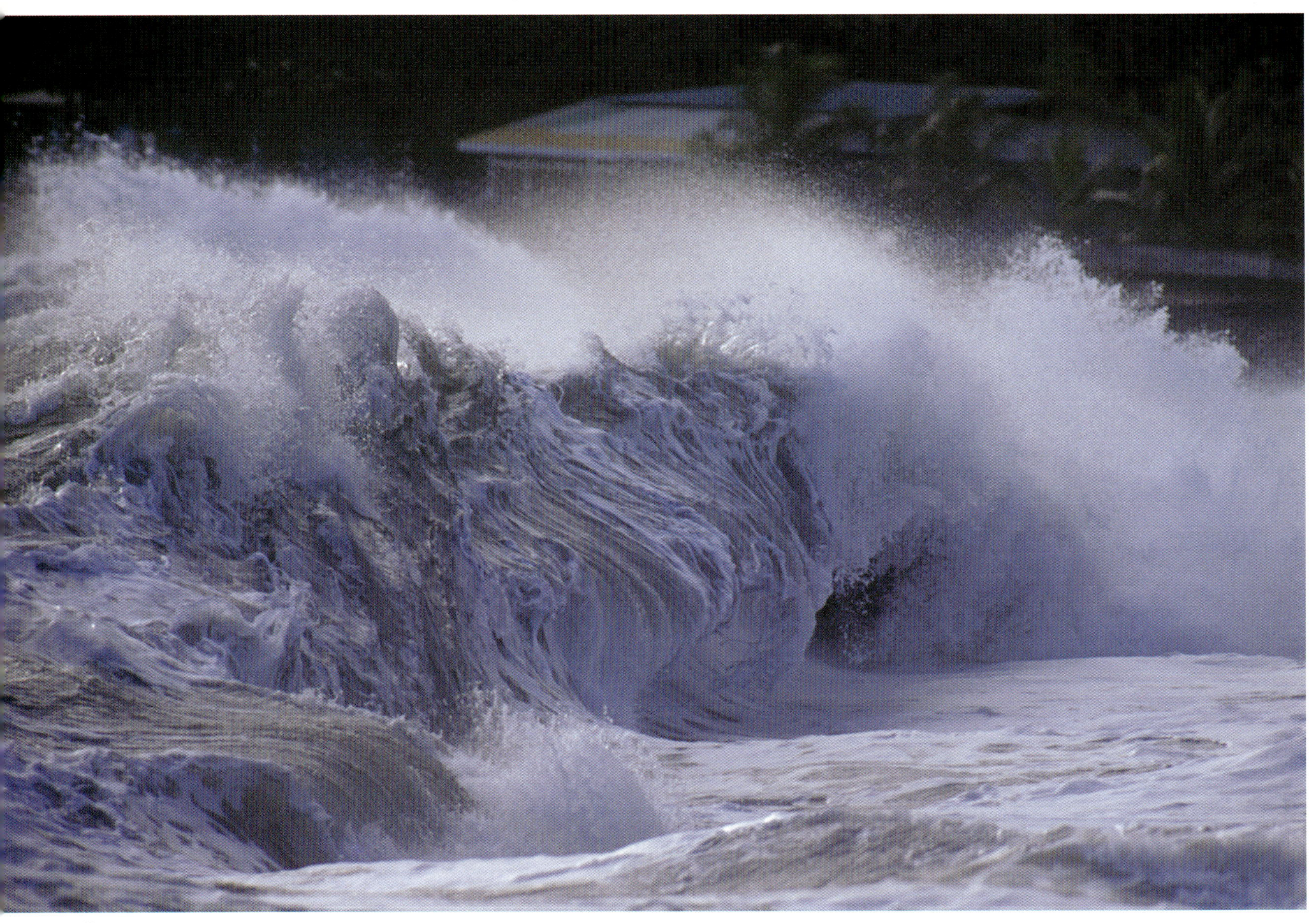

Surge
of the Tides and sand take apart this wave.

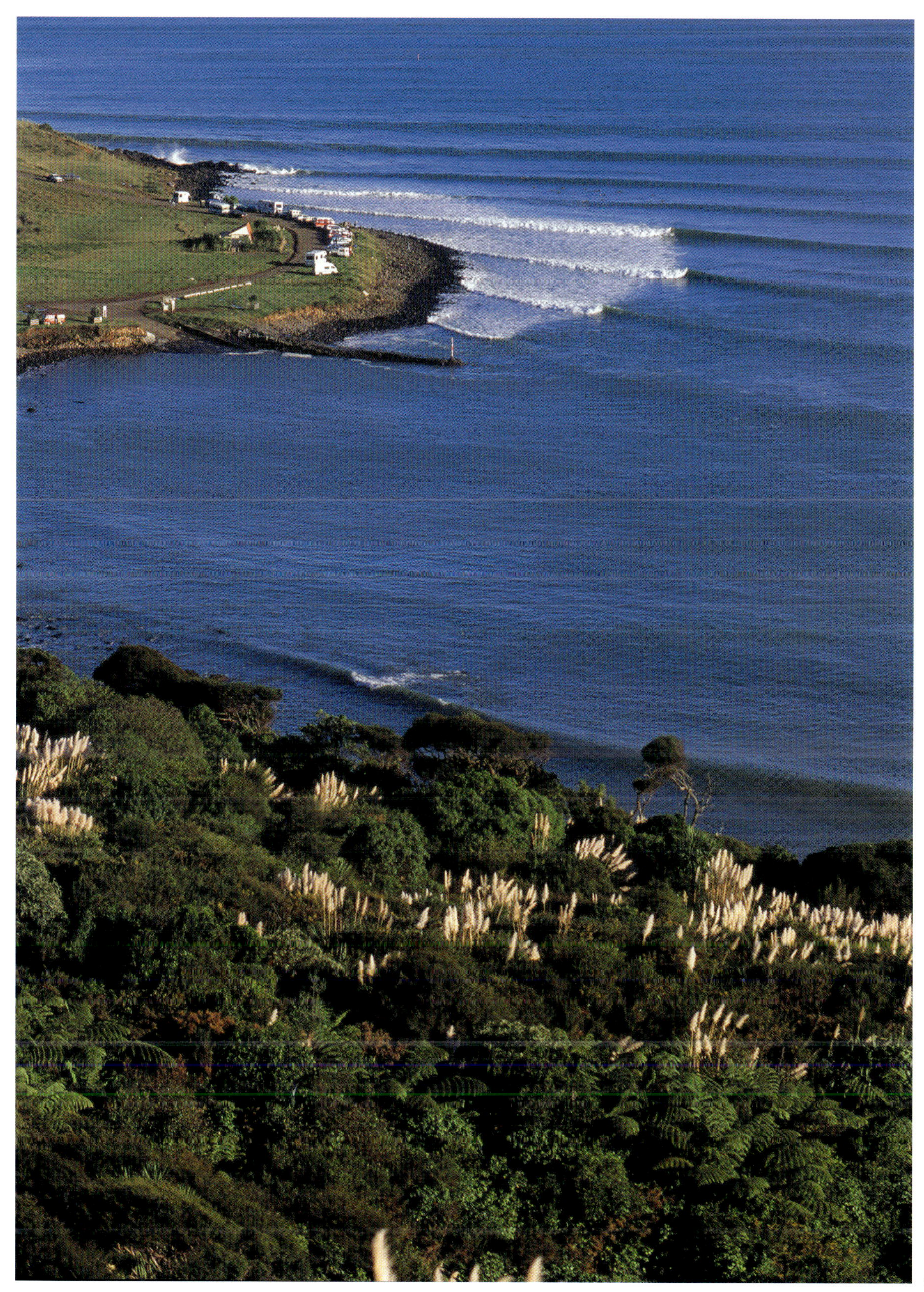

The Peace
of the Point in Ragland Bay, New Zealand.

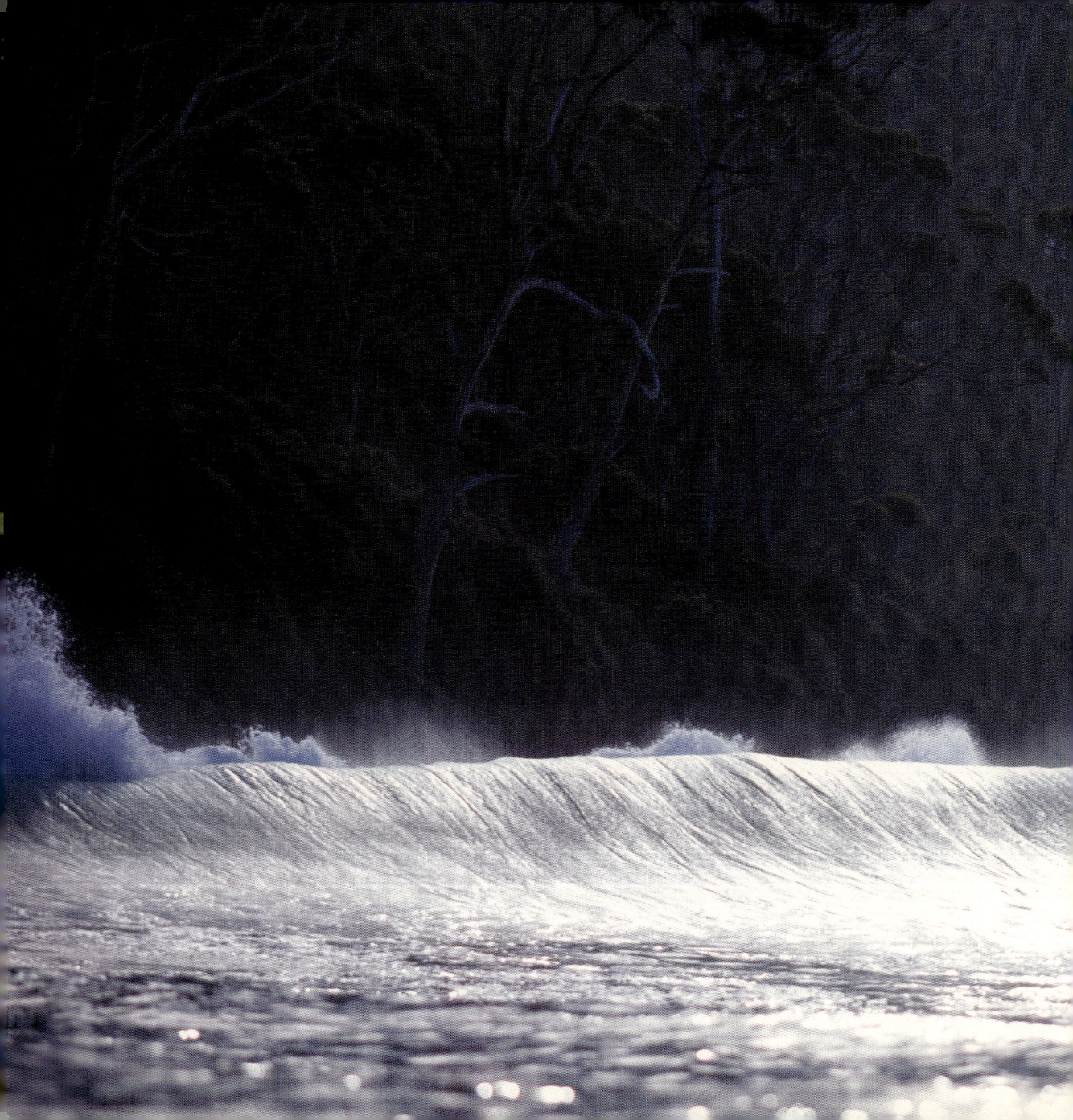

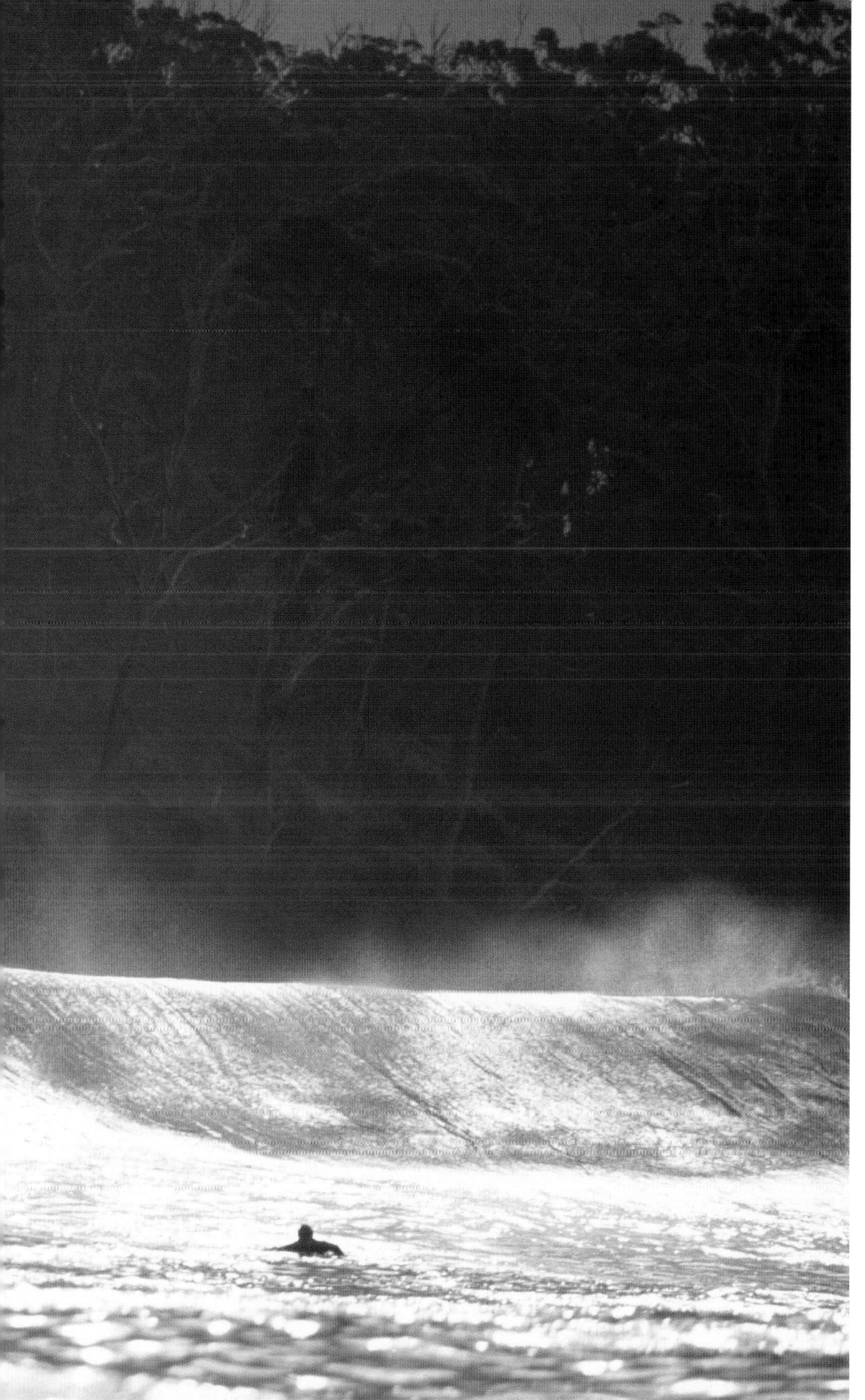

Dark Forest,
Deep and Disguised.

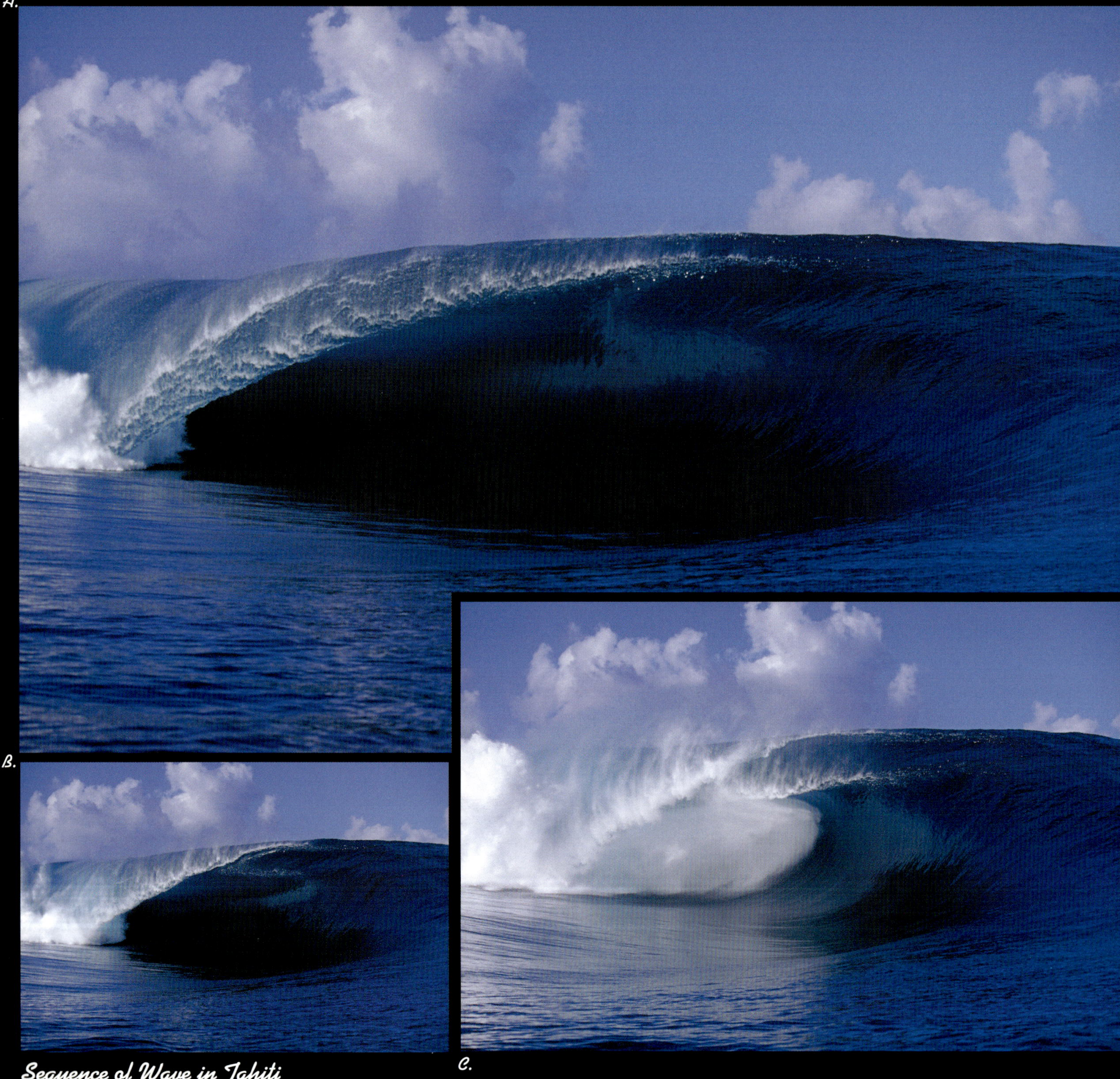

A.
B.
C.
Sequence of Wave in Tahiti

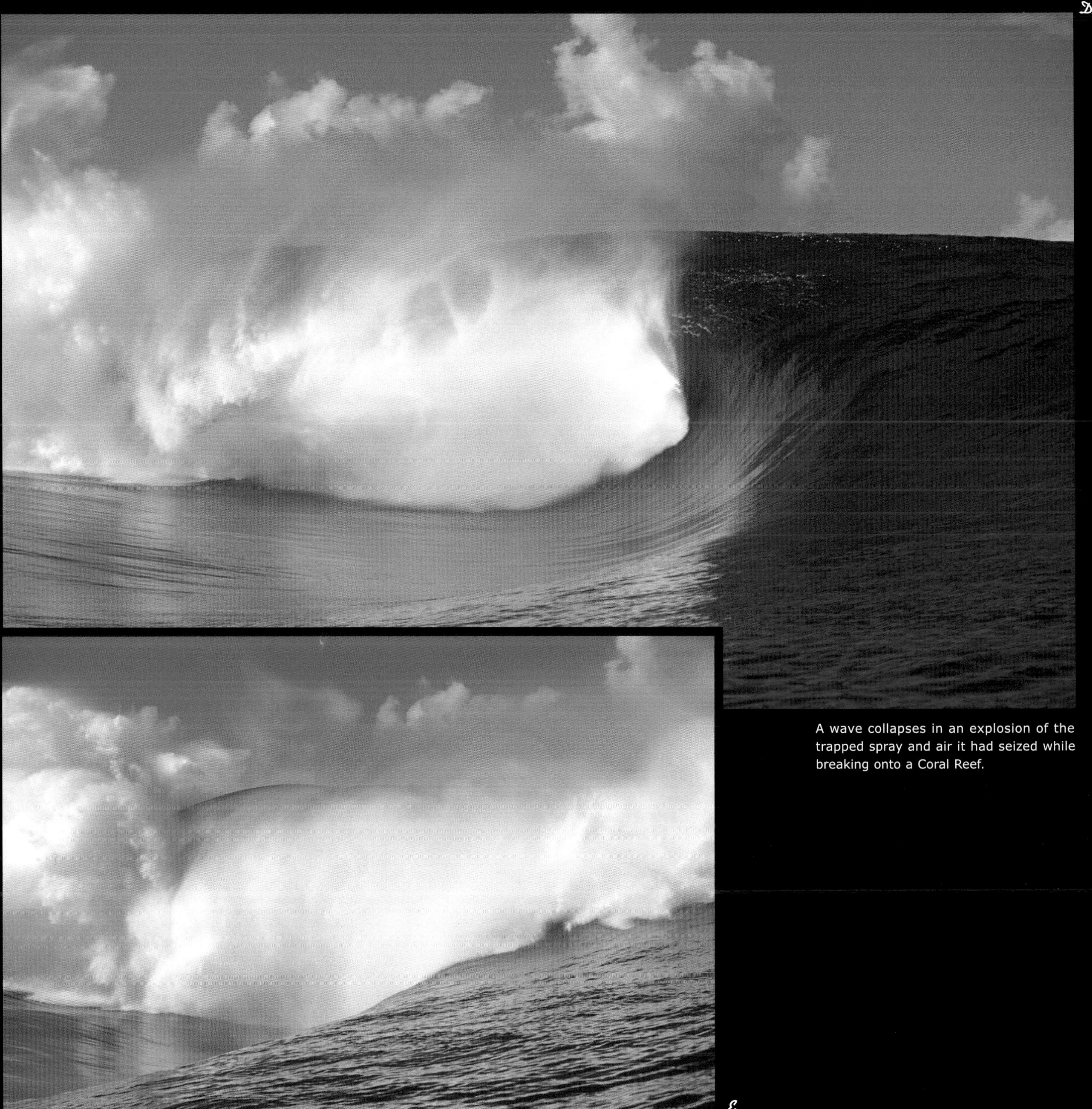

A wave collapses in an explosion of the trapped spray and air it had seized while breaking onto a Coral Reef.

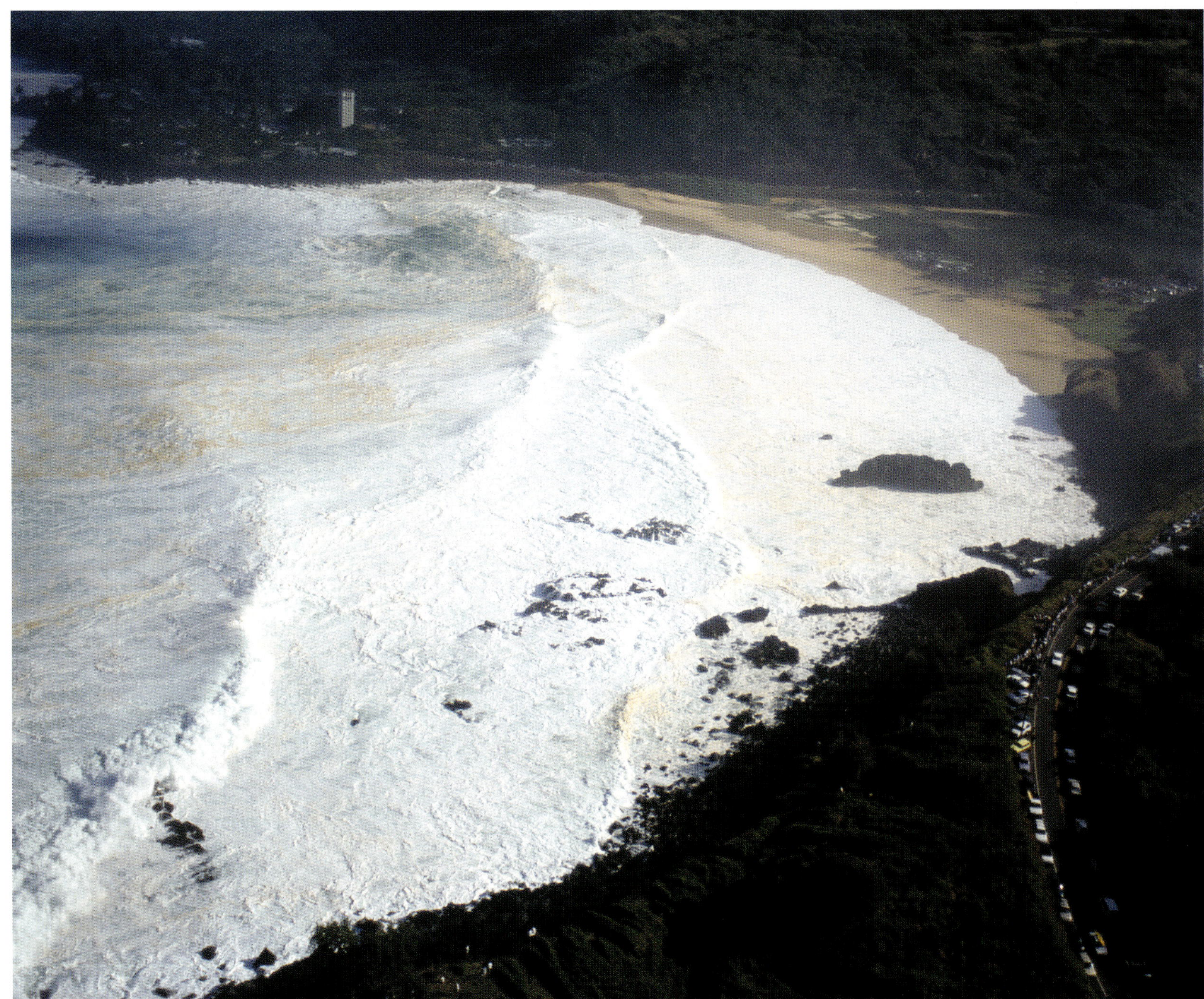

on the North Shore of Oahu, which is of the Hawaiian Islands.
What remains so distinct is that this Waimea Bay is considered
the premiere big-wave surfing spot on earth. But as this
photograph shows, it has 'closed out,' or cannot handle the
size of the waves the ocean has produced for it to display.

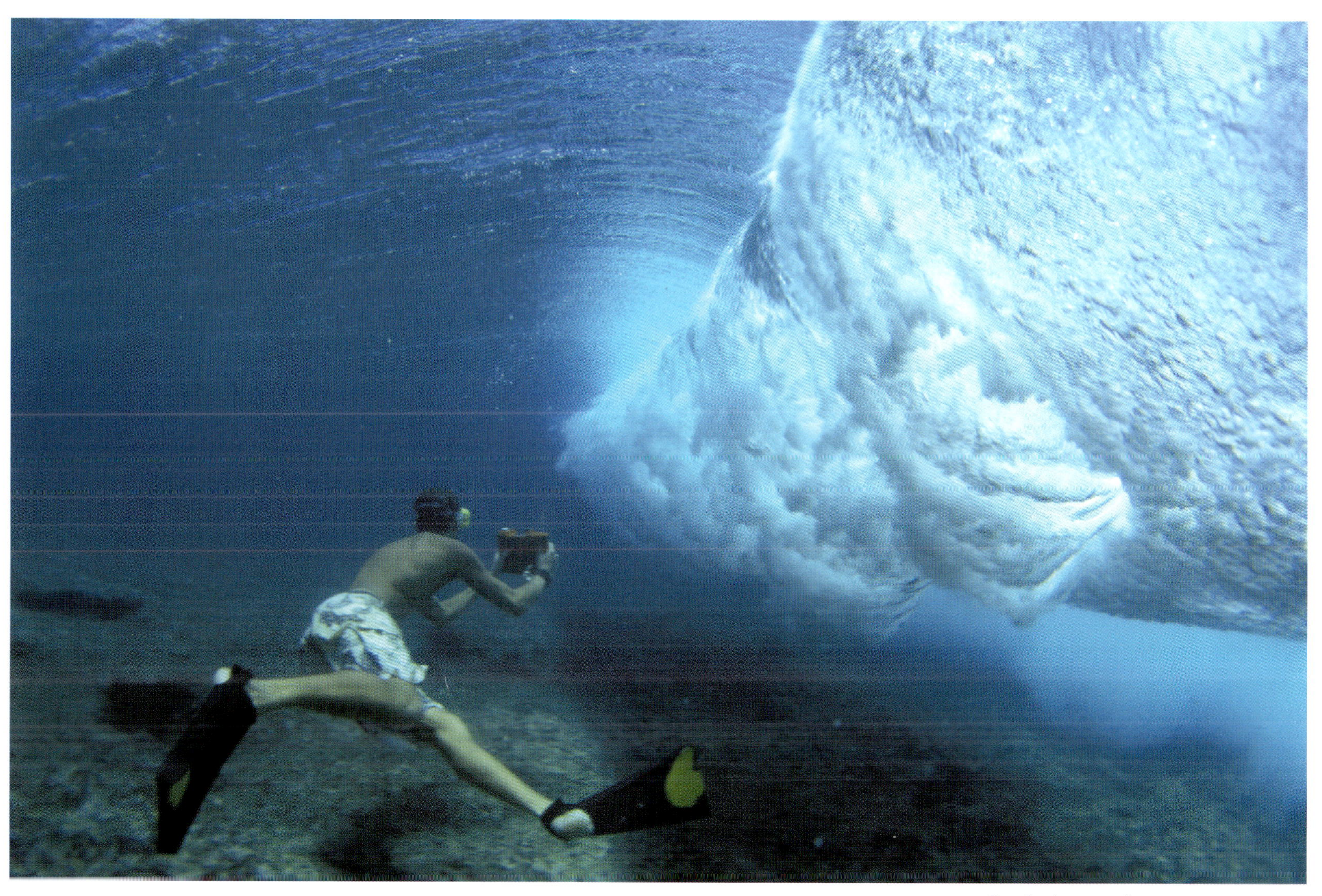

A photographer,
driven to capture what is not typically seen
by people, is, ironically, captured on film.

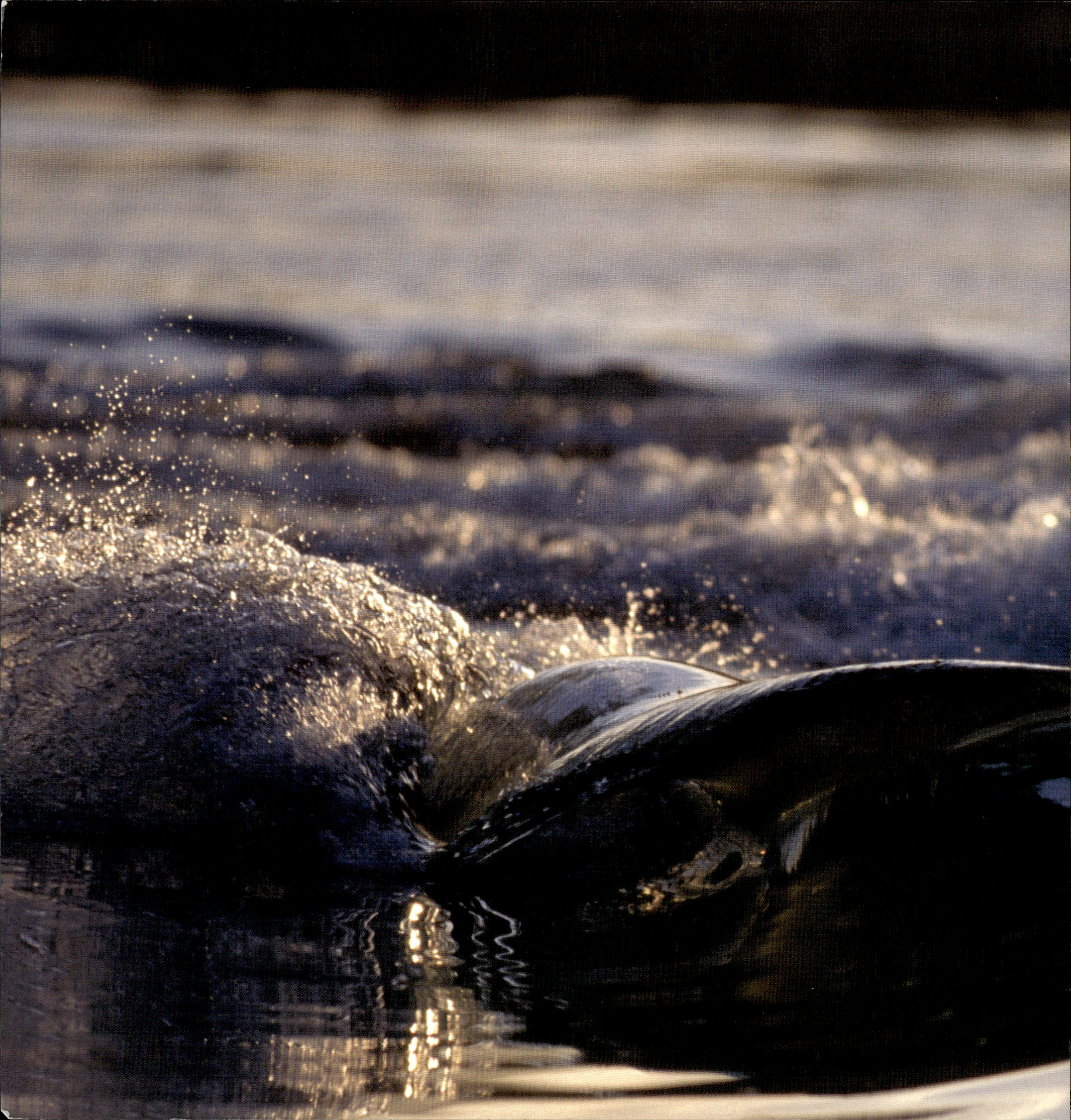

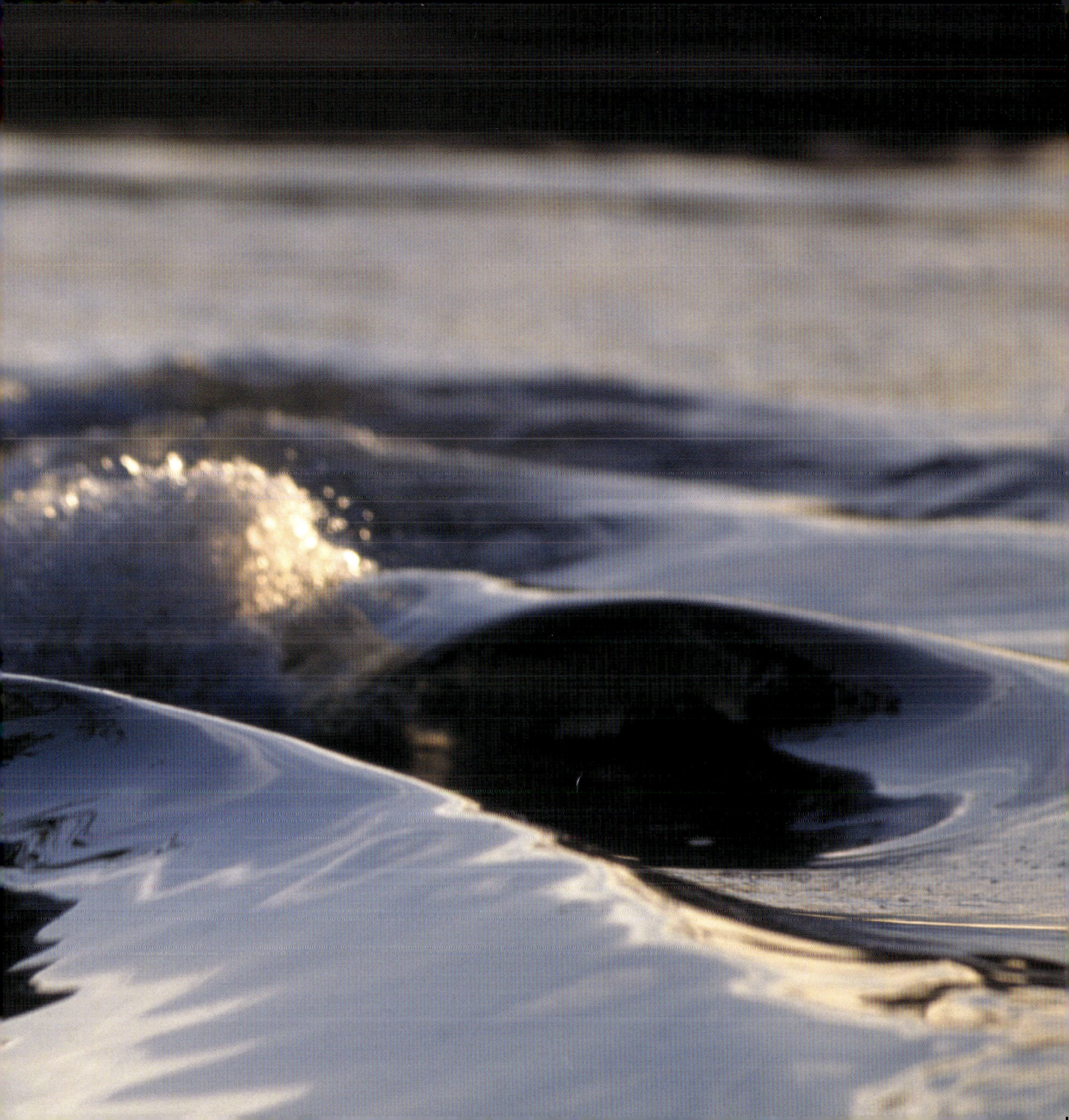